TRACKING POP

SERIES EDITORS: LORI BURNS, JOHN COVACH, AND ALBIN ZAK

In one form or another, the influence of popular music has permeated cultural activities and perception on a global scale. Interdisciplinary in nature, Tracking Pop is intended as a wide-ranging exploration of pop music and its cultural situation. In addition to providing resources for students and scholars working in the field of popular culture, the books in this series will appeal to general readers and music lovers, for whom pop has provided the soundtrack of their lives.

Listening to Popular Music: Or, How I Learned to Stop Worrying and Love Led Zeppelin
by Theodore Gracyk

Sounding Out Pop: Analytical Essays in Popular Music
edited by Mark Spicer and John Covach

I Don't Sound Like Nobody: Remaking Music in 1950s America
by Albin J. Zak III

Soul Music: Tracking the Spiritual Roots of Pop from Plato to Motown
by Joel Rudinow

Are We Not New Wave? Modern Pop at the Turn of the 1980s
by Theo Cateforis

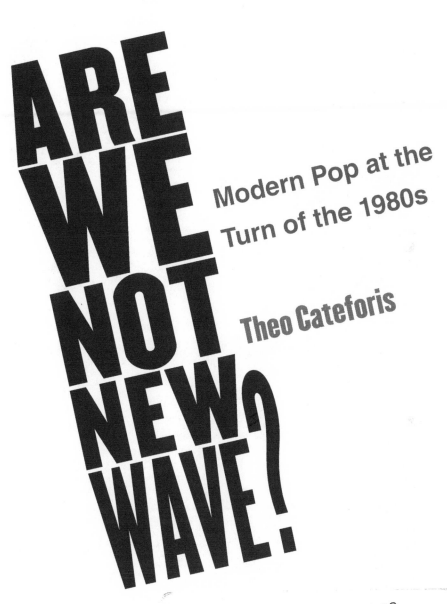

ARE WE NOT NEW WAVE?

Modern Pop at the Turn of the 1980s

Theo Cateforis

THE UNIVERSITY OF MICHIGAN PRESS

ANN ARBOR

Copyright © by the University of Michigan 2011
All rights reserved
Published in the United States of America by
The University of Michigan Press
Manufactured in the United States of America
⊗ Printed on acid-free paper

2014 2013 2012 2011   4 3 2 1

A CIP catalog record for this book is available from the British Library.

Library of Congress Cataloging-in-Publication Data

Cateforis, Theo.
    Are we not new wave? : modern pop at the turn of the 1980s / Theo
Cateforis.
        p.   cm.
    Includes bibliographical references and index.
    ISBN 978-0-472-11555-6 (cloth : alk. paper)
    ISBN 978-0-472-03470-3 (pbk. : alk. paper)
    ISBN 978-0-472-02759-0 (e-book)
    1. New wave music—History and criticism.   2. Popular music—
1981–1990—History and criticism.   I. Title.
ML3534.C37   2011
781.6409'048—dc22   2011000428

Acknowledgments

The idea for writing a book about new wave first came to me roughly fifteen years ago when I was pursuing my graduate studies in music history at Stony Brook University. It soon turned into the subject of my dissertation, which I completed in 2000, and ever since then new wave has been a constant companion of mine through three academic appointments, numerous conference papers and colloquia, classroom lectures, and late night revisions. Given the long journey of this project there are many people to thank.

First and foremost I would like to thank the Tracking Pop series editors at the University of Michigan Press for soliciting and believing in this project, and the anonymous readers whose insightful reports were of enormous help in my revisions. A special thanks to UMP music editor Chris Hebert, who had a timely answer for every one of my numerous e-mail queries. Likewise, my thanks to Susan Cronin and Mary Sexton at the Press, who relieved Chris of some of this burden.

Second I would like to thank the individual photographers, artists, and magazine editors whose work adorns the pages of this book. Robert Burger, Gerald Casale, Janet Macoska, Laurie Paladino, Ebet Roberts, Ira Robbins, Suzy Shaw, and William Stout all graciously granted permission to reprint their materials. Thanks as well to Michael Pilmer at Club Devo, and also to EMI Music Licensing, Hal Leonard Corporation, London Features International, and Music Sales Limited for the use of their holdings.

I received critical support to help complete this project at two important stages a decade apart. As a graduate student I was awarded the American Musciological Society's AMS 50 Fellowship in 1998–99, and as a faculty member at Syracuse University I was granted a research leave during the Spring 2009 semester that allowed me some much needed time for writing and reflection. I would also like to thank associate dean Gerry Greenberg in the Syracuse University College of Arts and Sciences, who generously provided financial support to assist with the book's permission fees.

At Syracuse University I have enjoyed the conversations, helpful feedback, research assistance, and technical support of many colleagues. In particular I would like to thank Carol Babiracki, Amanda Eubanks Winkler, Jeffrey Mayer, Stephen Meyer, Sascha Scott, Penelope and Stephen Singer, Vincent Stephens, and Carole Vidali. And a special thanks to Chris Jabot for his assistance with the musical examples.

Also I have not forgotten the expert guidance, judgment, and encouraging words that the faculty at Stony Brook provided many years ago when I was completing my doctoral work and dissertation. To Joe Auner, Judy Lochhead, Jane Sugarman, and Peter Winkler I offer once more my deepest gratitude.

The International Association for the Study of Popular Music (IASPM) has been a scholarly home for me for many years, and I have always valued its annual meetings as an opportunity to converse with colleagues and gain some much-needed perspective on my research. I especially would like to thank Bernard Gendron, Jason Hanley, Keir Keightley, Andy Krikun, Charles Kronengold, Nick Rubin, Carol Vernallis, and Steve Waksman for helping me to think through more clearly many of this book's issues.

In addition to the many conferences at which I presented material on new wave, I also delivered colloquia that allowed me to "road test" some of this book's material. My thanks to Anne Rasmussen at the College of William and Mary, Fred Maus at the University of Virginia, and David Yeardsley and Judith Peraino at Cornell University for extending these colloquia invitations.

An especially warm thanks goes to the members of the rock groups Bunsen Honeydew and Four Volts—Lisa Unander, Brian Rayman, and Danny Tieman—with whom I performed and recorded for many years while writing this book, and who have left an indelible imprint on the way that I think about music. Thanks goes as well to Robert Fanelli, whose unbridled passion and keen appreciation for the music of the new wave era runs deeper than anyone I have ever met. Our conversations and exchanges over the years have always left me feeling rejuvenated and inspired about my chosen subject.

Last of all, the biggest thanks goes to my family. To my parents, thank you for your unwavering support and for housing my vinyl LP collection for so many years (I promise I'll move them out soon!). To my wife Margaret, thank you for your incredible patience and comforting words, and your critical reading skills and proofreading prowess. I could not have written this book without you. And most of all, to our children Lester and Rhoda, thank you for bringing joy to my life and reminding me that there are much more important things than my shelves of books and records.

Grateful acknowledgment is made to the following for permission to reprint previously published materials:

Airlane
Words and Music by Gary Numan
Copyright © 1979 UNIVERSAL/MOMENTUM MUSIC 3 LTD
This arrangement Copyright © 2010 UNIVERSAL/MOMENTUM MUSIC 3 LTD
All Rights in the U.S. and Canada Controlled and Administered by UNIVERSAL—SONGS OF POLYGRAM INTERNATIONAL, INC.
All Rights Reserved Used by Permission
Reprinted by permission of Hal Leonard Corporation
Words & Music by Gary Anthony James Webb
© Copyright Universal/Momentum Music Ltd. (GB).
All Rights Reserved. International Copyright Secured.
Used by permission of Music Sales Limited.

Bombers
Words and Music by Gary Numan
Copyright © 1984 UNIVERSAL/MOMENTUM MUSIC 3 LTD
This arrangement Copyright © 2010 UNIVERSAL/MOMENTUM MUSIC 3 LTD
All Rights in the U.S. and Canada Controlled and Administered by UNIVERSAL—SONGS OF POLYGRAM INTERNATIONAL, INC.
All Rights Reserved Used by Permission

Contents

Introduction

Like many historical narratives, the story of rock music is one organized around a succession of cycles. The music's production, reception, and mythology are typically situated as part of a constantly renewing periodic phenomenon, intimately tied to the ebb and flow of adolescent or youth generations. This periodization finds its most conspicuous form in the shape of rock "invasions" and "explosions." Such events are characterized by a flurry of musical activity, as a number of related new artists and bands coalesce and the recording and media industries recognize a new popular music movement. We tend to associate these cycles with the spectacle surrounding a significant iconic performer or group: Elvis Presley serves as a lightning rod for the emergence of rock and roll in the 1950s; the Beatles head a British Invasion in the mid-1960s; a decade later the Sex Pistols and punk rock shock mainstream society; in the early 1990s Nirvana articulates a grunge style that solidifies alternative rock's popularity. In the most basic sense, any of these four dynamic outbursts might rightfully be considered a *new wave* of popular music. It is mostly a matter of historical circumstance that the actual label of *new wave* should be associated with the third of the aforementioned movements: the mid-1970s punk explosion.

In the 1970s critics credited punk bands like the Sex Pistols and the Clash with startling the rock industry out of its moribund complacency. But punk's raw sound, fueled in part by an anarchic rereading of 1960s garage rock and in part by a subversive political bent fashioned out of art school experimentation, was perceived in the United States as too confrontational for mainstream radio. To the major labels, punk appeared to be virtually unmarketable. In its stead, the music industry embraced new wave groups like the Talking Heads, Blondie, Devo, Elvis Costello and the Attractions, and Squeeze, all of whom shared punk's energy but tempered its vitriol with more accessible and novel songwriting sprinkled with liberal doses of humor, irreverence, and irony. Like their punk rock forebears, new wave musicians openly rejected the tired clichés of rock star abundance and bloated stadium extravaganzas that had come to dominate the 1970s. As Mark Kjeldsen of British new wave band the Sinceros put it: "We don't come on stage and pretend we're this immortal rock 'n' roll band full of sexist crap, and you're gonna partaaay, and do you feel like I do and every-one's gonna light candles and stick 'em up their arses."[1] Chris Stein of Blondie was decidedly more blunt: "Everything is bullshit in the '70s."[2]

One of new wave's most radical maneuvers was also one of its most sim-ple: new wave groups returned to rock music a direct, danceable energy that had largely been abandoned. By the mid-1970s, a listener was hard pressed to find up-tempo dance rhythms, as rock and roll's exuberant en-ergy had given way to slower, more contemplative singer-songwriter styles and more complex, deliberately paced progressive and hard rock structures. In America, popular groups like Led Zeppelin were characterized not as dance bands, but rather caricatured as "drinking-beer-in-the-high-school-parking-lot" bands.[3] As Kate Pierson of the B-52's explained, "When we first started and first came to New York there wasn't [sic] any dance bands. It simply wasn't the thing to do at the time, everybody was leaning against the bar looking bored in a leather jacket."[4] Bands like the B-52's jolted rock audiences back onto the dance floors by taking what would have been an exceptionally quick tempo for the mid-1970s, roughly 160 BPM (one of Led Zeppelin's fastest songs, "Rock and Roll," is 163 BPM), and making that the norm.[5] As such, the dance beat became integral to new wave. From songs (the Go-Go's' "We Got the Beat," the Jam's "Beat Surrender," Squeeze's "Farfisa Beat," and Elvis Costello and the Attractions' "The Beat") to album titles (Blondie's *Eat to the Beat*) to band names (the Beat was a name claimed by both an American and a British new wave band), the discourse of dance suffused the new wave style.

At its core, new wave signified the dissatisfaction that many musicians and fans felt with the rock status quo. Given this stance, it is not surprising that the movement quickly came to be characterized as "modern." Radio stations that began featuring new wave artists heavily in their rotations labeled their programming as "modern music" to distinguish themselves from the routine rock sounds of the day.⁶ Record labels promoted their new wave titles as the products of progressive modern artists. "Ultravox is modern music at its most accessible and creative level," declared the promotional blurb for their 1980 album *Vienna*. Two years later the advertisement for Duran Duran's album *Rio* promised "Musical Adventures for the Modern Age." In this colloquial sense, the modern label evoked a wide range of associations. To be modern is to be young. It is to be fashionable, to have a certain sense of visual style. To be modern is forward looking, futuristic. The modern is that which is contemporary, is now and therefore most relevant. To be modern is to stand out from the crowd in a novel way. To be modern is to be on the crest of a new wave.

This book explores the context within which new wave rose to prominence at the turn of the 1980s, when the music was conceived, promoted, and critiqued as a dynamic modern pop movement. While I detail how this transpired as part of a music industry easily swayed by the allure and marketability of the *new*, I also view the modern in new wave from a more historically and culturally situated vantage point. Modern, modernity, modernism—these are concepts that have a wide currency stretching across a variety of intellectual traditions and disciplinary perspectives.⁷ For social and political scientists, economists, and historians, the idea of modernity and the modern is tied to concrete sociohistorical conditions. Variously, the rise of urban centers, the industrial revolution, new technologies, and an accelerated consumer culture have all signaled distinctly "modern" eras marked most of all by rapid change. For those in the humanities, modernity is often intimately linked to new art forms that reflect our sensory experience of the new modern environment. Crucially, the modern is also "relational," rupturing with the immediate past and often turning to a more distant past as an inspiration of rebellion.⁸

As I argue, there are three modern historical eras that prove pivotal to understanding new wave's meanings. Two of them are past modernities that shaped the new wave in ways both subtle and obvious: (1) the emergence of a modern metropolitan American culture stretching roughly from 1880 to 1930 and (2) the period traversing the late 1950s to the mid-1960s, when first America and then England experienced a new affluence and rising youth culture. The third era is the modernity in which new wave itself emerged at the turn of the 1980s, or what is often referred to as a late modernity marked by deindustrialization and the rise of globalization. Significantly, each of these periods is associated with profound technological advancements that provoked responses both celebratory and cautionary. Whether it be the early twentieth-century Fordism of standardization and mechanized labor, the midcentury's new consumer culture and accompanying spread of mass-produced synthetic products, or the impending approach of a computerized society at the turn of the 1980s, the "modern" promised a better life just as it encouraged critiques of societal dehumanization. All of these different modernities figured into the new wave in one fashion or another.

There are some who have suggested that through its at times ironic and detached relationship to these various past modernities, new wave reflected the dawning of a new postmodern music sensibility. Such pronouncements emerged most forcefully in the middle to late 1980s as new wave was on the wane and postmodernism as an intellectual and academic debate was on the ascent. For example, noted critical theorist Fredric Jameson claimed that the recent punk and new wave music of groups like the Clash and the Talking Heads represented a striking postmodernist departure from the comparatively high modernist stance of late 1960s rock groups like the Beatles and Rolling Stones.[9] Others, like sociologist Jon Stratton, argued that the convergence of minimalist tendencies in both punk and new wave *and* the art music of composers like Philip Glass and Laurie Anderson represented a postmodern rupture of the distinctions between "low" and "high" culture.[10] As appealing as such propositions seemed at the time, they tended to locate postmodernism predominantly within the narrow realms of aesthetics and style, and furthermore were applied selectively to only a handful of new wave artists. There was less sense of *how* exactly this turn of events indicated a corresponding postmodern societal or historical shift.[11] Indeed many have argued since then that the idea of postmodernity can more rightfully be considered a variation upon, rather than a break from, modernity's long historical reach.[12] Given these circumstances, I am reluctant to consider new wave as a postmodern musical movement. At the peak of its popularity in the late 1970s and early 1980s, new wave was overwhelmingly recognized and labeled as a modern, *not* a postmodern, musical movement.

As an entryway into the connection between new wave and the modern, I would like to begin by briefly considering a representative song: "Video Killed the Radio Star." Although the song was first a hit for the Buggles (two British studio musicians, Trevor Horn and Geoffrey Downes) in 1979, most people know it as the answer to the perennial trivia question: what was the first music video to air when Music Television (MTV) launched on August 1, 1981? At the time of its original release, on the cusp of the 1980s, the song described the dawning of a new modern technological era while lamenting the passing of an older modern time, the golden age of radio.[13] Both these modern tropes emerge as an integral part of the song's intricately arranged production.[14] On the one hand, "Video" sparkles with a glossy modern and futuristic sheen thanks to the prominent use of synthesizers and processed filtering that transforms the acoustic drum hits in the song's bridge to sound as if they are electronic percussion. On the other hand, Horn's vocals are laden with heavy compression, an effect that suggests the timbral quality of a radio voice from the distant past. With the exception of a brief two-measure section following the song's bridge, "Video" eschews the conventional rock sonorities and riffs of the electric guitar in favor of a variety of disco tropes that by the end of the 1970s had emerged as a virtual shorthand for the sound of modern, contemporary pop. "Four to the floor" bass drum hits, open hi-hat accents, syncopated bass riffs, and stratified textures: all these elements suggest a strong link between disco and new wave's orientation as studio-based dance music.[15] Just as importantly, new wave's aesthetic alliance with disco also signified the music's growing distance from its punk roots.

The famed video for "Video Killed the Radio Star" elaborates upon the song's modern themes in numerous ways. It begins with a little girl seated in front of an archaic radio console; magically she awakens a glitter-haired woman clad in a leotard costume. Complete with a cape and belt, this science fiction heroine seems to have jetted out of a 1930s *Flash Gordon* serial, an obvious nostalgic nod both to her once glorious futuristic powers and her association with the vanishing radio medium. At the third verse, the video moves to a setting that appears to be a cross between a laboratory and a recording studio, where we see Downes playing a keyboard. A few feet away the heroine is encased and floating in what seems to be some sort of transportation tube. Horn wanders the set singing the lyrics while dressed in a white Nehru jacket suggestive of a lab coat and wearing oversized glasses with an antenna attachment that obliquely hints at his modern, scientific stature (see fig. 1). In the laboratory/studio's background, a television set is playing that shows two women dressed in matching outfits, wigs, and white-rimmed sunglasses who provide the chorus's background vocals. With their rigid bodies, stiff hand gestures, and clonelike appearance, they appear to be little more than singing robots (see fig. 2). Taken as a whole, the video's bewildering collision of scientist/musicians, an outer space heroine, transparent portals, and robotic background vocalists unfolds with little concern for any narrative cohesion. Like many early MTV videos, it places a far greater emphasis on its striking modern imagery than any underlying story.

The video plays upon these modern themes in ways that extend beyond its inventive fashion and set designs. Many of the images, for example, are mediated. We constantly find ourselves viewing the musicians, the heroine, and the background singers through television screens. There is a hint of surveillance, as if the video's participants are constantly under watch in a futuristic Big Brother state. The television's replication also raises questions about the very nature of these images. Are they the "real" thing, or are they—to borrow the philosopher Jean Baudrillard's term— simply all simulacra. The video solves this dilemma at the climactic turn to the song's final fade chorus when the laboratory setting splits apart to reveal the band performing in front of a stationary film camera reminiscent of a studio television stage. Horn and Downes are augmented by a third member, a keyboardist engulfed by a towering modular synthesizer unit that serves to underscore the band's modern, technological aura. Stationed at their instruments, and playing along to the song, there can be no doubt that this is the authentic, "real" Buggles.

As contemporary as "Video" undoubtedly was in its time, on second glance what is so striking is how much of its modern visual and musical style is pilfered from a previous era's version of modernity. Downes and Horn, who are both pictured at their instruments wearing skinny ties and matching synthetic blazers, represent a direct throwback to the mid-1960s

Figure 1. Trevor Horn sings, with the space age heroine in the backdrop, in a shot from the Buggles' "Video Killed the Radio Star" (1979).

"mod" style of the British Invasion. Likewise, the background singers' costumes—an assemblage of sharp angles, tight belts, restrictive turtlenecks, and blonde wigs—are a decade past their prime. They could be *Star Trek* uniforms, or direct descendants of the futuristic "space age" fashion styles popularized by 1960s designers like André Courrèges. Many of the song's vocal hooks look back toward an earlier rock and pop era as well. The female singers' staccato "oh-a-oh" refrain recalls the quirky glottal stops and hiccups of Buddy Holly's late 1950s rockabilly style, while the octave leap and descent of the ending legato "operatic" vocal melody—"you are the radio star"—nostalgically hints at the descant of an older novelty hit, the Tokens' 1961 chart topper, "The Lion Sleeps Tonight." Even the Buggles' name itself comes across as a willful misreading of the Beatles. For a band and song supposedly gazing toward the future technologies of the 1980s, surprisingly much of "Video Killed the Radio Star" is pasted together from var-

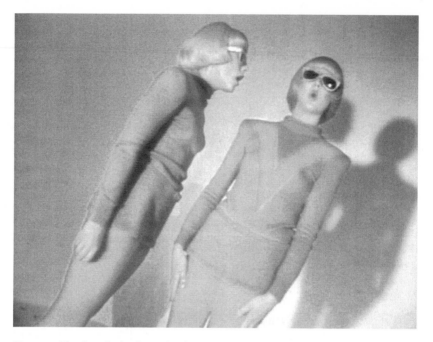

Figure 2. The Buggles' robotic background singers, in matching futuristic outfits, in a shot from "Video Killed the Radio Star" (1979)

ious pre-1970s musical and visual allusions, and sealed with the disco conventions of its present era.

But given the diverse backgrounds of the Buggles' two members, it should perhaps be expected that their vision of a modern age would emerge from so many different corners. Trevor Horn and Geoffrey Downes were both in their late twenties when they formed the Buggles in 1977, and by then had spent considerable time in the industry as studio musicians backing the British disco singer Tina Charles and penning songs for the likes of Dusty Springfield. Like many other experienced musicians who would become associated with the new wave—including groups such as the Police and Split Enz and artists like Joe Jackson and Marshall Crenshaw—it was mostly a matter of timing more than anything else that found them lumped in with the latest, most fashionable new rock movement. Horn and Downes had initially released "Video" in 1979 as a one-off single with only modest hopes of success. It was only after the song surprisingly

jetted to the top of the charts, first in England, then in sixteen other countries, that the two scrambled to put together a full album of material and
turn the Buggles into a more fully conceptualized new wave band. Released
symbolically on January 1, 1980, at the dawn of a new decade, the Buggles'
debut record played upon the various modern themes that had propelled
their hit single up the charts. The album title, *The Age of Plastic,* and songs
like "I Love You (Miss Robot)" and "Astroboy," picture the arrival of the
1980s as a novelty era of playful futurism. At the same time, the evocation
of plastic knowingly hearkens back to the 1960s, when "plastics" came to
connote both the ultimate attainment of modern manufactured consumer
comfort and depthless artifice. The album's cover, which features a digitally
animated rendition of Trevor Horn's head, complete with oversized "space
age" glasses, necktie and uniform, and a patch cord protruding from his
neck, further suggests the group's mechanized, technological orientation.
As an emblem of the new wave, *The Age of Plastic* portrays the dawning of
the 1980s as a peculiarly modern age informed equally by the ghosts of past
modernities and by visions of the future yet to come.

The Buggles' run at the charts would be short lived, however. *The Age of
Plastic* failed to replicate the success of its celebrated single, and by March
of 1980, merely months after "Video" had first appeared, Horn and Downes
retired the Buggles to join the progressive rock group Yes, with whom they
remained for a single album. Like many other artists, the Buggles' association with the new wave would come to represent only a fleeting, transient
moment in their longer musical careers. For Horn, however, new wave's
particular modern allure ultimately proved to be too much to resist. In 1982
he revived the Buggles moniker for one last album. Appropriately enough,
it was titled *Adventures in Modern Recording.*

Making Sense of the New Wave

To the best of my knowledge, this book surprisingly is the very first, scholarly or otherwise, to tackle the topic of new wave since the music drifted off
into the late 1980s sunset over two decades ago. For those familiar with
new wave's tangled and conflicted historical relationship with punk, however, this may not come as much of a shock. New wave originally emerged

as a term that was synonymous with the subversive sounds of the 1976–77 American and British punk rock explosions. But this relationship had changed by 1978 and 1979, when new wave was drafted out of its existing context and reclaimed as a safe harbor for those punk-related artists whose music derived from punk's caustic energy, but was rendered more stylish and accessible. New wave's commercial success came with a price. As Ira Robbins, the former editor of the new wave-oriented magazine *Trouser Press,* noted, after its split from punk, new wave became for many "a designation for watered-down bands who managed a hip style but were presentable enough for radio."[16] New wave's compromised reputation is perhaps most concisely summarized in the title of a retrospective CD compilation, *Punky but Chic.* Portrayed as a mollified, less dangerous version of punk's politicized confrontational rage, new wave's "posed" rebellion came to be seen by fans and critics alike as a more trendy and packaged rip-off of punk's supposedly "authentic" anger. Meanwhile, a virtual cottage industry of academic writings began to spring up around punk. Over the past three decades, scholarly books on punk have viewed the music through the lenses of subcultural theory, the avant-garde theatrics of Dada and the Situationist International, gender performance, left-wing and grassroots activism, and the identity politics of the straightedge wing.[17] Commentary on new wave, on the other hand, has largely been tucked away in the back corners of music video studies and the occasional article on pop artists of the 1980s.[18]

Part of the problem with new wave is that unlike punk, there has always been some confusion about precisely what artists and music the label actually encompasses. In principle, new wave's main unifying theme was its modern freshness and daring, and its separation from rock's conventions. But such blanket descriptions were not held together by any one specific sound or fan formation; the label of new wave accordingly could be thrown across a wide swath of quite disparate musical styles and practices. Thus one finds in the various new wave discographies, artist registers, and surveys that appeared throughout the early 1980s, a concession that the music was best thought of as a heterogeneous stylistic conglomeration. The cover of 1983's *The Trouser Press Record Guide to New Wave Records,* for example, advertises its new wave contents through a handful of divergent labels: power pop, technopop, rockabilly, electrofunk, art rock, two-tone, and others.[19] Likewise, 1981's *The New Music* divides its featured artists into trends such as power pop, rockabilly, synthesizer/electronic, ska/bluebeat, and mod.[20] This exercise in new wave classification reaches its dizzying zenith in David Bianco's sprawling 1985 discography *Who's New Wave in Music,* which separates its artist entries into over 130 discrete categories.[21] Many of these categories are relatively mundane, but there are also idiosyncratic head-scratchers like "percussion-oriented new wave disco," "nonrock progressive synthesizer," and "microtonal dance music." Clearly, new wave had a devoted connoisseurist following.

Like similar wide-ranging "new" music categories, such as alternative and indie, that have followed in its footsteps, the new wave label suffered the consequences of its seemingly inexhaustible stylistic breadth. Variously described as an "umbrella" or a "catchall" term, trapped between the idealized rebellious purity of punk and the compromised artifice of pop, new wave has been repeatedly branded as a label bereft of any concrete meaning. The *New Rolling Stone Encyclopedia of Rock,* for example, defines new wave as a *"virtually meaningless,* highly flexible form that arose shortly after punk in the late Seventies."[22] As a label that in the words of the *All Music Guide* website eventually came to describe "nearly every new pop/rock artist" of the early 1980s, new wave has seemed like an inviting topic, but one without a readily identifiable common thread.[23]

New wave, then, has been doubly disadvantaged. On the one hand it has been portrayed as a mild cousin to punk, an inferior substitute for some genuine sense of rebellion. On the other hand it has been cast aside as a "meaningless" label, a casualty of the far too numerous and disparate sounds gathered around its collective beacon. There is a memorable moment in Penelope Spheeris's 1980 documentary of the Los Angeles punk movement, *The Decline of Western Civilization,* where Claude Bessy, the editor of the punk fanzine *Slash* and singer for Catholic Discipline, summarizes in blunt terms the problems haunting new wave. Describing the riches of the then current new music explosion, Bessy leaves no doubt about new wave's apparent condition: its all too ubiquitous nature paradoxically ensures its very absence.

I have excellent news for the world. There is no such thing as new wave. It does not exist. . . . There never was any such thing as new wave. It was the polite thing to say when you are trying to explain you are not into the boring old rock and roll, but you didn't dare to say punk because you were afraid to get kicked out of the fucking party and they wouldn't give you coke anymore. There's new music, there's new underground sound, there's noise, there's punk, there's power pop, there's ska, there's rockabilly, but new wave doesn't mean shit.[24]

For all of Bessy's vitriolic polemics, his point is well taken. New wave seems to be nothing more than a container whose contents—such as power pop, ska, and rockabilly—are more substantive than the label of new wave itself. The more styles we add to the mix, such as art rock, technopop, or electrofunk, the more new wave becomes a mystifying assemblage that reads like a random and meaningless mess. By what logic can we group together rockabilly with technopop? How do art rock and electrofunk fit together? On the surface there appears to be no principle that unifies these styles. This book offers a corrective reading of the new wave era, one that proposes that for all its heterogeneity, the music was indeed unified by an overarching trope: simply put, new wave was seen as a *modern* pop music movement. On the surface, the concept of the modern is as potentially unwieldy and far-reaching as new wave itself, a jumble of contradictions and contested meanings. It is, like new wave, an impossibly large umbrella category. I propose then, in the chapters that follow, several lenses through which to view the modern in more specific and historically grounded contexts, each of which sheds light on a particular aspect of the new wave.

Taken collectively, the first two chapters provide a narrative that charts new wave's various modern guises vis-à-vis the music industry from the time that it emerged in the late 1970s to when it eventually faded away, or "died" by the mid-1980s. The two chapters are split along a historical divide that has long proven to be one of the most complicated aspects of defining the new wave. Chapter 1 deals with the initial new wave that emerged most prominently in the American music industry from 1978 to roughly 1981. Chapter 2 looks at the second new wave that emerged in 1981 through a series of "new" movements—the New Romantics, New Pop, and New Music—all of which corresponded with trends and developments in the United Kingdom and their trickled-over effect in the United States. Each chapter situates new wave's modern identity as part of a discourse that emerged through the interaction of musicians, record labels, radio, magazines, and critics, while also explaining the basic music stylistic dimensions that distinguished new wave from other contemporaneous genres.

The remaining chapters view new wave through a variety of sociohistorical and music-analytical vantage points, placing the movement within the context of different historical modernities. Chapter 3 examines in detail a specific musical and emotional quality that came to be seen as one of the new wave's most representative modern characteristics, that of *nervousness*. Associated with front men like David Byrne of the Talking Heads and Mark Mothersbaugh of Devo, nervousness in new wave can be traced back to the prominence of neurasthenia or "nerve weakness," a symptomatically modern disease associated with the rise of metropolitan society between 1880 and 1930. As this chapter argues, new wave's modern nervousness functioned not simply as a marker of modernity, but also served to reinforce the middle-class whiteness of the movement's performers and largest audience formation.

Chapters 4 and 5 both examine the new wave's fascination with the modern popular culture and music of the late 1950s to mid-1960s. To many, new wave's relationship with this period often appears to be distanced and heavily ironic. Chapter 4 considers this angle, focusing specifically on the B-52's and the ironic aesthetics of trash, kitsch, and camp, which in themselves were viewed as modern glosses on the debris of past modernities. Chapter 5, on the other hand, looks at those new wave groups who viewed the modern pop music of the mid-1960s, specifically the British Invasion, more reverentially. This nostalgia cohered most forcefully in a "power pop" genre exemplified by the phenomenal success of the Knack. In both of these chapters I show how the supposed purity of these respective attitudes—irreverent irony and nostalgic appreciation—were made problematic by the bands themselves, who wished to position their stances and motivations as more neutral or complex.

Chapter 6 offers a close look at the synthesizer, the musical instrument that came to represent above all new wave's status as a modern genre within the context of its own modernity, that of the late 1970s and early 1980s. I approach the topic by showing how new wave synthesizer players transformed the instrument's symbolic domain in ways that de-emphasized its status as a virtuosic solo instrument, while highlighting its properties of mechanization and artifice, and the blurred line between "man" and "machine." The chapter focuses much of its analysis on the new wave's first synthesizer star, Gary Numan.

Chapter 7 situates new wave on the precipice of a global modernity, specifically in regards to issues of globalization and cultural crossover that would come to dominate the 1980s. I look at one of the most hotly debated musical iterations of this globalization: the emergence of "world beat," a new genre whose name implied a blurring of races, ethnicities, and global boundaries. This chapter takes an extensive look into the formation and reception history of two new wave albums released in 1980 that act as compelling world beat case studies: Adam and the Ants' *Kings of the Wild Frontier* and the Talking Heads' *Remain in Light,* both of which deliberately announced their authentic borrowings of African music and culture. As I show through an examination of the recording techniques and critical discourses surrounding both albums, this imagined authenticity easily collapses back into new wave's overriding aesthetic of modern artifice.

The book concludes with a brief epilogue that examines new wave *after* new wave, specifically as the movement has enjoyed a considerable renaissance since the early years of the twenty-first century. Revivals as such are crucial to historians and scholars of popular music, for these moments reveal the ways in which genres accrue certain symbolic associations over time. Judging from the influx of *new* new wave bands, from the Killers to La Roux, the new wave of the past circulates most frequently these days as part of a retro-futurist fascination with the once modern technologies and pop culture styles of the 1980s.

Having laid out what this book hopes to accomplish, I should also mention what it will not. Throughout the late 1970s and early 1980s the new wave was a truly international phenomenon. From the "Neue Deutsche Welle" in Germany to the Russian "Novaya Volna," and bands like Japan's Plastics, the new wave could be found all across the globe. To tackle a history of new wave from an international perspective unfortunately lies far beyond the purview of what a single book can accomplish. For that reason I am confining my observations to the new wave as it occurred and was experienced in English-speaking countries, specifically the United States, and to a lesser extent England. Readers will also notice that I have opted not for a broad survey of all the movement's main artists, but rather for close analyses of a select few. My concern in writing this book is not to ensure that new wave's many notable artists and bands all receive equal attention, but rather to consider in depth the trends, styles, developments, and controversies that came to dominate the new wave, as exemplified by a handful of its most intriguing musical practitioners.

Last, I will conclude with a word or two about my own background, and how it bears on this book. My scholarly approach in writing this book is most of all informed by a multiplicity of methodologies and interests. This reflects, most of all, my long-standing participation in popular music studies, an interdisciplinary field where musicology, media studies, sociology, cultural studies, American studies, and numerous other areas meet and mingle freely. While I draw on many of these disciplines in my book, at its core this is a musicological study. I have therefore attempted throughout this book to address new wave along two folds. First, I have tried to sketch the music as a distinct historical formation, fleshing out the context through a variety of primary sources ranging from contemporary rock criticism magazines like *Trouser Press, Creem,* and *Melody Maker* to practicing musician magazines like *Keyboard* and *Musician.* Second, I have approached new wave through its most recognizable musical styles, as a subject worthy of close scrutiny and analysis, one whose musical details reveal illuminating elements about the movement as a whole.

This interest in new wave's musical stylistic dimensions stems not only from my training as a musicologist, but also from my background as a rock musician, having played in various bands, and in a variety of styles ranging from heavy metal to indie rock, from the 1980s through the early 2000s. Given this experience, I have a deep interest in performance practice and the means by which musicians approach their creative activities. One of my most driving curiosities in tackling the subject of new wave was to engage the question of *how* and *why* these musicians made the music that they did. How did their musical practices share similarities with, yet differ from, the prevailing trends of rock music-making that had become concretized by the end of the 1970s? How did they view their endeavors as part of, or separate from, a continuum of rock history? While one of this book's main goals is to illuminate the general social history and cultural formations under which the new wave arose at the turn of the 1980s as a "modern" style, my greatest hope is that dedicated new wave fans and curious initiates alike will be inspired to *listen* to this music. For it is the music itself—its rhythms, its arrangements, its tone, its often inventive songwriting strategies—that drew me to the topic of new wave in the first place. In the end, I am a subjective fan as much as an objective observer—one hopes—of this particular era of popular music history.

ONE

Tracking the Tide:
The New Wave Washes In and Out

The *Random House Unabridged Dictionary* defines a new wave as "a movement, trend, or vogue, as in art, literature, or politics, that breaks with traditional concepts, values, techniques, or the like."[1] There are numerous examples that fit this bill, ranging from the 1960s new wave of British theater and the influential early 1980s New Wave of British Heavy Metal to, of course, the music that serves as the subject of this very book. Regardless of how or where one encounters a "new wave," its signifying power traces back to the phrase's original etymology, that of the late 1950s French cinematic new wave.

In 1957, Françoise Giroud, the editor of the French cultural magazine *L'Express* coined the *nouvelle vague* (new wave) to describe a group of young filmmakers that she saw as poised on the edge of a cinematic revolution.[2] While the French directors who would become known as the core of the new wave—François Truffaut, Jean-Luc Godard, Eric Rohmer, and others—neither accepted nor promoted the label themselves, there nonetheless was a common cause that united their works. They were all critics, students of film, who had grown dissatisfied with the homogeneity and standardized division of labor typified by the era's major international studio productions.[3] Because movies at that time were bound to relatively conventional narrative practices, they believed filmmaking had failed to achieve its full potential as an art form. Only if directors were allowed the complete control and freedom of an *auteur*, they argued, could films approach the more fluid, rapid motion of poetic discourse and language. Truffaut's *The 400 Blows* (1959) and Godard's *Breathless* (1960) achieved international critical acclaim, and soon after *new wave* became a ubiquitous neologism. It has since been a label borrowed many times over to signify a collective group committed to realizing afresh the means of an artistic medium.

A concept like new wave, however, does not simply materialize out of thin air, and one can locate numerous historical and cultural precedents that anticipated the term's entrance into the language. One might point, for example, to the *Ars Nova* as an early example of a musical new wave. Originally a term found in the fourteenth-century writings and teachings of Philippe de Vitry and other French composers, Ars Nova was adopted by twentieth-century music historians to denote the institution of new music codifications in the 1320s and the subsequent flowering of French polyphony.[4] Granted this status, the Ars Nova has come to signify not only a movement, but, metonymically, an entire historical epoch. A new wave need not always be so large, though. It can also be a more ephemeral "trend" or "vogue." One might consider the fashion industry and its waves of rapid turnover as a cultural practice dictated by this type of new wave.[5] Newness, here, is written into the succession of competitive designs, such as Christian Dior's extravagant, controversial postwar *new look,* whose "huge, swirling skirts" and "cantilevered bust" revolutionized 1950s women's fashion before succumbing to the next stylish vogue.[6] While both these examples antedate the first known appearances of the term *new wave,* they share a theme central to the majority of its subsequent usages: a "new wave" serves as a shorthand for a pivotal turning point, and a progressive, modern change away from entrenched standards.

Throughout the 1960s, the new wave worked its way into all types of settings. It provided the title for a 1962 Dizzy Gillespie album and popped up again in the 1965 free jazz compilation *The New Wave in Jazz,* featuring the experimental works of John Coltrane, Archie Shepp, and others. In 1967 a singer-songwriter duo even released an album of conventional soft pop under the misleading moniker of the new wave. Over the years, the application of the new wave label has expanded far beyond these initial uses, drawing the new wave well outside the realm of the arts. A Google search for *new wave,* for example, returns over 55 million hits, many of them referring to high-tech businesses, such as New Wave Communications and New Wave Research, that draw on the label's cutting-edge connotations. Still other listings refer to innovative products such as New Wave Chess &

Checkers, a game board made unique by its lightweight insertable "3-D" player pieces. The game's creator, Paradoxy Products, was so smitten with its revolutionary design that they even placed the title "New Wave" under trademark. In every instance the use of a new wave sets apart the object as something fresh, exciting, and utterly modern.

Not all new waves come by their name as easily as the Chess & Checkers game, however, and in this chapter and the following one we will see precisely how convoluted a path the new wave label traveled as it wound its way through the music industry from the mid-1970s through the mid-1980s. Through this roughly decade-long period, a series of new waves would repeatedly rise and fall in brief two- to three-year chunks. Rock critic Greg Shaw, whom we will encounter again in chapter 5, often contended that rock's history could be broken down into precisely such a succession of short cycles, and in many respects new wave's repeated ebb and flow would seem to support his theory.[7] After new wave's initial appearance as part of the original mid-1970s British punk movement, the label was continually reinvented, and in some instances renamed, to designate a "new" flurry of musical activity. Whether it served as a rallying point or an object of derision, the new wave nearly always found itself at the center of some contested territory. And at each turn, its appearance raised the inevitable query: what does it mean to be "new"?

In order to address this question, I approach new wave as a cultural formation, one defined by an interaction of musical production, music industry practices, and critical reception. I look at how the nature of this formation changed over the course of new wave's history, which I divide into three main periods. This chapter deals with the first of these periods, specifically new wave's emergence in the middle and late 1970s. Chapter 2 turns to the second and third stages: the New Pop "second British Invasion" of the early and middle 1980s, and the rise of Modern Rock in the late 1980s and early 1990s, during which time new wave became a past historical genre. These three periods correspond with what cultural theorist Raymond Williams has referred to as "emergent," "dominant," and "residual" formations.[8] In its "emergent" phase, new wave was consistently identified as an up-and-coming modern genre, positioned against a rock and pop hegemony yet also considered as a potentially redefining new phase of this very same dominant formation. The second phase, that of the "new pop,"

was built off the ground that new wave had plowed, but also helped to popularize a new set of technologically oriented musical practices that soon became the definitive, "dominant" feature of the 1980s popular music landscape. By the mid-1990s these musical practices had receded from the
foreground, replaced by grunge and alternative's stripped-back guitar rock
textures. In this third and final phase, new wave became a "residual" style,
a reference to rock's past history, and this is where the music has remained
ever since.

To many, alternative rock's 1990s purging of the 1980s technopop
sound resembled a rebirth of the original punk rock's raw anger, which
nearly two decades earlier had similarly rectified in their eyes the accumulated wrongdoings of the 1970s popular music scene. Ironically enough, it
is with that same mid-1970s punk moment that new wave's story begins.

The New Wave Explosion

*New wave is the rock'n'roll of the '80s. What we are calling punk now, in the '80s we
will be looking back and saying that '80s music was invented in 1976.*

—Danny Fields, co-manager of the Ramones, speaking at a 1978 National
   Academy of Recording Arts and Sciences seminar on new wave[9]

To locate the exact first usages of the label *new wave* as part of the mid-1970s
punk explosion is a near impossible task. As early as 1973, music critics like
Nick Kent and Dave Marsh began applying the new wave tag to a variety of
New York groups who would prove influential to the punk explosion, most
notably the older 1960s avant-garde rock of the Velvet Underground and
the up-and-coming glam and glitter of the New York Dolls.[10] In 1975, toward the end of the Dolls' volatile and short-lived career, the band enlisted
Malcolm McLaren, the owner of a British fetish fashion store called SEX, to
act as its de facto manager. McLaren was with the group in the United
States for only a few short months, during which time he devised an elab-
orately subversive "outlaw image" for them and spoke excitedly of their future as "the new wave of rock'n'roll."[11] The band soon fell apart, however,
and McLaren returned to England to manage his shop, where his attention

soon turned to the formation of a new group that he would manage under the moniker of the Sex Pistols.

McLaren's experience with the New York Dolls would have a profound effect on his conception of the Sex Pistols. *Sounds* journalist Jonh Ingham recalls that in early 1976, before the Sex Pistols had even recorded a note, McLaren insisted that the music be called new wave.[12] The label held and by the fall of 1976 influential British punk fanzines such as *Sniffin' Glue,* as well as the major national weekly music papers *Sounds, NME* (*New Musical Express*), and *Melody Maker,* were constantly referring to a "new wave" centered on the activities of the Sex Pistols, the Clash, and other punk bands.[13] Back in the United States, one of the first punk-oriented magazines, *New York Rocker,* began using the new wave label as well with some regularity in late 1976, in reference to the cluster of New York bands and artists such as Television, Blondie, Patti Smith, and the Ramones that had gained a following in the downtown underground arts community through their performances at the club CBGB's.[14] While these New York groups would draw little outside attention over the next year, in England the punk and new wave labels rocketed into the headlines in early December, largely as a result of the Sex Pistols' infamous obscenity-laced interview with Bill Grundy on the Thames Television *Today* show. In the aftermath of this media scandal there seemed to be scarcely a household in England that had not witnessed punk's attack on the popular music landscape. The "new wave" was sweeping the country.

Given the tremendous impact that punk had both upon British society and the British recording industry in 1976 and 1977, it seems more reasonable to compare the British new wave, rather than the comparably slow-gestating American / New York movement, with the original French *nouvelle vague*. Indeed, the parallels between the two are manifold. Both were distinctly "youth" oriented. Both were politically charged. In the case of the French directors it was their goal to bring to the screen "the lived reality of the post-War citizen," to present to "the public an image of its identity" that the French national cinema had failed to capture.[15] The new wave directors moved their cameras out of the characterless controlled studio setting and instead developed their mise-en-scène in the natural, improvisatory environment of the street.[16] The British punks were similarly motivated toward a musical realism, exposing the impoverished, violent conditions of the dole queue that the upper classes would have preferred to keep hidden away. The names of punk bands and performers like the Sex Pistols and Sid Vicious rebelled against a popular music discourse that had traditionally self-censored themes of sexuality and violence behind sanitized language. Such music could only flourish at first outside the purview of the major labels, and like the French *nouvelle vague* directors before them, the punks developed a do-it-yourself, or "DIY," ethos built upon alternative channels of production, performance, and communication. Just as many of the *nouvelle vague* directors had financed their first films on minuscule budgets and found their voices writing as impassioned reviewers within the pages of the relatively young film journal *Cahiers du cinema*, British punk likewise emerged through independent labels like Stiff Records, and circulated its viewpoints through self-produced fanzines like *Sniffin' Glue, Bondage,* and *Sideburns.*

Neither *nouvelle vague* nor punk would have accrued such towering reputations, though, had they not eventually risen to financial success within the very industries that they both initially held in disdain. Only after Truffaut's *The 400 Blows* captured honors at the 1959 Cannes Film Festival, for example, and recouped its production budget many times over with the aid of substantial international distribution, did the stagnant French film industry realize the enormity of the new wave's potential. Conventional producers eager to revitalize their studios instantly sought out young directors with virtually any range of credentials. Likewise, only after British punk rock artists proved that they could push their songs into the Top 40 singles chart almost solely on the basis of grassroots fan support did the industry fully open up to punk. In the midst of a devastating national recession, British record companies saw punk as a potential answer to their troubling economic slump.

The impact of these two different new waves was so immediate and cataclysmic, however, that it was probably inevitable that they would each fall out of favor with both the critics and public as soon as their novelty had worn off. Just as suddenly as the *nouvelle vague* had created a sensation in 1959, during the next two years the movement's major directors failed to draw a large box office, and their brand of intellectually demanding cinema came under an "anti-new wave" attack.[17] It was no longer fashionable in

Figure 3. "New Wave R.I.P." October 1977. *Trouser Press* magazine laments the passing of the new wave of British punk. Portrait of Johnny Rotten by Robert Burger. Courtesy of *Trouser Press*, LLC.

France to be associated with the *nouvelle vague*. The backlash against punk emerged well before the music had begun to recede from the charts. In fact, much of it was aimed at the music's very success within the mainstream. In the United States, the Anglophile music magazine *Trouser Press* captured the increasingly bleak tenor of the times with an October 1977 cover article, which proclaimed "New Wave R.I.P." (see fig. 3).[18] The cover artwork, a portrait modeled on a notorious photo of Johnny Rotten assuming a Christlike crucifix pose, dramatically illustrated the fate that many believed had befallen the punk movement.

Surveying the events of the past year, *Trouser Press* editor Ira Robbins spread the blame for punk's failure to many quarters, but most of all to the apparent hypocrisy of a movement that espoused anarchy and revolution while chasing after the fame and fortune of major label success. Punks who had rejected groups like Pink Floyd as the establishment were now outperforming these very same acts on the charts.[19] Furthermore, the music's popularity had made a caricature out of punk's distinctive style and fashion, a point driven home by two accompanying photos in the article that showed mannequins in a Macy's department store clad in "punk rock rules" sweaters, complete with safety pins and chains. In bald terms, punk had "sold out." Or as sociologist Dick Hebdige would argue two years later in his 1979 analysis of the British punk scene, *Subculture: The Meaning of Style,* punk's shocking deviancy had been incorporated and "brought back into line" within the framework of the dominant culture.[20] As a commodity form, punk's codified meanings had become as stiff and "frozen" as the Macy's display window models.

For the major labels, however, the problem was hardly that punk had been commercialized, but rather that it was not selling enough. By late 1977 and early 1978, it was clear to the British major labels that the punk bands that they had signed in the wake of the Sex Pistols' media sensation would not amount to "the next big thing."[21] The industry was not about to be colonized by a new genre as it had been before in the wake of the Beatles' Mersey beat invasion nearly fifteen years earlier. The final blow came in mid-January of 1978 when the Sex Pistols, on tour in the United States, imploded and disbanded. The Sex Pistols' debut album, *Never Mind the Bollocks, Here's the Sex Pistols,* which had topped the British charts two months earlier in November, died on the vine in the United States, peaking at number 106 on the *Billboard* charts. While interest in punk would begin to wane in England, in the United States the music was a nonstarter, a style that was seen as virtually unmarketable. As Dave Laing writes in his study of the British punk movement, *One Chord Wonders,* punk had come to the end of its "heroic age."[22]

In the face of punk rock's demise, a splintering effect occurred, and the label of new wave began to drift away from its initial associations. In truth, hints of this split had been appearing in the rock press for some time. In November 1976 *Melody Maker* journalist Caroline Coon had argued that punk and new wave were *not* the same. New wave bands were, she claimed, less extreme than their "hardcore" counterparts in the punk scene. New wave was, for her, "an inclusive term used to describe a variety of bands like Eddie and the Hot Rods, the Stranglers, Chris Spedding and the Vibrators, the Suburban Studs, Slaughter and the Dogs, who are definitely not hardcore punk, but because they play with speed and energy or because they try hard, are part of the scene."[23] Throughout 1977 the new wave label continued to appear as a point of differentiation, distinguishing more melodic, pop-oriented groups like the Jam and the Stranglers from punk's increasingly politicized and violent realm.[24]

The decisive separation between new wave and punk would emerge most forcefully, however, in the United States through the efforts of Seymour Stein, president of Sire Records. Stein, who had signed such important New York punk bands as the Ramones, Talking Heads, Dead Boys, and Richard Hell and the Voidoids in 1976, had long chafed at the word *punk,* recognizing that its controversial connotations would impede attempts to market his roster to a broad American audience.[25] Finally, in October 1977, in promotion of their fall catalog of albums, Sire arrived at a new slogan: "Don't Call it Punk." This appeared in tandem with a promotional sampler issued under the title *New Wave Rock'n'Roll: Get Behind it Before it Gets Past You.* Additionally, Stein sent an open letter to FM radio programmers that made clear that *new wave* was now the preferred label: "One of the most significant trends in recent years has been 'new wave' rock, all-too-often wrongly referred to as punk rock. The term 'punk' is as offensive as 'race' and 'hillbilly' were when they were used to describe 'rhythm and blues' and 'country and western' music thirty years ago."[26] Stein was on a mission to rehabilitate the new wave and complete its divorce from punk.

Further splinters soon began to appear as well, especially in the British music weeklies, where the journalistic pressures of burying the old and unearthing new genres were particularly magnified. Throughout November and December 1977, *Sounds* magazine espoused the "New Musick" as an antidote to punk's stagnation. Writers like Jon Savage threw their loyalties behind the more overtly experimental and radical musical deconstructions of groups like Devo, Throbbing Gristle, Siouxsie and the Banshees, the Slits, and Wire. With their "harsh urban scrapings/controlled white noise/massively accented drumming," Savage saw these bands as a decisive "post-punk" maneuver that was moving well beyond punk's rather circumscribed garage rock roots.[27] The bands themselves were decidedly ambivalent toward punk, as the comments of guitarists Bruce Gilbert and Colin Newman of Wire reveal:

Gilbert: Punk was a confirmation for us of making music in a very simplified form, because of our technical inabilities.

Newman: From this point [late 1977] we already had an identity which was no longer "punk rock"; and so therefore the obvious things to do were to commit a series of heresies. To do things with the music which were not permitted in "punk rock," distort the song format, play with speed and chord shapes, and play with influences, particularly with those we weren't supposed to like and mash it all up into some kind of distorted stew.[28]

By juxtaposing the musical elements of rock, dub, funk, and electronics in discordant ways, groups like Wire sought to undermine "the idea of a direct line from social experience to musical form."[29] One of the most theoretical minded of the post-punk groups, the Gang of Four, even went so far as to suggest an analogy between their band's experiments and those of the original *nouvelle vague* directors, claiming that the jarring ambiguities in their musical textures and lyrics bore a similarity to Jean-Luc Godard's innovative use of split screen images.[30] As such, the post-punk movement brought a strong musical stylistic resemblance to bear on punk's relationship with the *nouvelle vague*.

By 1978 yet another splinter had materialized, this time populated by a second wave of punk bands such as Sham 69 and the Angelic Upstarts who had dedicated themselves to keeping alive the music's substance and sub-cultural rituals. These groups, which Laing categorizes as "Real Punk," shunted much of the sarcasm and outrageous behavior that had surfaced with the Sex Pistols, and instead embraced a distinct working-class street re-alism and politicized rhetoric.[31] To them, punk's turn toward a commercial new wave represented a traitorous betrayal of the music's idealistic values. At Sham 69 concerts, lead singer Jimmy Pursey would address the crowd, yelling, "We're not a New Wave band . . . we're a PUNK band."[32] The audi-ence had changed along with the music as well. Sham 69 and the other "real punk" bands attracted both a younger teenaged crowd (whom they referred to as the "kids"), as well as a sizable, and unwelcome, faction of racist skinheads. It was with "real punk," and the subsequent formation of Oi, that the music became irrevocably associated with youth, gangs, and vi-olent aggression. Within this new hardcore punk order, there was little space for a redefined new wave.

The three main splinters that had appeared in the wake of punk's col-lapse at the dawn of 1978—new wave, new musick (or post-punk, as it would soon be called), and real punk—would all continue to grow and prosper well into the 1980s. But of these three only new wave would take hold as a viable commercial entity. In the next section we cross the Atlantic and join new wave in 1978, the point at which the emergent genre would begin to assume a coherent identity as part of the American music industry, largely through its assimilation into radio programming. The discussion will focus on the Cars, the first new wave group to find success on both the *Billboard* Top 40 singles chart and AOR (album-oriented rock) radio rotations.

The "New" New Wave: The Modern Sound of AOR

On January 14, 1978, the very date that the Sex Pistols' American tour and short-lived career finally collapsed following their disastrous performance at the Winterland in San Francisco, *Billboard* magazine presented its first full-blown coverage of the punk / new wave movement with a twenty-page "spotlight" feature entitled "The New Wave Coming of Age."[33] On the face of it, this coincidence would seem to be dripping with irony. Just as the American music industry had belatedly awakened to the new wave's potential, the movement was losing its most recognizable, and presumably bankable, commodity. Reading through the *Billboard* feature, however, one is struck by the number of artists *other* than the Sex Pistols that are prominently featured, as well as the deep inroads that had already been forged to establish new wave as an emergent cultural formation within the industry. As the magazine's regular contributing punk and new wave reporter Roman Kozak observed, nearly every major record company had already signed at least one new wave band, and lying in wait was a vast expanse of well-stocked independent labels that essentially could serve as a new wave farm system. Typical of such *Billboard* features, the magazine also surveyed radio, record distributors, and key retailers whose testimonials served as evidence of the new wave's vitality. The movement's main industry torchbearer, Seymour Stein, also weighed in, specifically to debunk the negativity and myths that had accrued around the music and to ensure readers that "new wave is not, as many seem to think, equivalent to 'punk rock.'"[34] Rather, new wave was by his estimation an industry-changing movement whose impact would approach and perhaps equal that of 1950s rock and roll and the 1960s British Invasion. Most of all, the *Billboard* feature made clear that new wave had a solid infrastructure in place, and thus its chances of success were virtually guaranteed.

Over the first half of 1978 new wave artists did indeed begin to garner more airplay and shift more units, but it was hardly the breakthrough that the music's supporters had been anticipating. Elvis Costello had placed his first two albums in the Top 40, and Patti Smith's *Easter* had made the Top 20 largely on the strength of her Bruce Springsteen–penned single "Because the Night." Blondie had broken into the Top 100, and the Ramones were stalled just on the outskirts. But outside of these meager advances there was little indication that new wave would threaten the chart positions of such soft rock artists as Pablo Cruise or Barry Manilow. In August, however, there was a hint that the new wave's fortunes might be changing. The Cars' debut single, "Just What I Needed," became the first song specifically marketed as new wave to crack the Top 40 singles chart, a rare feat for a genre whose most serious inroads had thus far been on the AOR radio format. The album produced a further Top 40 single with "My Best Friend's Girl" and would eventually go on to achieve multiple platinum sales, providing proof that a new wave group could successfully navigate the mainstream.

As Joey Ramone would later comment, "After The Cars broke, people were saying, 'Well, new wave, this is all right.'"[35]

From the very beginning, early reviews of the Cars routinely painted them as a band balanced on both the avant-garde and traditional sides of rock, a description that would become common for those new wave bands that began to fill the charts. As *Creem* opined in its typical irreverent fashion, the Cars' debut was "at once both *tres outre* and rootie kazootie accessible."[36] In other words, as modern as "Just What I Needed" sounded, it would not have succeeded had it not been able to mingle freely with the typical AOR fare of the day. As with most emergent formations, new wave's presence was defined vis-à-vis the dominant formation, represented most visibly by the powerful AOR format. By the late 1970s AOR had become the most prominent venue for rock bands on FM radio. The format had emerged out of the legacy of "progressive" or "free form" FM stations that had revolutionized the industry in the late 1960s when renegade disc jockeys broke away from the strictures of the Top 40 singles playlist and instead began to play lengthy album cuts that better reflected the experimental ethos of the new rock counterculture. It was inevitable, however, that such a radical format would eventually be tamed, and for many it was hard not to see the resultant AOR format as a compromise. While the "album oriented" designation was a clear link to the progressive days, many AOR stations were also beholden to playlist conformities that mimicked some of the worst tendencies of Top 40 radio. Rock critics saw the subsequent rise of pop-conscious AOR favorites like Foreigner, Journey, and Boston as a bleak omen of the times, and demonized them in the press as examples of soulless, formulated "corporate rock." Negative *Rolling Stone* reviews notwithstanding, the same fans that were listening to these groups were purchasing the Cars' debut as well, which suggests that for all the obvious differences between AOR and new wave, the line separating the two was in truth rather thin.

In one of the few scholarly essays that deals with new wave, music theorist and rock historian John Covach has acknowledged this gray area between AOR and new wave, specifically by comparing Foreigner with the Cars.[37] Placed side by side, the initial similarities between the two actually are quite striking. The basic instrumentation of each group—lead and rhythm guitar, keyboards, drums, and bass—is identical, as are the presence of guitar and synthesizer solos, thick vocal harmonies, and composite song forms. Both groups, while new to the late 1970s rock scene, were comprised primarily of journeymen rock musicians who had been in various other bands since the early 1970s. The two groups even toured together in 1978, with the Cars opening for Foreigner. By 1979 they were also both using the same producer, Roy Thomas Baker. Furthermore, should there be any doubts that the Cars' record label, Elektra, was aiming the new wave band at a young male AOR audience, one need only glance at the tacky, sexualized cover of their debut album, a tight close-up shot of a glamorous, heavily lipsticked model that was foisted upon the band against its wishes and gave little hint at their underlying modern identity.

As musicologist Charles Kronengold has noted, both AOR and new wave were "impure" genres, mongrel entities that emerged out of a pronounced stylistic pluralism.[38] Covach takes up this line of reasoning as well in his comparison of Foreigner and the Cars, but mainly to demonstrate that the key differences between AOR and new wave resided in their musical frames of reference. Analyzing Foreigner's first single from 1977, "Feels Like the First Time," Covach locates the band's main influences in bluesy hard rock (which comes across in the song's distorted guitar tones and singer Lou Gramm's bends and ornamentation) and progressive rock (which can be heard in the arpeggiated synthesizer and chaconne-like bass pattern that dominates the song's first bridge). Given that Foreigner guitarist Mick Jones had logged time in the early 1970s with British blues rockers Spooky Tooth and that guitarist-keyboardist Ian MacDonald had been with the progressive outfit King Crimson, such a lineage makes sense. Covach's main point is that AOR bands viewed their music as a teleological development and evolution out of their direct predecessors. Bands like Foreigner had simply distilled the hard edge and virtuosic complexity of the early 1970s into song forms and arrangements that were more immediately palatable to the FM radio formatting of the late 1970s.

If Foreigner's sound clearly drew from the 1970s, Covach sees the Cars as rooted more in a grab bag of pre-1967 rock styles that ranged from late 1950s hand claps and rockabilly guitar lines to the cheap combo organ sound of mid-1960s garage bands, a slew of references that emerged most fully on "My Best Friend's Girl." As Covach argues, for groups like the Cars these references to earlier styles were significant precisely for what they were *not*. They allowed a way out of and around the posthippie rock conventions that had taken hold in the 1970s, which most new wave bands viewed with an unwavering suspicion. Rather than assuming their place in an uninterrupted rock lineage, the Cars deployed rock's distant past in order to escape the hegemonic rock styles of the present. As important as such maneuvers were to the Cars, however, they did not serve to obliterate the 1970s from the group's sound. Instead, as the band members duly noted in their interviews, they were simply engaging a *different* 1970s lineage, one that stretched back to the simplicity of punk, the detached minimalist art rock of Roxy Music, and the electronic synthesizer textures of experimental German groups like Kraftwerk. At the same time that the Cars were looking backward to an earlier classic period, they were also exploring a side of the 1970s that had not yet found its way into AOR radio.

The significance of these stylistic differences surfaced most of all as a contrast in tone and emotional articulation. Where Foreigner's roots in the blues and hard rock steered the group toward an authentic realism, the Cars' background led to a lyrical and vocal palette that was laced with ambiguity and a dispassionate uncertainty. Consider, for example, the chasm separating Foreigner's 1978 summer hit "Hot Blooded" from "Just What I Needed." The former is a chugging riff rocker, an unrestrained celebration of singer Lou Gramm's heroic, unquenchable lust. Slurring and bending his notes throughout with a soulful, gravelly tone, Gramm leaves no blues cliché untouched, addressing his sexual advances to a "baby," "honey," "girl," "mama," and "child." The extended "improvisatory" fadeout call-and-response chorus throws Gramm's salacious asides fully into the spotlight.

Like "Hot Blooded," "Just What I Needed" is, at its core, a song about the singer's desires. But where Gramm's exhortations amplify the male libido to its breaking point, vocalist Ben Orr of the Cars maintains an aloof stance that views a relationship simply as something *to do*. Eschewing any hint of the blues, Orr delivers the lyrics as a deliberately paced, spoken melody, a distanced approach that underscores the ambivalence of a line like "I don't mind you coming here and wasting all my time." By depicting romance through an air of detachment rather than insatiable physical attraction, "Just What I Needed" borders on the cynical, highlighting the conflict that many new wave musicians felt in dealing with rock's well-worn tropes of sex and love. This lyrical tension and ambiguity is deftly mirrored in the song's harmonic construction as well. Each verse is based on a repetitive four-chord cycle that begins with a tonic–dominant statement in E major, but then shifts directly to the tonic–dominant in the relative key of C♯ minor, refusing to commit to either fully. The turn to the chorus appears at first as if it is securely in E major, but its phrases cadence on the C♯ minor chord, a gesture that further emphasizes the song's harmonic ambivalence.[39] By the third verse, the drummer has even joined in as well, as he periodically flips the backbeat onto beats 1 and 3, a final complementary nod to the song's lyrical air of hesitancy and confusion.

As crucial as such lyrical, harmonic, and rhythmic ambiguities were to establishing "Just What I Needed" as a modern new wave song, an even more important, if less commented upon, element resided in the band's stripped-back overall sound. On first glance, to consider the Cars in these terms would seem laughable. Listening to the stack of seventy-eight vocal tracks that blare out the title of "Good Times Roll," for example, one easily hears the similarities between the Cars and other 1978 AOR favorites like Boston and Van Halen, who liberally peppered their recordings with comparably thick vocal arrangements. Roy Thomas Baker, who had risen to fame with his work on Queen's "Bohemian Rhapsody," was particularly well known for his powerful ornate vocal productions. But as he explained in a 1982 interview with *Trouser Press* magazine, with the Cars he sought to emphasize the space in between these vocal flourishes: "The thing that was appropriate for The Cars, and not at the time appropriate for those other bands, was a thing called *air*. Staccato notes with air in between them."[40] This extended beyond the vocals and into the overall instrumentation. One hears this most of all in the introduction to "Just What I Needed," where the rhythm guitar stands alone, picking out a clean, crisp eighth-note line that soon pervades the entire texture of the song. By allowing the music to breathe, so to speak, Baker's production accentuated the group's distinctive rhythmic emphasis, which placed the rhythm guitar and drums in the foreground, while using riffs more as coloring than foundational elements.[41] This approach would soon proliferate throughout the new wave.

As with the Cars' other modern elements, the significance of the "air" to their overall aesthetic is best understood within the context of 1970s popular music as a reaction to the prevailing trends of the time. To listen to popular mainstream acts of the mid-1970s, such as Steely Dan, Fleetwood

Mac, or the Eagles, was to encounter a dry, clinical sound that was almost completely devoid of any breathing room. Partly this production standard had evolved as a matter of necessity. As the spacious recording studios of the 1960s gradually disappeared over the course of the 1970s, they gave way to smaller, more economical studios, with "drum booths the size of a toilet," that lacked the resonance of their predecessors.[42] While these new spaces were, by comparison, "dead," they also allowed producers to more easily isolate instrumental sounds and separate them into thick, overflowing layers within the new twenty-four-track and forty-eight-track mixing boards. In setups such as these, producers purposefully placed close microphones to the instruments, shutting out the ambient room sound in the studio, and effectively giving "the impression that there was a rug over everything."[43] Many new wave producers like Richard Gotterher, who worked with Blondie, the Go-Go's, and Marshall Crenshaw among others, revolted against the dullness of the dead studios by seeking out alternative spaces and pursuing a more "natural" live sound. Whether it was through their efforts or Baker's introduction of space and air back into the mix, new wave's novel, energetic timbral quality would eventually emerge as the standard for the late 1970s modern rock sound.

There is one final aspect of the Cars that deserves comment and that is their image. Dressed in slimmed, angular clothing—with a predominantly red, black, and white color scheme—their attire mirrored the stripped-back demeanor of their music. As with their musical referents, their fashion was most important for what it was not. No denim, no bell-bottoms, no ornately patterned Hawaiian shirts, no sports jerseys. Instead, they appeared in photos and on stage in complementary solid colors accented with lines, dots, and stripes. The architect of the group's look, drummer David Robinson, credited their coordinated colors most of all to serendipity ("Everybody had a lot of black and white clothes").[44] But intentionally or not, the group had arrived at a fashion design that tapped into a wealth of associations. On the one hand, the colors red and black evoked an array of avant-garde artistic movements, from the solid metallic, industrial reds and blacks favored by 1970s minimalist artists like Donald Judd and Tony Smith to the angular red and black designs of the 1920s Russian Constructivists, whom Kraftwerk parodied on the cover of their 1978 album *The Man Machine*.[45] On the other hand, the dark reds and blacks and geometric forms

Figure 4. The Cars, standing abstract in red, black, and white. Ben Orr, Greg Hawkes, Ric Ocasek, Elliot Easton, and David Robinson (*L–R*), photographed in Memphis, Tennessee, in 1979. © Ebet Roberts.

of their clothes had an even more general resonance, easily suggestive of the very hues and shapes of the modern urban city, with its endless succession of brick buildings and dark skyscrapers. Whatever its particular resonance, the red and black color scheme would come to define the new wave over the next two years. From the Romantics' matching red suits and Devo's red flower pot hats to Gary Numan's black and red belted jumpsuit and Chrissie Hynde's red leather jacket, seemingly everywhere one turned in 1980 new wave album covers were saturated in red and black fashion. It had become a de rigeur component of new wave style.

In late 1978, however, such visions of a stylistic hegemony still seemed rather distant. With the exception of the Talking Heads' "Take Me to the River," no new wave songs had followed the momentum of the Cars into the Top 40 chart. To many within the new wave scene, the music's failure to win over a larger audience, and specifically to crack radio playlists, represented a bleak moment of crisis. As Alan Betrock noted in a September

New York Rocker panel devoted to the future of the new wave, all of the movement's most staunch supporters had "backed off" their original prediction that the new wave would become the "next big thing."[46] Not everyone viewed new wave's fate in such a dismal light, however. Despite the sluggish sales, 1978 had indeed seen an unprecedented steady stream of highly regarded new wave albums. In the year-end *Village Voice* Pazz & Jop poll, new wave artists had captured nearly two-thirds of the magazine's celebrated Top Thirty Albums list, prompting the magazine's music editor, Robert Christgau, to herald 1978 as the "Triumph of the New Wave."[47] There was no doubt that new wave had won over the rock press. Over the next two years the emergent genre would grab the attention of a larger rock audience as well.

New Wave in America, 1979 to 1981: The First Rise and Fall

While anyone looking at either *Billboard*'s singles or album charts needed to squint to spot a new wave artist in 1979, for those who were paying attention to such things, the few that *had* made an impact offered signs that the genre's fortunes were on the rise. Elvis Costello's third album, *Armed Forces*, was in the Top 10, as was Blondie's third album, *Parallel Lines*. Two new British artists, the Police and Joe Jackson, had also cracked the Top 40 singles chart, and better yet had also each placed two separate releases in the Top 40 albums chart. Two albums in particular, the Cars' *Candy-O* and the multiplatinum debut from Los Angeles power pop quartet the Knack, had sold remarkably well and had swept *Billboard*'s end-of-the-year "Reader's Rock Polls."

In many respects, the increase in new wave sales during 1979 was simply a case of a slow-building genre with deep roots that was beginning to gain more momentum. At the same time, new wave's heightened presence must also be understood within the more complicated context of a desperate American music industry that was facing its worst financial crisis in decades. To a large extent the troubles befalling the industry were symptomatic of a larger national recession, compounded by the oil crisis and skyrocketing gasoline prices. In such a climate CBS Records president Walter Yetnikoff may have exaggerated only slightly when complaining, "Our customers literally ran out of money."[48] An industry accustomed to yearly upward profits was sent reeling, and, faced with a sea of abnormally large overstock returns and sharply declining sales, the major record labels panicked. Companies began to lay off employees at an alarming rate. In August, *BusinessWeek* reported that the music industry had cut one thousand employees in a workforce of only fourteen thousand.[49] Five months later *Rolling Stone* estimated that the number had increased to two thousand.[50] The result was a bloodletting that had decimated a significant portion of the industry's workforce. The year ended in what R. Serge Denisoff has called "The Great Depression of '79."[51]

Many in the industry were quick to point their fingers in blame, and inevitably they were directed at disco. The year 1978 had been a banner year, largely thanks to the *Saturday Night Fever* soundtrack's unprecedented sales and the rise of disco dancing as a mainstream pop culture phenomenon. The industry had gotten drunk on the genre, however, as labels expanded their disco department staffing and pursued new artists with reckless abandon. Throughout the first half of 1979 disco continued to dominate the singles charts thanks to radio programming and the club scene, but a glance at the more highly prized album charts, where disco's profile was comparatively modest, told a different story. Disco, which was more a producer-oriented than artist-oriented style, and which thrived on extended remixes and twelve-inch singles rather than albums, was having difficulty prospering within the industry's standard rock-driven marketing model. *Billboard* bemoaned the relative anonymity of the music and the movement's "dearth of superstars."[52] The problems, however, extended beyond just disco. Even the proven superstar rock acts that the labels rushed for a fall release, hoping that they would help offset disco's lost potential revenue, managed relatively disappointing returns. As Fleetwood Mac's *Tusk* and Led Zeppelin's *In Through the Out Door* fell far short of the bands' previous triumphant sales, it appeared that the recession was resistant to any convenient remedies.

In such an atmosphere, labels were understandably anxious to resuscitate their failing health. Even though members of the industry looked upon disco's failure with disillusioned eyes, they still held out hope that they could harness the music's selling power in some way. Most of all they were looking for some magical genre that could fuse disco's formula of "high rates of turnover and low production costs" with the consistently high sales that the top rock albums provided.[53] New wave appeared to fit this bill in many different ways. For one, the music had already assimilated some of disco's familiar turf, specifically through the spectacular boom in urban clubs known as rock discos. The first of these, the former New York City discotheque Hurrah, switched over to playing predominantly rock music in May 1978 and flourished as a space where disc jockeys could spin new wave records for a dance audience, and where bands could also occasionally play live.[54] The concept soon spread, and by the summer of 1979 New York alone boasted at least seven similar clubs.[55] Undoubtedly the rock disco helped in breaking the year's first new wave / disco crossover hit, Blondie's chart-topping smash "Heart of Glass," and there would be many more such success stories to follow as rock discos began to spread to nearly every metropolitan center throughout North America.[56] Even more importantly, the major labels noticed that new wave was incredibly cheap to produce. At a time when the average rock album cost anywhere between $70,000 and $100,000 of studio time and blockbuster productions like Fleetwood Mac's *Tusk* and the Eagles' *The Long Run* could run well over $500,000, a new wave group on an independent label could record an album for $2,000 to $4,000.[57] The Police's 1977 debut single, "Fall Out," had only cost the band $300.[58] Such numbers were hard for industry representatives to ignore.

The band that finally realized the major labels' wide-eyed dreams was the Knack, a Los Angeles guitar rock quartet decked out in British Invasion era Beatles suits, whose danceable debut *Get the Knack* would spend five weeks at the top of the album charts. I will look at the Knack in more detail in chapter 5, specifically at how their nostalgia for mid-1960s power pop played a significant role in defining a new wave musical style, but for now it is the narrative of their rise to success that is most relevant to the present discussion. The Knack's rapid ascent from Los Angeles club act to rock star sensations provided a model that many bands and record labels alike hoped to replicate. The group had first generated interest by playing to increasingly large crowds in Los Angeles, which essentially acted as showcase performances. With evidence of a proven audience, the Knack became the subject of an intense bidding war, one that saw Capitol Records pay the band what was at that time the largest signing sum in the label's history.[59] Most importantly, the group took just eleven days to record their album, for a total of $18,000, which allowed the label to shift more of its budget and focus to promotion. Upon its release, the album met with immediate success, reaching gold status (500,000 sales) in just two weeks. Likewise, the lead single, "My Sharona," became the fastest U.S. debut single to achieve gold sales since the Beatles' "I Want to Hold Your Hand" fifteen years earlier.[60] Equally successful on AOR and Top 40 radio, the Knack seemed to be a model for the type of rock artists who could penetrate the pop market that the major labels hoped to cultivate.

It is impossible to understate the significance of *Get the Knack*. In many ways it proved to be as important to the new wave as *Saturday Night Fever* was to disco, inasmuch as its overwhelming success validated the genre in the industry's eyes and sent the major labels on a massive signing frenzy in search of comparable talent. Well aware of the post–*Saturday Night Fever* fate that had befallen disco, Ray Caviano, head of Warner Brothers' dance music division, noted with a tinge of ominous foreshadowing the labels' shift in attention and resources toward the new wave: "Anybody who walks in with a skinny tie seems to get a contract right now . . . a year ago it was anybody with a whistle and a tambourine."[61] Word travels fast among musicians in such a climate, and a whole underclass of amateur and semiprofessional hopefuls had soon made the switch to new wave. As Will Birch of British power pop band the Records noted while on tour in the United States in support of the AOR single "Starry Eyes," the Knack's influence had permeated the Los Angeles scene with awkward results:

> We had a few days off in LA and went clubbing 'round. Every bar we went into we saw bands with three guitars and drums, three minute songs, Beatle haircuts, the whole bit, doin' pop. Most of 'em were appalling. They were all good musicians—the drummers were always great—but it was almost as if they were all session musicians who couldn't get gigs, telling the bands, "I'll get the haircut but I keep my Octa-plus drumkit." So you get these older guys with dyed hair and huge drum kits doing these flashy licks, hoping some record company will discover 'em as "their" pop group. You can look good and have the hype, but it's down to the song. Most of 'em don't have 'em, and they'll fall by the wayside.[62]

Birch's estimate of the situation would prove to be prophetic, but in late 1979 and 1980, the music industry was too enthralled with new wave's potential to notice. In the wake of the Knack's success, *Billboard* issued numerous optimistic announcements that signaled new wave's breakthrough into a larger marketplace. The most impressive of these was a cover feature announcing that "New Wave Rock [was] Catching Hold All Over [the] U.S.," which consisted primarily of quotes from a nationwide survey of AOR program and music directors who had begun adding a handful of new wave artists into their stations' rotations.[63] Unsurprisingly the most positive reactions to new wave programming resided on the coasts and in liberal college cities like Austin, Texas, while many midwestern and southern stations reported less enthusiastic responses. Most stations were easing (sometimes reluctantly) new wave artists into their rotations, but some, such as KROQ Los Angeles and WPIX New York, were now devoting roughly half their programming to the new genre. Other AOR stations relegated their new wave programming largely to late-night shows, with appropriate titles such as KSJO San Jose's *Modern Humans* or KZEW Dallas's *Rock and Roll Alternative* that indicated the genre's progressive status.

New wave's infiltration into AOR programming was complemented by its expanded coverage in the rock press, and not just in small-scale East Coast publications such as *New York Rocker* and *Trouser Press* that had been linked with the music ever since punk's emergence in 1976 and 1977. Nonpartisan rock gossip and pop culture magazines like *Circus* and *Hit Parader* began to place new wave artists on their covers, as did the more estimable *Rolling Stone.* Detroit-based *Creem,* which had been feeding readers with a steady diet of hometown heroes Bob Seger and Ted Nugent and other hard rockers for much of 1978, gradually devoted more and more of its space to the new wave, to the point where over half of the magazine's 1980 covers featured new wave artists. *Creem* readers responded to the magazine's mixed genre allegiances in kind, flooding their mailbox with both anti-new wave and pro-new wave letters that soon spiraled into a virulent debate over the merits of the Clash and its fans on one side and Led Zeppelin and its fans on the other. Even a publication like the solidly Deadhead-oriented *Relix* was not immune to the new wave's influence. Faced with plummeting sales, the magazine turned to a new editor, who placed Blondie's Debbie

Harry on the cover and began to feature new wave articles with increasing regularity. The magazine's fortunes took a turn for the better.

As with disco before it, perhaps the strongest indicator of new wave's passage into the mainstream was the large number of high profile *non*-new wave artists who began releasing new wave-inspired albums. Just as the disco craze of 1978 had precipitated such 1979 disco-fied rock crossover novelty singles as Rod Stewart's "Do Ya Think I'm Sexy" and Kiss's "I Was Made For Lovin' You," so the 1979 emergence of new wave would attract in 1980 such wandering pastiche stylists as Billy Joel (*Glass Houses*), Linda Ronstadt (*Mad Love*), and Robert Palmer (*Clues*). Unsurprisingly, Joel and Ronstadt, both of whom were in their early thirties, claimed to be less intrigued by the new wave's modernness or sense of difference than by its reenactment of an energetic rock and roll spirit that was deeply embedded in their own personal and artistic histories. In particular, Joel's hit single "It's Still Rock'n'Roll to Me" amounted to an adamant defense of his intentions. As he explained to *Rolling Stone* magazine, there was nothing *new* about the new wave:

> New wave songs, it seems, can only be about two and a half minutes long. . . . The sound has to be limited to what you can hear in a garage. A return to that sound is all that's going on now, so don't give me any of this New Wave—using a Farfisa organ because it's so hip. . . . I grew up on jukebox music, and everybody in the band has played this music all their lives.[64]

Others, like seasoned art rockers Peter Gabriel and Pete Townshend, were less sheepish or defensive about their admiration for the new music and their solo albums (Gabriel's third eponymous album, *Peter Gabriel*, and Townshend's *Empty Glass*) willfully embraced the movement's more progressive and experimental tendencies. Likewise, veteran British groups like King Crimson and Yes overhauled their sound, exploring the meeting ground between progressive rock's virtuosic complexities and new wave's layered minimalist textures and synthesized tones. King Crimson's new front man, Adrian Belew, had spent time recording and touring with the Talking Heads, while Yes replaced departed vocalist Jon Anderson and keyboardist Rick Wakeman with Trevor Horn and Geoffrey Downes of the Buggles.

By the close of 1980, the emergent new wave formation had become seamlessly integrated with the dominant rock formation. *Creem* magazine acknowledged as much when it dispensed with the separate new wave categories in their year's end reader's poll with the justification that the music had finally assimilated itself into the mainstream. As had happened with punk, however, new wave's newfound popularity brought to the fore familiar concerns over the music's incorporation. These debates surfaced in the critical reception surrounding the August 1980 Heatwave festival held in Toronto, a one-day event that brought together such notables as the B-52's, Pretenders, Talking Heads, and Elvis Costello & the Attractions for an estimated 50,000 fans. Reporting for *NME*, Richard Grabel questioned the logic of moving what was a club-based music out into the fields. A new wave rock festival was "a contradiction in terms," and a sign that the rock industry was "a big-bellied whale, capable of swallowing anything."[65] James Henke of *Rolling Stone* likewise structured his entire review around the haunting question of whether or not the new wave had sold out and compromised its original ideals.[66] Could the very event that seemingly legitimized the new wave also be the one that symbolized its death? In the end, these questions of co-optation proved to be moot. While both critics agreed that compelling sets, especially from the Talking Heads and Elvis Costello, had made the Heatwave festival a creative and artistic success, from a financial standpoint it was a disaster. With ticket prices ranging from twenty to thirty dollars, the organizers had hoped to draw double the number of fans that ultimately paid their way for the event. The Heatwave festival ended with substantial losses that guaranteed it would be the first and last such mass new wave gathering.

Heatwave's failure to match its advance billing as the new wave "Woodstock of the Eighties" was not lost on the industry. While rock critics were wringing their hands over the genre's dance with the big-business devil, the major labels were noticing that the majority of bands that they had signed in their post-Knack moment of infatuation were managing only modest returns on their investments and in many cases were complete stiffs. Worst of all, the Knack itself, like the bands that were intended to follow in its footsteps, was faltering badly. The band's second release, *. . . But the Little Girls Understand,* had run drastically over budget (reportedly reaching in excess of $500,000), negating the expectations of a cheap overhead that their first release had promised.[67] To make matters worse, the album peaked at only number fifteen on the charts, while its lead single, "Baby Talks Dirty," barely scraped into the Top 40. By the time of its third album for Capitol in 1981, the Knack was essentially a nonentity reduced to playing half-filled clubs rather than the coliseums it had packed on their first tour.

As the Knack fizzled, the image of the British Invasion skinny tie became a new wave albatross, a representation both of the movement's most heavily corporatized musical act and the legion of copycat "poseur" bands who had planned to cash in on its success. *Skinny tie* had become a derisory term, a modern fashion accessory as damning as John Travolta's white leisure suit and choreographed dance routines had been to disco's credibility. As with punk and as with disco, new wave had died a double death, one attributed to selling out and becoming a fad, and another ironically from its inability to gain a secure commercial foothold.

Two years after proclaiming the genre's breakthrough into radio, *Billboard*'s September 1981 headline, "AOR Cuts New Wave Shows," signaled the industry's waning interest in the music.[68] AOR directors were starting to curtail their new wave programming because they were fearful of how the new genre would blend with their established formats and audiences. The perception of new wave was that it was music favored by an audience primarily in their teens and early twenties. For AOR stations such audiences were suspect because they failed to match the purchasing power of the "plum over-25" demographic.[69] Reliant upon advertising sponsorship, AOR stations could ill afford to disturb the cash flow that they believed a more established "classic rock" style promised. *Billboard* summarized the programmers' decision to cut back on new wave in brutally honest terms, naming "apathy on the part of the listeners, the desire not to be associated with the music because of the risk of listener tuneout and the willingness to let noncommercial college stations program [new wave.]"[70] College radio would indeed pick up much of the new wave programming that AOR dropped and in a few short years would prove to be a major influence on the recording industry, but in 1981 it was still largely viewed as a noncommercial ghetto.[71] By banishing new wave to the college radio ranks, most in the industry concurred that the music had run its course as a marketable genre.

R. Serge Denisoff has characterized new wave's "invasion" of the American music industry as an unfortunate "Bay of Pigs," and based on *Billboard* reports and chart action, it is easy to see why.[72] The labels had lunged for new wave in 1979 in the midst of an economic collapse, but the passage of two years had failed to alleviate the industry's financial ailments. Label executives laid the blame on numerous sources, from home taping to the intrusion of new formats such as video games and movie rentals that were stealing away the audience's leisure time and money.[73] Whether the effect of these demons on the industry was real or imagined, they nonetheless reflected a discouraging situation. Within this paranoid industry climate, new wave bands with shaky sales histories were viewed as expendable.

At the same time, there is a danger in charting the course of a genre such as new wave through its depiction in the weekly music industry papers. To be sure, this reception reflects a certain reality, but it is a narrow one. Looking beyond the dim assessments of AOR programmers and jaded industry insiders, one could easily find evidence to the contrary in 1981 and 1982 that new wave was a sustainable, growing movement. New wave's most successful acts—groups like the Cars, the Police, the Talking Heads, and newcomers the Go-Go's—had established themselves among the upper echelon of critically acclaimed and top-selling rock artists. Additionally, the occasional new wave novelty, such as Toni Basil's "Mickey" or Trio's "Da Da Da," still found its way into the Top 40 rotation. A number of important independent new wave labels had emerged, such as I.R.S., Slash, and 415—all of which by 1982 had signed distribution deals with major labels—and Ian Copeland's Frontier Booking International had formed a national circuit of new wave–friendly clubs in which these artists could perform. Even if the music had not transformed AOR and conquered the charts, there was still a tremendous amount of energy emanating from the new wave.

The continuing interest in the new wave was especially evident with the launching of the New Music Seminar in 1980, an event that explored through a series of panels the means and measures of evaluating, producing, marketing, and selling progressive, modern music to an indifferent industry. By its second year, the Seminar had expanded nearly threefold, and it would soon become a requisite professional meeting ground for industry representatives as well as a coveted showcase opportunity for up-and-coming artists. The New Music Seminar would stand as one of the new wave's strongest legacies until its folding in the mid-1990s, but ironically one of its

most significant contributions was the shift in nomenclature that it encouraged away from new wave to that of new music. As a genre label, new
music differed only slightly from new wave, and any fan of the bands gathered underneath their respective wings would have readily noticed that
they were referring to essentially the same thing. But for an industry still
smarting from a post-Knack fallout, it was prudent to create some distance
from new wave's troubled past.

As we will see in the next chapter, in the early 1980s many "new" vari-
ants would come to compete with the new wave as descriptors for the modern pop music of the time. More than just simple name changes, these
shifts in labeling would reflect a new expanded range of styles. Most
significantly, these newest of the new waves would finally come to dominate the Top 40 realm that had generally proven so elusive to the first new
wave. As a result, new wave would be transformed from an emergent cultural formation into a dominant one.

TWO

The Second British Invasion and Its Aftermath: From New Pop to Modern Rock

Ever since the new wave label had been thrust upon radio programmers, record retailers, and consumers via Seymour Stein's aggressive marketing campaign for Sire Records in the late 1970s, the genre had been intimately intertwined with the machinery of the American music industry. In England, however, new wave's presence was much more fleeting. The genre label did not enjoy the same industry cachet as it did in the United States. There are many reasons why new wave assumed a different shape in the United States than it did in England. For one, new wave's relationship to punk was much more in the foreground in England than in the United States. British punk had infiltrated the British pop charts and been a topic of seemingly endless scandal in the mainstream press in 1977; the new wave that survived its collapse was thus doomed to exist in the shadow of the Sex Pistols and their ilk. Punk in the United States, however, had always been a more vague threat, one that the major labels had assiduously avoided, and one that rarely if ever penetrated the news headlines. While most knowledgeable American new wave fans knew of the music's connection to punk, successful groups like the Cars, the Knack, and the Police, whom Joey Ramone drolly dubbed "middle-of-the-road" new wave, introduced the genre to a general audience for whom punk meant very little.[1] New wave was thus allowed to circulate as a genre on its own separate accord.

The difference between new wave in the United States and England also stems from the very different roles that radio and the music press play in the two countries. As we saw in chapter 1, in the United States the new wave genre was defined in large part by its relationship to the AOR radio format.

While there were new wave songs that crossed over into the Top 40 as well, it was assumed that the music catered to a relatively stable album rock audience, and it was to this demographic that the music was most heavily promoted. By comparison, the national BBC programming of the late 1970s and early 1980s was much less fragmented along formatted genre lines than its commercially driven American counterpart. The BBC's contemporary popular music station, Radio One, allowed its disc jockeys more freedom and in general encouraged a less restrictive interplay among genres that reflected the BBC's aim to entertain a broad general audience.[2] New wave was thus heard as one of many contemporary pop and rock musical styles, and its supposed modern "otherness" was much less of a divisive issue.

This contrast between American stability and British free play, to reduce it to crude terms, was even more exaggerated in the functioning of the music press. In England, the persistent rhythm of the British weekly music press has always allowed for a more flexible relationship to new musical developments and genres than the comparatively glacial flow of the monthly American music magazines or the biweekly *Rolling Stone*. The influx of punk into *Melody Maker, NME,* and *Sounds* only sharpened this distinction. As Jason Toynbee has observed, after punk the British weeklies collapsed their traditional critical standards of musical taste into a focus on lifestyle, fandom, and identity that sought to captivate a series of readerships rather than a singular rock audience.[3] The focus on the "new" was accelerated, and as to be expected a parade of emergent genres—each of them evocative to some extent of the stylistic freedom that British punk had originally promised but then seemingly betrayed—soon marched forth from the music press pages. A fledgling mod revival, a Two Tone ska revival, a rockabilly revival, neopsychedelia, and a steady stream of innovative independent label releases from the likes of Factory, Rough Trade, and Cherry Red records kept the covers of the weeklies revolving at a fast clip throughout 1979 and 1980.

Each of these new musical developments could be viewed in its own way as an emergent cultural formation, and one could even argue that taken as a whole they represented a dominant post-punk formation that validated punk's impact upon the music industry. As tempting as such an analysis might be, it ignores the economic reality that this parade of subgenres largely emanated from an independent underground, one that deliberately positioned itself as ideologically resistant to a dominant rock and pop mainstream. The very strength of its musical statements was dependent upon its subordinate relationship to the music industry's hegemonic values. The true heir to new wave's commercial aspirations would emerge from elsewhere, and it would eventually succeed where the original movement had failed, as it redefined the very ground rules by which the dominant musical culture operated.

New Romantics and New Pop

Given the British music press's new focus on style, it should come as little surprise that the one post-punk genre, "New Romantics," that would eventually precipitate a major commercial landslide was at first centered on a group of fantastically dressed fans whose captivating presence clearly outshone the music associated with the scene. The genre had grown out of a gay Soho nightclub named Billy's, where promoter Steve Strange and DJ Rusty Egan organized a "Bowie Night" that attracted numerous fans dressed up in tribute to the various phases of the singer's career. By the time that Strange and Egan moved to the Blitz club, the patrons were dressing in increasingly imaginative and original costumes that cut across a seemingly inexhaustible range of historical periods, ethnic influences, and gender boundaries. The music press and their photographers were quick to notice, and descriptive labels ranging from the Cult with No Name and the Blitz Kids to Peacock Punk and finally New Romantics began to accrue around the scene. A reporter covering a large 1981 St. Valentine's Day New Romantics gathering at London's Rainbow Theatre captures perfectly the carnivalesque spirit of the phenomenon at its height:

> There was a rich masquerade of Regency fops, Kiss-me-Hardy sailors, medieval princesses, Afghan dervishes, swashbuckling Robin Hoods, white-faced Pierrots, Bertie Wooster twits and Somerset Maugham planters in white ducks. There were monocles, pince-nez, Malacca canes, Japanese fans, pillbox hats, tutus and even the beak and veil worn by Arab women (here, though, by a man); only the incredulous horde of photographers sported denim.[4]

Where the new wave movement had drawn much of its inspiration from the 1960s mod youth culture, the New Romantics, or the "new New Wave," as Bowie offhandedly referred to them, ransacked a realm of more distant styles that had lain virtually untouched in the late 1970s.[5] To further underscore this difference, they claimed not to be modern, but "moderne," a reference to the *style moderne* of the 1920s art deco movement. With its extravagant and sleek designs, art deco had wiped away the cold austerity of World War I, a dichotomy that in the New Romantics' eyes perfectly paralleled their own celebratory rejection of the uniformly gray fashion and doom-laden songs that had come to define a grim post-punk aesthetic. The New Romantic tag soon became synonymous with a wildly eclectic and unabashed emphasis on style, one that was welcomingly attached to fashion conscious bands like Spandau Ballet, Visage, and Duran Duran, as well as artists like Adam and the Ants, who had no real connection with the scene. While the New Romantics label would eventually begin to fade from the magazines by the end of 1981 as the scene itself dissipated, its influence would continue to be felt as "style" became a watchword for most new British pop artists.

Likewise, the music emanating from the New Romantics club scene would leave its mark as well. The New Romantics' rise out of the London club scene between 1979 and 1981 was more or less simultaneous with the growth of the rock disco in the United States, and as with those venues the music that populated spaces like Blitz was heavily indebted to the synthesized textures and beats of disco. Rusty Egan's DJ playlist at the Blitz featured not only experimental British synthesizer-dominated bands like Ultravox, Cabaret Voltaire, and the Normal, but also an international array of similar-minded artists that included Telex (Belgium), Kraftwerk (Germany), Giorgio Moroder (Italy), and Yellow Magic Orchestra (Japan).[6] By 1981, the number of synthesizer artists had expanded well beyond the New Romantics London club scene to include British groups with a more pop-oriented bent such as Orchestral Manoeuvres in the Dark (OMD), Depeche Mode, and Soft Cell, all of whom soon landed singles in the Top 10. The group that would finally broker a true breakthrough for these new synthesizer pop bands was the Human League, specifically their single "Don't You Want Me," which first topped the British charts at the end of 1981 and then repeated the feat six months later in the United States. The success of the

Human League had a tremendous impact, and in the band's wake a new genre label soon emerged that would come to take precedence in 1982 and 1983: *new pop*. As with most such radical generic shifts, the new pop's ascendance was facilitated by developments in the music industry on both sides of the Atlantic. The rest of this section will consider the Human League and "Don't You Want Me" in more detail, as a means to understanding the nature of these industry changes.

The British music press was especially drawn to the Human League in 1981 for a number of reasons, but most of all because their newfound popularity was predicated on a dramatic reinvention of style and purpose that made for a compelling story. The group had begun in 1977 as an all-male synthesizer outfit from Sheffield, whose live shows featured an experimental cut-and-paste slide show. With harsh drum sounds constructed out of filtered white noise and dark songs such as "Circus of Death," the Human League fit well with the gritty industrial post-punk textures and lyrical topics that at that time were in step with the antipopulist stance of the British music weeklies. After two albums the group disbanded in late 1980. Faced with a contractual tour obligation, however, singer Philip Oakey and film projectionist Adrian Wright decided to retain the band name and quickly recruited two female teenagers to dance and sing backup vocals at the front of the stage. Placed alongside Oakey's androgynous image, they lent the group a new visual dimension, one that crucially drew attention away from the ubiquitous tape recorders that provided the majority of musical backings for their live shows. After the tour, Oakey drafted two new synthesizer players on board, recorded some new, more accessible, songs and before long was giving interviews that espoused the group's love of Abba and their designs on commercial stardom. Given the band's bold reinvention, it was easy for critics to paint the Human League as a distinct dividing point between the supposedly failed isolationist experimentations of late 1970s post-punk and the dazzling populist promises of an early 1980s new pop.

As with the Cars' reception in the American market three years earlier, when they were lauded for blending rock traditionalism with avant-garde experimentation, part of the novelty surrounding the Human League hinged on its hybrid identity. Much as the band was praised for the glamour of its pop appeal, the press equally fetishized the advanced modern technology of its musical arrangements. As journalist Dave Rimmer com-

Figure 5. The Human League display the new pop's mix of style and technology on Britain's Top of the Pops, April 30, 1981: lead singer Philip Oakey flanked by dancing girls, tape recorders, and synthesizers.

mented in late 1981, "*Everybody* wants to talk to them . . . from *Sun* and *Mirror* newshounds gasping for details of Philip's love life to specialist electronics magazines enquiring about the frequency modulations of their synthesizers."[7] Much of the technological discussion surrounding the band's modern identity focused on their prominent use of two new instruments: the digital Roland Microcomposer, which could create detailed sequencer patterns, and the Linn drum machine, a synthesizer that allowed one to construct electronic beats in "real time" out of samples from actual acoustic drum sets. At the same time, the Human League was wary of the synthesizer's potentially gimmicky status and sought to emphasize the very commonness and craft of their endeavor, a move no doubt intended to underscore their musical legitimacy. As Oakey explained, "People in Britain think we're very new and outrageous, whereas in fact, we're very, very old-fashioned. We're a pop group; just forget that we're using synthesizers."[8] Such were the tensions that the band navigated in their dealings with the press.

Oakey was well aware that as important as its improved sound was to dance club and radio airplay, it was most of all the band's visual appeal that would ensure its success. Indeed significant changes in the British music press, specifically the introduction in late 1978 of the weekly teen fan magazine *Smash Hits,* had made a band's appearance all the more important. Whereas the broadsheet paper "inkies" like *NME, Sounds,* and *Melody Maker* typically featured stark black-and-white live photos of sweat-stained musicians, *Smash Hits* offered a glossy full-stock color format. Complete with stylish fold-out studio photos designed for wall display, song lyrics, and witty, irreverent tabloid gossip, the magazine was perfectly tailored to photogenic new pop groups like the Human League who gleefully embraced the chart success, glamour, and celebrity status that had been anathema to the punks. So fully did *Smash Hits* reconfigure the music press hierarchy that by 1984, when the new pop was at its commercial peak, the magazine was selling just over half a million copies, nearly double the *combined* sales of its three major rock weekly competitors.[9] In addition to *Smash Hits,* a crop of monthly "style bibles," including the wildly influential *The Face,* gravitated to the new pop as well and helped shift the emphasis in their coverage even further away from text and criticism toward image and provocation.[10] Seamlessly integrating studio photos of the latest pop stars with similarly framed lifestyle advertisements, *The Face* celebrated the ambiguous dividing lines between creativity and commerce so essential to the pop experience.

New pop bands like the Human League were a natural fit for magazines like *The Face* because they themselves had embraced the language of style, fashion, and advertising as part of their overall creative presentation, often to a similarly ambiguous effect. The Human League designed the cover for its 1981 album *Dare,* for example, as a parody of *Vogue,* partially mimicking the fashion magazine's tight facial close-up and utilizing a similar graphic design that highlighted the shared lettering between Lea**gue** and Vo**gue.** Whereas the *Vogue* magazine cover of the early 1980s unfailingly focused in on the full face of a gorgeous female model, however, *Dare* presents a more closely cropped image that throws the gender of the face into doubt. Gazing at the cover art, one is met by a set of eyes and lips, meticulously detailed in mascara and lipstick. On first glance, it is unclear whether the face belongs to Philip Oakey or one of the group's female singers, though a closer look reveals that it is indeed Oakey. Over the course of the next two years, this ambiguous gender play of fashion, style, and androgyny would become even more closely associated with the new pop, culminating with the striking imagery and cross-dressing of Culture Club's Boy George and the Eurythmics' Annie Lennox, who emerged as two of the genre's most recognizable cover stars.

The Human League released *Dare* in the U.K. in October 1981, and in three months time it had achieved platinum sales. Such rapid ascents were fairly common in England, where the concentrated effect of exposure through the weeklies, dance clubs, Radio One airplay, and appearances on the weekly television chart show *Top of the Pops* could saturate the marketplace. *Dare*'s rise toward the American Top 10, however, was more slow building, not the least because the album was available only as an import until the spring of 1982, when A&M picked up the release for distribution. In general such lag times were typical of the new pop's importation to the United States. The second British Invasion—or synthpop, electropop, or technopop as it would come to be called in the American music press—was not a quick strike, but rather the result of a gradual, accumulated effect spread across a wide range of media.[11] As we will see, the trenches along which these British bands traveled had been furrowed for some time, but also represented some significant changes in the industry.

The British Are Coming

The first inklings that a surge of new British synthesizer bands might have some impact in the United States came late in 1981. Surveying New York City's well-established live venue and rock disco scene, *New York Rocker* warned of an encroaching "Anglophilia" that was crowding out local acts specifically, and American underground rock in general, from vital gigs, club and radio play, and sales. As the magazine noted, only eight of the Top 30 records in a recent *Rockpool* national dance-rock chart had been by American groups. The problem was particularly acute in Manhattan, where the easy availability of the British music weeklies and specialty import record stores had elevated the new British bands who "sound good over a p.a. system . . . to the level of deities."[12] This impact could be seen as well in *Billboard*'s more inclusive Disco Top 80 charts from late 1981, where, nestled among familiar R&B royalty like Kool and the Gang and Thelma Houston, one found such British twelve-inch single imports as A Flock of Seagulls' "Telecommunication," Pete Shelley's "Homosapien," and Soft Cell's "Tainted Love / Where Did Our Love Go." The Human League's "Don't You Want Me / Open Your Heart" was there too, and it would remain on the chart for an astounding forty weeks as the song began to receive more notice outside the rock disco venues.

As important as the rock discos were to exposing new British bands, they admittedly reached a narrow audience. Radio was still a more primary means of breaking an artist, and here the Human League would benefit from a changing of the guard in formats. Whereas new wave bands of the late 1970s had too often been at the mercy of conservative AOR consultants and programmers who viewed the music with suspicion, the new pop was attractive to a different range of formats. Specifically, new pop found a large audience through revamped, youth-oriented Top 40 formats such as "Hot Hits" and "Contemporary Hits Radio" (CHR) as well as the numerous "Urban Contemporary" stations that had emerged to replace the failed disco radio format. The new pop's relationship with Urban Contemporary is of particular interest. These stations were considered by and large to be "black stations," but at the same time they closely followed dance club charts and retail sales to determine their programming and were thus receptive to music that regardless of genre or race fit into the station's overall sound and aesthetic.[13] Songs that enjoyed great success on Urban Contemporary, such as "Don't You Want Me," benefited from what music critic Nelson George called a "reverse crossover," attracting a substantial African American audience most of all because they were novel records that worked well on the dance floor.[14] As AOR stations found their ratings slipping dramatically throughout 1982, Top 40 and Urban Contemporary picked up larger audience shares, propelled in part by their willingness to program the new pop.

While club play and radio were both crucial to exposing bands like the Human League in the United States, one scarcely reads about these connections anymore, largely because their importance has been dwarfed historically by the revolutionary medium that would become most associated with the new pop: MTV (Music Television). Much has been written about MTV's launching in 1981, and how the channel routinized the music video as a standard music industry promotional tool that would eventually come to usurp radio's power. Ironically, in its initial planning stages, MTV director Robert Pittman and the head of talent and acquisitions, Carolyn Baker, had sought to market the new video network as if it were a traditional "AOR channel," one whose music videos would cater to an already well-established white rock radio audience.[15] Pittman found, however, that not only were many U.S. record labels skeptical of the new format's potential and thus uncooperative with the fledgling network, but also that the majority of American rock artists who had relied on the surefire publicity of radio were not even prepared with promotional clips that MTV could air. The British new pop bands, on the other hand, had been experimenting with the emergent medium for some time and arrived with stylish videos in hand. They found themselves in a serendipitous position, and MTV was eager to welcome them into its rotation.

As Andrew Goodwin points out in his study of MTV, *Dancing in the Distraction Factory,* the new pop groups were in many respects especially well suited to the nature of the video format.[16] Because bands like the Human League were so reliant on sequencers and drum machines, often appearing on stage with little more than a couple of synthesizers and perhaps a tape machine, audiences had come to accept that they were mostly "miming," simply singing over prerecorded sounds that were identical to the record. These groups did not suffer the same pressures as rock artists to prove that their recordings were not illusory, and that they were indeed authentic creative musicians. This had two consequences. First, it served to naturalize and legitimize the lip-synching that would become the video's main mode of performance. Second, the displacement of the musician from the role of the instrumentalist freed the new pop bands to move away from the constricting stagelike settings and clichéd poses of the typical "performance video" to a more varied and exploratory array of dramatic scenarios, intertextual allusions, and devices lifted from the filmic avant-garde. Such is the case with the video for "Don't You Want Me," a self-reflexive pastiche of Francois Truffaut's movie-within-a-movie, *Day for Night* (1974), which unfolds with the shadowy implications of a love triangle between Oakey and the two female singers, copious lip-synching, and nary a musical instrument in sight. Videos like these stood apart on MTV and generated further interest in the wave of new British bands.

MTV's influence grew throughout 1982, especially after September

Figure 6. Human League singer Susan Sulley lip-synchs as she strolls through the movie set of the band's self-reflexive "Don't You Want Me" video (1981).

when the network expanded from its original test markets into the larger New York and Los Angeles metropolitan areas. British videos were receiving more and more exposure on the channel, and the results were beginning to trickle over into radio. In January 1983, when *Billboard* implemented its first Video Programming chart in recognition of MTV's impact, the corresponding Top 40 singles chart featured seven singles by British artists. By mid-July, that number had exploded to eighteen, or nearly half of the Top 40, shattering the previous record of fourteen that had been established in the summer of 1965 when Beatlemania was at its height.[17] References to a second British Invasion were soon ubiquitous in the press, and MTV was credited as the most important factor.[18] Many noted that the network had essentially served as an ambassador for Britain's biggest musical sensations, groups like Duran Duran, Culture Club, and ABC. But an even better measure of MTV's impact lay in its ability to make stars in the United States out of relatively minor British new pop acts like A Flock of Seagulls, the Fixx, and Thomas Dolby, all of whom were virtually ignored in their own homeland. MTV's influence trickled over into the new surge of popular teen-oriented cinema as well, where films like *Valley Girl* (1983) incorporated soundtracks prominently featuring new British groups like the Psychedelic Furs and Modern English. This trend would continue well into the mid-1980s as teen movies like *Sixteen Candles* (1984) and *Pretty in Pink* (1986) emphasized a strong relationship between new British music and alternative youth fashion and culture.

It had taken two slow years, but the summer of 1983 finally provided indisputable evidence that the wave of new British bands was now a dominant force in the United States music industry. *Billboard* recognized their achievements with a twelve-page spotlight feature on the "New Music," the generic description that had increasingly become the industry's label of choice since the institution of the New Music Seminar in 1980.[19] Commenting on MTV, the club scene, and the increasing technological and stylistic crossovers between black R&B and the white new pop, *Billboard* heralded the new music as the dawn of a "modern era" of music making. At the same time, the shadows of punk, new wave, and disco all lingered over the feature's pages, rendering the new music not so much a new genre but rather the result of a five-year dance floor cross-fertilization that had resulted in an experimental, pluralistic, polyglot mass. Given that the new music's multiple stylistic allegiances roamed from Motown to minimalism, the label seemed nearly impossible to contain. It had come to encompass nearly any new white artist whose music employed synthesizers or sounded particularly good on the dance floor.

Regardless of *what* exactly the new music signified, its arrival represented an important structural shift in the music industry culture, one that reversed the 1970s rock paradigm by placing a greater value on singles than on albums. As media studies scholar Will Straw has noted, this resulted in a dramatic acceleration and turnover of new acts and artists.[20] In the 1970s record labels had emphasized career development and longevity. An artist might start slowly, even releasing several albums before achieving a bona fide Top 40 hit, but labels anticipated that with each successive release the artist's audience would grow. The labels thus endorsed a view of rock music as a "career," the center of which was based around the durability of the full-length album. The new music artists of the second British Invasion, on the other hand, were attractive to U.S. record labels precisely because there was no need to invest in developing a career. Labels could now simply license the rights to a preexisting foreign product and promote it first through established singles and then later a full-length album.[21] Singles, in both seven-inch and the newly circulating twelve-inch and mini-E.P. (extended play) formats, enjoyed increased sales, and Top 40 radio stations and video clip showings became the most crucial elements in marketing artists. To be sure, the new music artists sold their fair share of albums, but it was more the high velocity of singles that propelled a stream of fresh faces into the charts. As 1983 came to a close, *Billboard*'s year-end Top 100 singles chart showed that fully half of the new artists had come out of the new music invasion.[22]

On the whole, 1983 was a triumphant year for the overlapping genre domains of new pop and new music, both of which validated the original new wave's staying power. In celebration of the genre's rich history, *Trouser Press* magazine issued *The Trouser Press Guide to New Wave Records,* a brave attempt to provide an encyclopedic critical review of every new wave album that had been released in America and England. While the editor, Ira Robbins, admitted that the impossibly broad variety of bands included in the volume rendered new wave a "pretty meaningless term," the book was nonetheless a strong testament to the long strides that the genre had made since its punk origins. By 1984, however, that optimistic outlook had changed. *Trouser Press* magazine folded in the middle of the year, a victim of Robbins's waning enthusiasm, impending "fiscal insecurity," and a growing sense of irrelevance in the face of MTV's reach and its young "teenybopper" audience.[23] Robbins would return in 1985 with an updated second edition of *The New Trouser Press Record Guide,* but he had removed the *new wave* label from the book's title. As he explained, new wave had not only lost its musical specificity, it was also no longer in use by most music writers. The music had spread and splattered in so many directions that the genre label had seemingly become pointless.

Today, more than two and a half decades after the fact, there does indeed seem to be a consensus that the arrival and popularization of new pop and new music in the mid-1980s is the point at which new wave's historical narrative draws to a close. For example, Rhino Records' definitive fifteen-volume new wave anthology, *Just Can't Get Enough*, grinds to a halt in 1985. The anthology gives no explanation, however, for why the genre should end there. What exactly was it that killed new wave? Why did the genre label no longer seem appropriate? One thing is certain. Unlike new wave's previous iterations, it was not incorporation that led to the new music's demise. Unabashedly commercial groups like Duran Duran and Culture Club, who had announced their pop star ambitions from the very beginning, were hardly capable of "selling out." Their arrival had helped to transform the very workings of the industry in a new video-dominated age. As we will see in the next section, the proposed reasons for new wave's death lie elsewhere.

The Death of New Wave?

There's definitely going to be a new music backlash. Everyone is going to stop using electronics and mechanical stuff and go back to just being bands.
 —Mike Score of A Flock of Seagulls, September 1983[24]

If 1983 was the year that new wave had finally and fully crossed over into the mainstream via the new music explosion, few events appeared to be more symbolic of the stature the genre had attained than the highly publicized three-day "US Festival" that took place in Devore, California, over Memorial Day weekend. In consideration of the potential audiences, the festival organizers decided to devote each day to a separate genre. The first day was specifically reserved for "new music," with a cross-section of bands—ranging from the American rockabilly revivalists Stray Cats and the new pop synthesizer music of A Flock of Seagulls to iconic punks the Clash—that displayed both the genre's history and stylistic diversity. Day 3 was intended for a more general rock crowd, but here as well the influence of new wave, post-punk, and synth rock revealed itself in sets from the Pretenders, U2, Berlin, and Missing Persons. It was the second day, however, that would come to dominate the festival's coverage in the music press. With performances from Quiet Riot, Mötley Crüe, Ozzy Osbourne, Judas Priest, Triumph, the Scorpions, and Van Halen, "Heavy Metal" day attracted an estimated audience of 250,000, which was nearly more than the first and third days combined.[25] Viewed as a battle between genres, heavy metal's victorious performance at the US Festival carried clear implications for the music industry. As Mötley Crüe's Vince Neil commented afterward, "It was the day that new wave died and rock and roll took over."[26]

It is tempting to follow Neil's lead and recognize the US Festival as a moment of deep symbolic significance. Such historical events are naturally compelling because they conveniently frame in one brilliant flash of lightning the heroic ascendancy of one genre vis-à-vis the tragic decline of another. In this case, the US Festival seems to validate heavy metal's incredible cultural impact, showing how the genre's overwhelming grassroots audience response and fan commitment eventually won out over new wave's fabricated marketing exposure of radio and MTV airplay. At its root, new wave's death at the hands of heavy metal can be reduced to a basic myth absolutely germane to the writing of rock's history: the triumph of authenticity over artifice.[27] In such a scenario heavy metal's authentic representations of power—guitars, virtuosic display, sweat-stained leather, and male communal headbanging—emerge as correctives to new wave's artificial mélange of synthesizers, rudimentary musicianship, androgynous fashion, and feminized dance music. To be sure, such genre boundaries mirrored an undeniable social reality routinely reinforced in heavy metal-oriented magazines like *Hit Parader,* where musicians commonly dismissed new music groups as "faggots."[28] At the same time, such hostilities were not capable of killing off an entire genre of music; they could only help further define each warring genre's constituencies. In the end, it would be foolish to swallow Vince Neil's rhetoric whole.

Still, as one looked around the 1983 popular music landscape, there were ample examples elsewhere of critically acclaimed bands that strategically pitted themselves against the new music, generally in the (unspoken) name of authenticity. U2's The Edge vehemently insisted that his group not be categorized with "the very poppy, very disposable" new music.[29] The Smiths' Morrissey explained, to virtually anyone who would listen, his disdain for the soulless polish of the new British pop. As he made clear in an interview with *Sounds* magazine: "There was nothing more repellant than the synthesizer."[30] In the United States, guitar-based underground rock bands like X similarly blanched at the stifling omnipresence of the British Invasion, "a glitter-disco-synthesizer-night-school" trend that in their eyes had knocked more deserving American bands off the airwaves.[31] By 1984 this revolt against the new music had grown into what many critics perceived as a genuine American "roots rock" revival that encompassed bands like R.E.M., the Dream Syndicate, the Del Fuegos, and the Long Ryders, who drew their inspiration from such 1960s sources as the Byrds and psychedelic garage rock. Appraising this new American "post-punk" uprising, music critic David Fricke stressed the familiar dichotomies of rock/pop, guitars/synthesizers, and humans/machines that underscored the presumed divide between authenticity and artifice:

> It seems strange, then, to think America's post-punk flowering also owes a debt of begrudging thanks to the British fashion groove thing of Duran Duran, Culture Club and Spandau Ballet. The endless parade of comely English faces with their undisguised teen appeal and glossy soul inventions infuriated Yankee youngbloods. They felt it was practically their patriotic duty to play their *rock*—as opposed to pop's tick-tock electronics and casual disco glide—that much harder, to cut away every ounce of naïve fat from their songs.[32]

In England the press's enchantment with the new pop began to sour in 1984, and by 1985 had turned fully to disappointment and even disgust. Writing in the independent "pop journal" *Monitor,* Simon Reynolds addressed many of the main issues, most pointedly in an article entitled "What's Missing: The State of Pop in 1985." In his view, the new pop was suffering from many problems. Reynolds found the music's main stars—late twenty-something artists like Paul Young, Annie Lennox, and Howard Jones—to be too "adult," presenting a luxuriant lifestyle of money, status, and leisure that was unapproachable to a younger generation. In his view, their music, a mongrel appropriation of funk, soul, and R&B, reeked of marketing strategies rather than artistic depth. And their songs consisted of a "flattened-out approximation of real life . . . just lowest common denominator humanist platitudes" (one thinks, for example, of Jones's 1985 single "Things Can Only Get Better") that lacked any poetry, passion, or raw feelings.[33]

As an antidote, Reynolds proposed the Smiths, a band that he felt had grasped a more genuine emotional state: the awkward misery and romanticism of youthful adolescence. To him their music represented a "new white

bohemianism" bleached of the studied and stilted black musical affectations that had held white British pop in its grips for the better part of the
decade. In later articles Reynolds would expand upon these sentiments further, railing against the mainstream "health and efficiency" of the new
pop, and praising the return to a shambling, childlike innocence and
naïveté that the Smiths and a new crop of white guitar bands on independent labels had embraced.[34] As with the American roots rock revival, these
groups drew from the fashion and sounds of the 1960s, which represented
a distinct nostalgic purity in the face of the 1980s' technologically advanced dance music. They would eventually come to be lumped together
under a variety of names ranging from "cutie" and "twee" to C86 (after a
compilation cassette that appeared as part of a 1986 *NME* issue), but the one
that would stick is "indie."

Even more than Vince Neil's claims for heavy metal's dominance at the
US Festival, the emergence of both American underground "roots rock"
and British "indie" has come to assume a certain agency in the narrative of
new wave's demise, their mere presence seemingly ensuring a closure to the
genre's brief history. This is the tack that the *All Music Guide* website takes
when it contends that "new wave finally died out in 1984 . . . and a new
crop of guitar-oriented bands like the Smiths and R.E.M. emerged to capture the attention of college-radio and underground rock fans."[35] The 2007
BBC documentary *Seven Ages of Rock* similarly uses the Smiths' November
1983 debut on *Top of the Pops* to symbolize the overthrowing of a decadent,
decaying new pop hegemony. After panning across a shot of new pop star
Paul Young performing on the same show, the camera turns to former
Smiths guitarist Johnny Marr, who recalls with measurable disdain that "it
was all about people in headbands, with a bright red jacket and three backing singers and a keyboard player, and that kind of thing."[36] The implication is that only through the death of new wave's artifice could an authentic genre like British indie experience its true birth.

Such clearly drawn, self-contained dichotomies are naturally attractive
not only to documentary filmmakers, but teachers, historians, journalists,
or anyone who seeks a memorable and economic means of telling a historical story. As convenient and tidy as such stories are, however, they inevitably paper over the complexities of how genres actually intermingle
and share spaces. They reduce genres to either-or equations—guitars or

synthesizers—and privilege ideological reductionism and the agendas of music critics over the lived realities of most listeners' experiences. A glimpse at how these musical genres actually circulated during the mid-1980s reveals a different picture. For example, as music critic David Fricke acknowledged in his assessment of the 1984 American roots rock uprising, even though groups like R.E.M. were seemingly at the polar stylistic extreme from Duran Duran or Culture Club, many fans nevertheless perceived them all as part of the same new wave formation, as an alternative to "the lumbering AOR giants."[37] Rock discos and clubs routinely played British new pop dance mixes and videos, while also featuring live sets from local American guitar bands. In England, tracks from the Smiths seamlessly rubbed shoulders on the dance floor with such synthpop chart regulars as Depeche Mode and Erasure. Simply put, while some fans undoubtedly championed the Smiths and R.E.M. as the dawn of some new musical horizon, many more welcomed them into an existing new wave formation and saw little ideological or aesthetic difference between them and their supposed rivals.

Rather than seeking out new wave's demise at the hands of another genre, I would suggest that there arrived a point at which the label no longer sufficiently communicated a coherent sense of newness. This breakdown resulted largely from the significant shift in the genre's terrain that occurred with the arrival of new pop and new music. As an "emergent" genre in the late 1970s and early 1980s, new wave had assumed a modern, oppositional stance to the traditional "dominant" rock culture, which was manifest—sometimes subtly, sometimes obviously—in the music's irony, irreverence, experimentation, and appropriation of earlier, unfashionable rock styles. Where new wave was defined by an attitude and its link (however tangential) to punk, the new music of the early 1980s largely broke with these connections and instead came to be identified by its modern synthesized instrumentation, as evidenced by the names under which it frequently circulated: electropop, synthpop, and technopop. While at first this technological focus stamped the genre as an exciting, unique development, as the new music became a "dominant" cultural formation, its mode of production ceased to be special; it became the lingua franca of popular music. Furthermore, by 1984 and 1985 the rise of digital synthesizers such as the Yamaha DX-7, with its numerous built-in factory "preset" sounds, and the popularization of both drum machines and heavily modified "gated" drum sounds, had introduced a "timbral conformity" that spread across the popular music landscape.[38] Former disco producers and engineers like Nile Rodgers and Bob Clearmountain were in heavy demand, not just for pop chameleons like David Bowie and Madonna, but also for icons of rock authenticity like Bruce Springsteen, who even leased his singles "Dancing in the Dark" and "Cover Me" to hip-hop DJ Arthur Baker for dance club remixes. As more and more artists gravitated toward these new marketable sounds, the specificity of the new music genre became increasingly difficult to discern.

This is not, however, to say that the democratization of musical technology in the mid-1980s wiped away existing genre distinctions. Springsteen's "Dancing in the Dark" may have employed the synthesizer timbres and textures of technopop, but there was no disguising the song's guitar power chords and driving backbeat or Springsteen's distinct rock vocal identity. Similarly, the Human League's unexpected turn toward distorted electric guitar and bass riffs on the otherwise synth-dominated 1984 single "The Lebanon" did not suddenly obliterate the group's past history and make it a rock band. Rather, the confusion surrounding the new music arose more from the arrival of brand new groups and artists who took the new musical technology as a foundational element, but ventured into any number of stylistic directions that bore little relation to new wave. Thus one could easily market Corey Hart, Mr. Mister, or Cutting Crew as "new music" on the basis of their strong synthesizer textures, but at the same time their melodramatic hard rock mannerisms were equally, if not more, suggestive of an aggressive AOR sound. Likewise, many found it difficult to find any connection between a heavily synthesized new music British teen idol pop group like Wham! and the punkish new wave that had directly preceded it. As music critic Bill Flanagan wrote in 1989, looking back on the developments of the first half of the 1980s:

> Bit by bit the last traces of punk were drained from new wave, as new wave went from meaning Talking Heads to meaning the Cars to Squeeze to Duran Duran to, finally, Wham! And that was a sad day, the day you turned on MTV and saw George Michael dancing around in a white sweatshirt singing "Wake Me Up Before You Go Go." You couldn't kid yourself that this was

anything remotely progressive. All of a sudden Michael McDonald seemed pretty good after all.[39]

In the bouillabaisse of mid-1980s MTV, where heavy metal, R&B, rock, pop, and rap videos freely intermingled, the synthesizer had become the main ingredient that held the stew together. As the new music technology's presence became standardized across many genres, it was no longer unique to new music. Having largely severed its ties to new wave's original oppositional stance, the new music category had little else on which to hang its generic claims.

It was not, however, just the proliferation of styles and genre confusion that rendered the new music label problematic. Changes within the music industry also steered labels away from the new music's steady parade of singles-based artists toward the more heady profits of album blockbusters and superstars.[40] As it turned out, the model of success from 1983 that the industry tried to emulate as it finally climbed out of its lengthy recession was not that of the second British Invasion, but rather the unprecedented sales of Michael Jackson's *Thriller*. From the labels' perspective it made more sense to throw one's weight fully behind a mammoth seller than to gamble on the success of many smaller acts. For example, after Warner Brothers witnessed Prince's 1984 album *Purple Rain* outsell all its other titles combined, it promptly dropped thirty artists from their roster. As a steady stream of video hits from Bruce Springsteen, Madonna, Whitney Houston, Lionel Richie, and Janet Jackson flooded MTV, the mid-1980s were defined by a small handful of multiplatinum albums that dominated the charts for months on end. A striking number of new superstars were African Americans, a fact that further accentuated the distance the industry had traveled since the early 1980s when MTV had shunned "black" music and musicians in favor of the white British new pop's postdisco and R&B interpretations.

By 1988 it seemed as if most any remnant of new wave or new music had been fully eradicated from the *Billboard* singles and album charts. The majority of the original new wave bands—groups like Blondie, the Police, the Cars, the Pretenders—had broken up or lay dormant. And those who *had* soldiered on—such as Squeeze, Devo, and the B-52's—had seen their sales plummet drastically. Likewise, while the charts had a healthy proportion of British performers, they generally were not the survivors of the second

British Invasion. Rather, they ran the gamut from first invasion old-timers like George Harrison and Steve Winwood and heavy metal acts like Def Leppard and Whitesnake to glamorous pop stars like Samantha Fox. While new wave appeared to have vanished from *Billboard,* however, this was not entirely the case. As we will see, it had simply graduated to a different location and a different genre label, one that after all these years finally and officially acknowledged new wave's "modern" status.

New Wave in Memoriam: Modern Rock

In its September 10, 1988, edition, *Billboard* magazine announced the introduction of a new "alternative" album track chart that was to run under the heading of Modern Rock Tracks.[41] While the magazine offered no explanation of the "modern rock" label itself, clearly its lineage dated back to the many repeated "modern" references that had been used to promote and market new wave in its various manifestations. Approximately ten years after the Cars had entered the *Billboard* charts as the first Top 40 new wave act, the movement had belatedly received its first official, albeit indirect, industry recognition. As *Billboard* described, the chart would be tabulated based on weighted reports from nearly thirty radio stations. They included such respected "standard-bearer" stations as KROQ Los Angeles, which had begun programming new wave in 1978, and WDRE (the former WLIR) Long Island, which had switched to a "new music" format in 1982, as well as a select group of noncommercial college stations. Taken as a whole they represented the diverse radio pathways along which new wave had traveled during the 1980s.

Part of what had made the early 1980s new wave and new music in the United States seem so "modern" was the intrigue and allure of lesser-known import releases and foreign artists whose underground cachet positioned them outside the mainstream of the predominantly North American AOR radio. *Billboard*'s inaugural Modern Rock chart confirmed that this element continued to define the music. Of the tracks comprising the Top 30 chart, only seven were by American artists, while sixteen were from the United Kingdom. Many of the names, such as Siouxsie and the Banshees and the Psychedelic Furs, were well-known bands familiar to new wave and post-punk fans from earlier in the 1980s. Stylistically, however, the music bore little resemblance to that era. The modern rock of the late 1980s was gathered together out of numerous streams, ranging from guitar-oriented British indie influenced by the Smiths to the second-generation reggae of Ziggy Marley & the Melody Makers. Nonetheless, there still remained one basic similarity: modern rock was, much as new wave had been, associated with rock discos and dance clubs. Through all of new wave's many 1980s manifestations, this proved to be the genre's one consistent quality: the music never shed its up-tempo dance floor legacy.

The Modern Rock charts changed very little in their overall character over the course of the late 1980s and early 1990s, as they continued to be dominated by foreign, predominantly British, artists and dance-oriented tracks. This began to change, however, in 1992 as the emergence of grunge and alternative rock initiated a stylistic avalanche that would reconfigure the 1990s American music industry and effectively wipe the majority of British artists off the airwaves. Dressed in tattered jeans and loose flannel shirts, and wielding an unadorned distorted guitar sound, alternative rock bands brought to the mainstream an abrasive look and sound that had been brewing throughout the American music "college rock" underground in the 1980s, but which had been relatively absent from commercial radio. The new stripped-down alternative sound emerged as a statement against the highly stylized imagery of the British dance artists, but even more so it rebuked the superstar preening that still dictated so much hard rock and heavy metal music. As Chris Cornell of grunge rockers Soundgarden explained, the arrival of alternative truly represented a watershed moment:

> The commercial rock bands of the late '80s—every single band, regardless of their sound—did very specific things. They had videos where they showed excess as much as they could. They showed up to their concerts in helicopters. The songs didn't matter at all, but their hair mattered a lot. The clothes mattered. The girl in the video was always a big, big story. The successful bands of our era were all about leaving that out, and putting the focus back on songwriting.[42]

Given the discontent that bands like Soundgarden felt with the prevailing trends that had come to define the major music industry, it is little wonder that more than a few observers compared the early 1990s alternative explosion with the original punk movement. To many it represented a colossal cleansing of the 1980s' "Age of Excess."

The biggest catalyst behind alternative was Nirvana, a former indie label group whose 1991 major label debut *Nevermind* dislodged Michael Jackson's *Dangerous* from the top of the album charts, an achievement that has since come to symbolize a momentous changing of the guard. *Nevermind's* success was sparked in large part by the enormous popularity of the single "Smells Like Teen Spirit," which eventually cracked the Top 10 of not only the Album Rock and Modern Rock charts, but the pop-dominated Hot 100 singles chart as well. Given the stratified industry and audience demographics that Nirvana seemed to have transcended, the group's widespread success stood as a remarkable crossover achievement.[43] Nirvana's influence was monumental; so much so that Gary Gersh, president of Capitol Records, could justifiably refer to "a pre-Nirvana and post-Nirvana record business."[44] In the wake of Nirvana, as well as the success of Pearl Jam, Soundgarden, and other groups, alternative would move from an emergent formation in the industry to the dominant rock formation, essentially reaching a point of saturation similar to what the new music had achieved a decade earlier.

As alternative reached this point of dominance over the course of the early to mid-1990s, it pushed aside the older AOR groups that had been successful throughout the late 1980s, while simultaneously colonizing the modern rock label of the previous generation. One can see this transformation simply by comparing the makeup of the Album Rock Tracks and Modern Rock Tracks charts, which *Billboard* conveniently published side by side throughout the early 1990s. In January 1992, the month that "Smells Like Teen Spirit" first reached the Top 10 of both charts, the Album Rock chart, which was essentially a legacy of the AOR format, had a particularly "aged" quality. It consisted primarily of male-dominated North American hard rock, progressive rock, heavy metal, and classic rock artists like Van Halen, Rush, John Mellencamp, Metallica, and Bob Seger & the Silver Bullet Band, all of whom were well into (at least) the second decades of their careers.[45] By contrast, the Modern Rock chart still featured a heavy British influence, many more females, and a higher proportion of newer artists. The two charts were worlds apart, sharing only four artists in common (U2, Nirvana, Pearl Jam, and the Smithereens).

Over the course of 1993 and 1994 these older AOR artists and British artists began to disappear from the charts as the influx of alternative artists caused a substantial ratings spike in the Modern Rock format, which had a consequent "snowball effect" on Top 40 and AOR radio.[40] Numerous stations reconfigured their rotations, either adding alternative artists or switching entirely to a modern rock format. Record labels started to recognize the value in promoting new artists under the modern rock umbrella, and began to market a disparate array of singles and albums accordingly. Just as most any new white rock artist of the mid-1980s who fell outside of the blues or heavy metal's domain was heralded as "new music," so the definition of "alternative" and "modern rock" by the mid-1990s had expanded to encompass an impossibly wide range of artists. A "neo-classic rock band" like the Counting Crows, who only a few years prior would have been introduced via AOR, was now suddenly pitched as modern rock, as were guitar-oriented "roots rock" artists like Sheryl Crow, Blind Melon, and Cracker.[47] Two years after Nirvana's breakthrough, the January 29, 1994, Album Rock Top 40 and Modern Rock Top 30 *Billboard* charts now showed eight shared artists between them. Perhaps even more significantly, the number of British and foreign artists had dropped precipitously on the Modern Rock chart, as more than two-thirds of the entries were from North Americans. The last vestiges of the new wave were beginning to disappear from the modern rock category.

By 1996 alternative and modern rock had fully assumed the mainstream position that AOR once enjoyed. The Album Rock Tracks and Modern Rock Tracks now overlapped to a staggering extent, as the two routinely shared at least half of the same songs. Alternative had also made significant inroads into the Hot 100 singles chart, where one often found at least a dozen of the Top 40 Modern Rock chart's tracks residing. As all these formats increasingly elided with one another over the course of the mid-1990s, and modern rock assumed a dominant yet aesthetically vague commercial role in the industry, rock critics and jaded fans alike found it difficult to speak of alternative and all that the word implied, without adopting a tone that was ironic or cynical.[48] If alternative *was* the mainstream, then it begged the question: "Alternative to what?"[49] In a gesture that illustrated the perverse absurdity of alternative's situation, in April 1996, *Billboard* renamed the Album Rock Tracks chart as Mainstream Rock Tracks.[50] Placed alongside the Modern Rock Tracks chart in the magazine, the virtually identical

Mainstream Rock Tracks chart now showed conclusively that "mainstream rock" and "modern rock" were essentially the same thing.

As alternative and modern rock moved from an emergent to a dominant formation, whatever random new wave remnants that might have been lingering about were finally put to rest. The contemporary American rock of the mid-1990s featured a heavier sound, dominated by guitars and almost completely devoid of both the foreign and dance influences that had been so crucial to the original new wave. And many of those foreign artists who *did* manage to break into the charts—groups like Bush and Silverchair—were virtually indistinguishable in style from such American grunge forebears as Nirvana, Pearl Jam, and Stone Temple Pilots. In this context new wave became a "residual" style, both an acknowledged tributary feeding into the current modern rock moment and a distant moment in rock's past history that was available for resuscitation and reevaluation. Dance clubs began hosting '80s nostalgia nights, new wave CD retrospectives and anthologies appeared, and "classic modern rock" stations started up that leaned heavily on early 1980s "oldies" like Soft Cell and Duran Duran.[51] With the smell of nostalgia money in the air, groups like Blondie reformed and recorded new material and audiences swarmed to revival flashback tours like 1998's "Big Rewind," which featured Howard Jones, Human League, and Culture Club.

But it was not just the reappearance of older or forgotten acts that jostled people's memories of the 1980s. As a residual style, new wave became a touchstone through which brand new artists could forge a link to a past formation, just as the new wave had originally done through its evocation of mid-1960s garage rock and the British Invasion. In 1994, the British music press cobbled together a number of new fledgling groups such as S*M*A*S*H and These Animal Men under the ungainly banner of "The New Wave of New Wave," a designation meant to suggest a revival of the original mid-1970s British punk rock new wave's spirit of outrage and anarchy. The contrived "movement" fizzled out rather quickly. In the United States, artists like the Rentals and the Pulsars turned to a different new wave and focused on the one musical element that signified the most remote aesthetic distance from the current rock scene: the synthesizer. Specifically employing various vintage analog keyboards from the 1970s and early 1980s, they placed their residual musical technology in the foreground, where it quickly served to set them apart. As Matt Sharp of the Rentals explained: "It's weird . . . we'll play a show, and afterwards people will come up and they don't know what synthesizers are. 'What are those?'"[52] In the years since then, the synthesizer has become more normalized as a representative icon of the 1980s technopop era. Whether invoked as an homage, a form of resistance, or an ironic reference, the synthesizer provides the easiest passageway into a recognizable new wave style, and the most immediate reminder of the genre's once prominent position.

Over the course of the first two chapters, I have sketched a history of new wave, examining the genre as a cultural formation and showing that its designation as a form of "modern" popular music was tied to specific musical practices and their relationships to the music industry. With this chronological context in place, I turn in the following chapters to a more detailed analysis of new wave's modern identity. To be sure, the label of "modern" undoubtedly circulated around new wave as a handy marketing catchphrase, one that distinguished the music from more conventional or traditional rock and pop. But as I will argue, new wave also enjoyed deep connections with a host of different historical modernities, whose presence—in one way or another—informed the music's very meanings. Through the lens of the modern, I will examine the creative process behind the music and how it was interpreted and received, while also considering why new wave attracted certain audiences while repelling others. Most of all I will ask, how did the connection with the modern mark new wave as something special, unique, odd, or different within the sea of popular music styles that flooded the turn of the 1980s.

THREE

From Neurasthenia to Nervousness:
The Whiteness of the New Wave

The Talking Heads' 1984 concert film *Stop Making Sense* remains one of new wave's definitive artistic statements, an adventurous cinematic portrait of a band long associated with the genre's most experimental proclivities. As conceived by the Talking Heads' front man David Byrne and director Jonathan Demme, the movie intentionally unfolds as a three-act theatrical play. In the first act, we are introduced to the Talking Heads' four main members, who enter the stage one song at a time. They are then followed by the auxiliary musicians: first, two female background singers and a percussionist, and then a keyboard player and a guitarist, all of whom, unlike the Talking Heads, are African American. In the second act, the collective nine-piece ensemble plays a number of songs, each of them exhibiting different cinematographic touches that highlight Byrne's unusual choreographed dances and stage props. For the climactic third act, Byrne appears on stage in a specially designed oversized "Big Suit" that leaves him looking like a ridiculous cartoon character, with "a teeny little head and teeny little arms and feet stickin' out."[1] Byrne's meticulous attention to the visual and physical details of his bizarre stage persona seizes the viewer's attention throughout the film and reminds one of why new wave was frequently labeled as a form of art rock.

Unsurprisingly, the uniformly glowing reviews that accompanied *Stop Making Sense* focused their comments mainly on Byrne's inventive, avant-garde screen presence. Writing about the film in the journal *Artforum,* Carter Ratcliff applauded the constructed nature of Byrne's stage character as a subversive renunciation of the rock-star fiction of naturalness and easy

71

expression. An "emblem of selfhood plagued by self-consciousness," Byrne presents to the audience a fractured "Frankensteinian" identity constantly aware of its artificial design. At every turn the Talking Heads' stage show reflects his "awkwardness, rawness, [and] android angst," all of which communicate an intense sense of alienation and *difference:*

> [Byrne's] an outsider and he knows it; signaling his knowledge with a dazzling repertory of alienated moves: grimaces straight out of low-style, brand-X cartoons; mad-scientist leers; sudden fits of the shakes; hyperkinetic lopes around and around the two platforms; a pas de deux with a tilting, lit-up lamp; running in place; hoedown stomps that induce the backup singers, Lynn Mabry and Ednah Holt, to join in. They show good spirits but their grace can't help looking like mockery, as they try to mirror Byrne's ecstatic clunkiness. Guitar player Alex Weir never tries. His moves are as loose and warmed-up as Byrne's are tight and cold and wound-up. With his human immediacy, Weir reminds you of all that Byrne's stage presence has renounced.[2]

Ratcliff plays Byrne's "tight," "cold," and "wound up" gestures against the "loose" and "warmed up" body language of guitarist Alex Weir for strategic effect. This stark contrast helps to underscore just how far removed Byrne's constructed persona was from the typical performing bodies that had graced popular music concerts throughout the 1970s. There is an unspoken subtext in Ratcliff's review, however, that is crucial to understanding the significance of Byrne's performed awkwardness. Simply put, Byrne is white, while Weir is African American. Viewed in this context *Stop Making Sense* is more than just a three-act play; it is, as Talking Heads biographer David Bowman suggests, "the spiritual journey of a hapless white guy . . . trying to 'get down,'" who by the end of the show "finds his mojo."[3] In this respect *Stop Making Sense* is nothing less than a musical and visual commentary on what it means to be white.

While Byrne's performance in *Stop Making Sense* is obviously an exaggeration, it nonetheless underscores a fundamental characteristic of new wave as a whole: it was overwhelmingly perceived as a white genre of music. Little has been made of new wave's specific racial constitution, but even a cursory examination reveals that in the United States especially the ma-

Figure 7. David Byrne of the Talking Heads with lamp, performing at Forest Hills in Queens, New York, on August 21, 1982. © Ebet Roberts.

jority of the genre's performers were white, and more precisely white middle class. Many new wave bands, such as the Talking Heads, were formed by graduates (or dropouts) of art schools, universities, and colleges, traditionally white middle-class institutions that provide a far different background than the more typically romanticized portrait of rock's working-class genesis. As such, new wave was often characterized as "intellectual" or "progressive," possessed of a substance and depth that distinguished it from the standard blue-collar AOR rock fare with which it shared the airwaves. It was not simply that new wave's whiteness served to distance the music from other genres, however. Those fans that identified with a performer like Byrne latched onto new wave because it also presented them with a smart, misfit persona, one whose quirky mannerisms signified a rupture with the middle class's increasingly faceless anonymity. In its own way, new wave's most important rebellion was the one it enacted internally against the staidness of its own middle-class self.

It is one thing to acknowledge that new wave was predominantly performed and consumed by white middle-class musicians and fans. It is quite
another to claim that the genre itself connoted whiteness. This is the line
of reasoning, however, that I will follow in this chapter. My argument will
focus on a single musical and emotional quality, one that dominated the
critical reception of Byrne's persona and other male new wave singers as
well, and one that became virtually synonymous with a type of white new
wave masculinity: nervousness.[4] Byrne's nervousness is one of *Stop Making
Sense*'s strongest visual tropes. He develops this idea from the film's opening scenes, when he appears alone playing a scaled-back version of the
band's first hit, "Psycho Killer," on acoustic guitar accompanied by an electronic drum beat emanating from a boom box. Dressed in white shoes, a
floppy cream-colored suit that hangs off his frail frame and a shirt rigidly
buttoned all the way to the collar, Byrne bobs his head and neck awk-
wardly, assuming the role of the song's "tense and nervous" protagonist.
Toward the song's end, the boom box accompaniment interrupts the
steady beat with a series of skittering drum fills. Byrne responds to these
sonic cues by stumbling across the stage, as if suffering from a nervous col-
lapse brought on by the overwhelming stimuli of his environment. Later in
the film, with the full group assembled around him, Byrne's nervousness
takes a different form. In "Once in a Lifetime," now sporting thick horn-
rimmed glasses, Byrne staggers and shakes convulsively to the music. His
erratic bodily motions match the disorientation and alienation of the
lyrics, a portrait of a modern man wracked by the fragmented, confusing
details of his very own identity and selfhood.

It is clear from watching Byrne in *Stop Making Sense* that his nervousness is inseparable from his whiteness. It is one of the qualities that sets
him apart from the loose and exuberant African American musicians that
surround him. But why should nervousness and whiteness be interlinked
in this way? And why should nervousness so readily signify a sense of white
modern alienation? The answers, I will suggest, stretch far back to an earlier modern American era at the turn of the twentieth century, when discussions of nervousness dominated medical and cultural discourse. If we
are to understand how the nervousness of the new wave could cut a distinctly white path through the heart of rock's African American roots, we

must begin by examining how nervousness itself came to be a defining feature of white cultural identity over a century ago.

The Roots of Nervousness

*I haven't done many interviews recently, but when I do, I make it a point to
mention that I've never seen a psychiatrist.*

   —David Byrne, 1979[5]

Throughout the Talking Heads' early career, Byrne's persona was a magnet for all manner of psychological musings among music critics, who much to the singer's chagrin alternately pigeonholed him as neurotic, paranoid, schizophrenic, and psychotic. Consider, for example, Lester Bangs's 1979 *Village Voice* review of the Talking Heads' third album, *Fear of Music*. Bangs depicts Byrne as a hypersensitive observer, acutely attuned to his environment, a kind of "every-neurotic, wandering through the world encountering ouch-producers every step and breath he takes."[6] Through his reactions to his modern environment—from the hustle and bustle of city life to the very air that we breathe—Byrne acts as "a sort of dowser's wand for neuroses and trauma."[7] While these conditions could be seen as debilitating, Bangs suggests quite the opposite. Describing the full weight of Byrne's nervousness and sensitivity to his environment, he claims that "to feel anxiety is to be blessed by the full wash of life in its ripest chancre—everything else is wax museums."[8] For Bangs, Byrne's portrayal of an anxiety-ridden subject is a sign of intellectual distinction. To be nervous is to have the gift of a refined sensibility, a heightened awareness and reception to the world around us.

As tempting as it is to lunge for the jargon of Freudian psychoanalysis in explaining Byrne's peculiar state, Bangs's descriptions point elsewhere. Based on his observations, had Byrne been diagnosed in, say, the 1880s the singer would have been labeled not as a troubled or mentally ill patient, but rather an overly sensitive one, and his suffering would have been traced to a modern psychosomatic disorder known as neurasthenia, literally "nerve weakness" or "nervous exhaustion." Neurasthenia's symptoms were vexingly vague and numerous, and included everything from "insomnia, cerebral irritation, and a feeling of profound exhaustion" to "convulsive movements, fear of society, and lack of decision in trifling matters."[9] In many ways neurasthenia enjoyed a strikingly broad currency among practicing physicians of the late nineteenth century precisely *because* its diagnosis allowed for an incredible flexibility. Nervousness as such could be used to explain all manner of problems that might be troubling a patient.

While neurasthenia's physical and mental symptoms were impossibly wide in their scope, the reasons offered for the illness's manifestations came grounded in much more concrete cultural and social explanations, and it is here where its connection with new wave becomes particularly important. The American neurologists who first identified neurasthenia in the 1870s—particularly George Beard and his colleague A. D. Rockwell—proposed from the very start that neurasthenia was a uniquely modern disease. A prominent New York practitioner, Rockwell asserted that "the primary cause of neurasthenia in this country is civilization itself, with all that the term implies, with its railway, telegraph, telephone, and periodical press intensifying in ten thousand ways cerebral activity and worry."[10] Neurasthenia reflected the rapid growth of modern urban and industrial centers in the Northeast and the corresponding sensory overload that these new environments precipitated.[11] As the noted philosopher and sociologist Georg Simmel suggested in his 1903 essay, "The Metropolis and the Mental Life," urban life had resulted in an "intensification of nervous stimulation."[12] In short, for many people the increasingly frantic tempo of modern life, the varied demands of social interactions, and the economic pressures of time management and business production had become overwhelming. Much like attention deficit hyperactivity disorder (ADHD) for a more recent generation, neurasthenia's appearance had no concrete physiological basis, but rather was explained as an unfortunate by-product of stressful environmental circumstances.[13]

Neurasthenia diagnoses would eventually recede in the second and third decades of the twentieth century as the popularization of Freudian psychoanalysis suggested a new means for treating neurosis. But by then the idea of nervousness and the recognition of the neurotic personality type had become normalized as part of American society. From the 1920s on, the discourse on nervousness and modernity would graduate rather seamlessly into the notion of the nervous breakdown, a phrase that in keeping with the modern mechanized tenor of the times implied that people were equivalent to machines, capable of breaking down. Like neurasthenia, the nervous breakdown was a vague designation, a catchall for a variety of symptoms lacking any standardized medical explanation. Similarly, the nervous breakdown was linked to the problems of a hectic modern lifestyle, affecting both the overworked corporate businessman and the idle, underworked housewife vulnerable to "frivolous worries" and "temptations."[14] This portrait of nervousness would come to be seen as symptomatic of the underlying tensions in the post–World War II suburbs, not only as a reflection of the pressures of modern living but as a measure of the pervasive anxiety linked with Cold War panic and societal paranoia. By the late twentieth century, nervousness was generally recognized as a malady both peculiarly modern and American.

This modern zeitgeist forms the core of new wave's nervousness at the turn of the 1980s in a variety of ways. Certainly many new wave songs such as the Humans' "I Live in the City"—with its pulsating tempo, ominous diminished chord tritones, and lyrics depicting an "intense," "loud and fast and high energy" modern lifestyle fraught with frustration—draw on the long-standing association of the urban metropolis as a site of dangerous, nervous excitation. New wave musicians drew attention as well to the array of new modern technologies that had transformed every walk of life. From a burgeoning video game industry to such new electronic household commodities as videocassette players and recorders, answering machines, and the portable Walkman, electronic gadgets had begun infiltrating various facets of everyday life at an alarming rate in the late 1970s. No advancement signaled society's widespread technological modernization as thoroughly as the arrival of the personal computer (PC), which emerged from its status as a fringe technology to become an accepted domestic appliance, eventually earning *Time* magazine's "Man of the Year" honors for 1982. With the popularization of computers there arose corresponding fears that technology had become an alienating force and a source of social anxiety.[15] Unlike the easy accessibility of today's computer technology, the computers of the early 1980s were associated most of all with cumbersome programming. Their true usefulness could only be invoked through a series of complex, seemingly mathematical instructions. Their daunting interface was compounded by their new roles. As repositories of vital security information or as the new automated face of robotic factory production, computers fed into dystopian fears of human obsolescence in a new mechanized society.

1979's "Computer Games," the lone hit single from Australia's Mi-Sex, captures the modern nervousness surrounding the complexity of the new computer culture in a memorable fashion. The whole song pulsates along on a repetitive arpeggiated sequencer pattern and synthesized drum rhythm that suggests a computerized mechanization while also securing the song's strident dance floor beat. The singer assumes the role of a worker overwhelmed by a hodgepodge of technical imagery—fidgeting with "digit dots," connecting with an "XU-1" and an unresponsive "matrix grid"— which leaves him crying an "anxious tear." The vivid abstract hyperstimuli of the lyrics bleeds over into the vocals, as the singer alternates between monotonous drones on a single pitch and wild, erratic melodic leaps that mimic the computer's random numerical operations. The singer's theatrical, mannered delivery creates a playful nervousness, one amplified by the verses' open C major (I), F major (IV) harmonies and bluesy, reverbed guitar riff/hook. But the chorus, which moves to the darker relative A minor harmony, and a tense repetitive vocal stutter hints at the potential discord and alienation lingering beneath this dizzying technological surface.

This darker tone completely subsumes Wall of Voodoo's 1981 song "Back in Flesh." Singing in a tremulous deadpan voice, front man Stan Ridgway presents himself as a nervous worker "on the edge" chained to the punch card schedule of an unfeeling corporation. Ridgway seeks a way out of this modern bureaucratic nightmare through acts of leisure and relaxation, but only meets with frustration, as background vocalist Chas Gray thwarts his desires through a series of stifling call-and-response exchanges: "Well, I'd rather go bowling" (The lanes are all closed) . . . "Well, how about some golfing?" (The greens are overgrown). A repetitive slow-pulsed A minor melodic loop in the bass (a–f–b–e) that moves one pitch per measure signifies the mundane, deadening workday life of the corporation; the exposed dissonant tritone (f–b) within the loop further emphasizes Ridgway's unbalanced state of mind. During the verses an accelerated arpeggiated sixteenth-note pattern appears in the synthesizer, clearly intended to depict the corporation's modern machinelike efficiency. Played largely around a black note pattern (c♯–f♯–g♯–a♯), and slightly out of time with the ground bass pattern, it clashes dissonantly with the song's repetitive melodic and rhythmic textures. The synthesizer's thin, staccato timbres and closely clustered rhythms signify in abstract terms the imagined mathematical precision of a computer. The "brains" behind the corporation, the synthesizer/computer also signifies the modern hyperstimuli that drive the singer to nervous exhaustion.

"Back in Flesh" deals with the overwhelming effects of a modern environment, and it is easy enough to link its troubled nervous protagonist both to the 1950s corporate nervous breakdown as well as the neurasthenic patients that had proliferated in the early twentieth century. But the connection extends far beyond the mere recognition of nervousness as an environmental malady. What is perhaps more revealing is *who* the nineteenth-century urban neurologists believed to be most susceptible to the disease's symptoms. As George Beard explained, nervousness was a peculiarly American disease, a reflection of the country's rapidly developing urban centers and competitive marketplace. Nervousness was thus most likely to occur among "the business and professional men who were most committed to the competitive ethic."[16] Beard and his neurological colleagues argued that neurasthenia was a diagnosis to be reserved for a select class of America's "brain-workers"—that is, those among the upper, urban professional classes, as well as teachers, intellectuals, and men and women of a particularly sensitive, refined nature. In Beard's view, such people shouldered the greatest burden and stresses of America's push toward a higher level of modern civilization. It is a short step from Beard's modern urban professional to the late-twentieth-century corporate man, his nerves frayed by the abstract logic and random programming sounds of the synthesizer/computer "brain."

As was clear from Beard's descriptions, neurasthenia also served as an elitist sign of distinction. The typical nervous subject was, in his words, "distinguished from the coarse (person) by fine, soft hair, delicate skin, nicely chiseled features, small bones, tapering extremities, and frequently by a muscular system comparatively small and feeble."[17] As historian Julian B. Carter points out in his study *The Heart of Whiteness,* the language of Beard's portrait made clear the racial and class dimensions along which neurasthenia was drawn. This was not a disease to be found residing among brawny laborers, ex-slaves, or Indians. The racialized lower classes were not deemed to be nervous because "they lacked the physical, intellectual, and moral sensitivity and self-discipline that moderns had evolved."[18] Nervousness as such not only reinforced the separation between the middle or upper class and the working class, but also served to distance "civilized" whites from "barbarous" blacks and the growing immigrant population. Neurasthenia was so closely connected with the elite modern classes that in some respects it became a "marker of status and social acceptability."[19] By the 1930s neuroses had in many respects even become glamorized, as evidenced by Dr. Louis Bisch's book of 1936, *Be Glad You're Neurotic*.[20]

It is this legacy—that of nervousness as a marker of intellectual sensitivity and whiteness—that provides the backdrop against which new wave's nervousness should be read. New wave's whiteness generally went without comment, but the coded critiques that emerged around the music—aligning the genre with intellectuals and minimalist machinelike efficiency, and distancing it from the "natural expression" of rock's blues-based roots—left little doubt about how the music signified within rock's racialized sphere. Cast within this context, the nervous new wave front man stood as a recognizably white modern trope. As a marker of whiteness, nervousness allowed new wave's white performers a space within which they could both celebrate and critique their cultural backgrounds, and also present a version of whiteness quite different from what had come to typify the societal norms of the 1970s.

Wound Up Tight

There's a streak of defiance in David Byrne; he hates anything that's clichéd in modern life. When he's nervous he shows he's nervous because that's not a cliché.
    —Tina Weymouth of the Talking Heads, 1979[21]

New wave's nervousness drew obvious attention from rock critics for its novelty and freshness. In order to understand its full significance, however, this nervousness must be placed in a specific context and read as a deliberate reaction against the prevailing societal and musical norms that had become entrenched by the end of the 1970s. In his book *Getting Loose,* sociologist Sam Binkley reveals a postcountercultural "self-loosening" discourse that took hold in the 1970s.[22] A range of advice manuals and books encouraged white middle-class Americans to loosen up and throw off the shackles of social and sexual mores that inhibited true self-expression and intimacy. A mode of expressive behavior emerged, one that valued directness, openness and a connection with a more natural self. This quest for individuality and an authenticity of feeling manifested itself in a variety of ways, ranging from longer hair, flowing sideburns, open collars, and looser, more sexually revealing clothing to such popular phrases as "Let it all hang out." Such maneuvers deliberately aimed to vanquish, once and for all, the image of the stressed-out, uptight white Establishment 1950s "organization man," whose lingering specter still haunted the white middle class. As one loosened up, relaxed, communed with nature and engaged the inner "swinger," so the nervous self inhibited by the demands of the work force would disappear.

As Binkley points out, the white middle class strove to be loose in part by embracing a "hipness," adopting, for example, the slang, fashion, and bodily expressions of African American culture. New musical styles like funk, and songs like Sly and the Family Stone's 1969 hit "Thank You (Falettinme Be Mice Elf Agin)," entreated listeners to get loose and be themselves, and came to signify the sense of individuality that was central to the post-countercultural movement. To be groovy was to be loosened up, and funk's musical groove, with its celebration of the individual instrumental voice within the seamless textured whole, provided the ideal soundtrack. Funk's celebration of the loosened, expressive self reached its apex in the decade's second half with its mainstreaming via the explosive popularity of disco. Here the consumerist individuality of the loose style found its most notorious representations through the hedonistic media-sensationalized discotheque extremes of Studio 54 and the expressive sexualized routines of couples' disco dancing.

Other music styles demonstrated a loosening as well. The white middle-class singer-songwriter genre stressed a new honesty and autobiographical expression. The movement's most celebrated artist, James Taylor, communed with his audience in songs like 1970's "Fire and Rain," opening up about the traumas and tribulations of his past personal history. Taking to the stage in dressed-down denim, long, flowing hair and playing an acoustic guitar, Taylor exuded a loose, comfortable image that suggested an acceptance of intimacy and experience. On the other end of the spectrum, the popularity of the Dionysian "cock rocker" represented the ultimate attainment of rock as a lifestyle of hedonism and uninhibited sexuality. Surveying the links between rock and sexuality in 1978, Simon Frith and Angela McRobbie described the white cock rocker's symbolic domain—one extending from Elvis Presley to Robert Plant and Roger Daltrey and hard rock groups like Thin Lizzy—as an integral part of rock's iconic mythology. Much of it, they claimed, was based on an image of power and sexual conquest, whether through the figurative phallic thrust of guitars and microphone stands, the physical display of the male body or the music's objectification of female bodies. These images were most obvious in cock rock's live staged performances, where the genre's various visual and musical codes forcefully denoted rock's hardened masculinity:

> Cock rock performers are aggressive, dominating, and boastful. . . . Their stance is obvious in live shows; male bodies on display, plunging shirts and tight trousers, a visual emphasis on chest hair and genitals . . . the music is loud, rhythmically insistent, built around techniques of arousal and climax; the lyrics are assertive and arrogant, though the exact words are less significant than the vocal styles involved, the shouting and screaming.[23]

Much of the overt sexuality and expressive power on display in cock rock's rituals derived from the music's connection with the rhythm and blues tradition. In this regard, it emerged as yet another example of rock's oft-commented-upon minstrel heritage, of whites performing as liberated bodies by co-opting and channeling a distinct musical and cultural blackness.

Set against this "cock rock" stereotype, the appearance of new wave's nervous front man in the late 1970s offered nothing less than an alternative masculinity, one whose greatest power derived from the ways that it diverged from or contradicted what had become rock's normative performative stance. If the cock rocker embodied an unsubtle realization of rock's working-class rebellion, espousing a hardness born of the street, new wave's contrasted this with a middle-class bookish intellectualism and collegiate, art school pedigree. Where the male cock rock singer was emotionally, physically, and sexually direct, the nervous persona was constricted, distant, and detached. The fraternal bonding of the male cock rock group was contrasted with the nervous singer as an isolated narrator wrestling with his own mental and physical constraints. Lastly, if the cock rocker was presented as an authentically powerful individual, one possessed of confidence and self-assurance, the nervous persona was viewed through an ironic lens where the artificial construction of this nervousness was made obvious and transparent, an element of play in which the singer had chosen to engage.

Most of all, the nervous persona enacted a performance of the sexualized body on which was mapped the exuberances as well as the anxieties of self-control rather than the liberating potential of getting loose. This relationship between sexual activity and self-discipline figured prominently in the original late-nineteenth-century discourse on nervousness, which is unsurprising given the restrictive Victorian culture in which neurasthenia initially appeared. As Beard, Rockwell, and other neurologists conceived the disease, neurasthenia resulted in large part from an excessive expenditure of nervous energy. They also argued that one of the largest reserves of human energy was located in the sexual organs. To waste that energy, whether through masturbation or profligate sexual activity, would result in a depleted body. This condition, for which physicians reserved the specific category of *sexual neurasthenia,* was believed to afflict males and not females, who physicians viewed as reproductive rather than sexual beings.[24] The prescription for a male sexual neurasthenic called for a focused self-restraint. Such discipline was intended not only to channel the body's energies properly, but also to separate white civilized society from the wanton sexual hyperpotency ascribed to "Negroes" and the laboring class.

This relationship between neurasthenia and self-control underwent a crucial twist during the second and third decades of the twentieth century, however, as the treatment of nervousness and neuroses graduated into the Freudian realm of psychoanalysis. Freud had studied Beard's writings on neurasthenia, but as he explained in his essay "Civilized Morality and Modern Nervousness," he saw the role of discipline and restraint not as a cure but as potentially the actual root of neuroses.[25] Nervousness as such was the result of *too much* control, the body straining and bubbling over at the repression of desires. In this view the blockage of sexual expression could have damaging effects, resulting in male impotence. This conflict surrounding self-control has never truly been resolved. On the one hand, the practice of self-control still provides the stabilizing center for arguments of moral standing and decency in society. On the other hand, it remains as the scapegoat for many stress related maladies, nervousness among them.

Regardless of how one chooses to read the relationship between control and nervousness, as with neurasthenia the discourse that emerged around the two was one that reaffirmed certain assumptions about what it meant to be white. As the cultural theorist Richard Dyer has observed in his book *White,* the self-denial and self-control required to maintain a moral decorum (and also distance oneself from the physicality of others) highlights the "triumph of mind over matter" that has long constituted a white cultural ideal.[26] Dyer explains how white European and American cultures for centuries have had extremely uncomfortable and conflicted relationships with their bodies. He gives as an example white society's strong cultural basis in the tenets of Christianity, which has stressed the strength of spiritual transcendence over the weaknesses of bodily temptation. Historian Peter Stearns has echoed this image of the body as a site of discipline and control in his multivolume study of twentieth-century white American middle-class emotional ideals, depicting the white body as a "battleground of desire."[27] Understood within this specific context, the troubled, malfunctioning nervous persona can be viewed as one of the white body's most prominent "battleground" casualties.

From a visual perspective, new wave performers realized this portrait of repressed self-control in numerous ways, consciously rejecting the flowing and revealing clothing that had become the trademark of 1970s rock superstars. The new waver's suit jacket and skinny tie, borrowed from mod style, accented the shape of the body, while at the same time concealing it from view. Collars buttoned fully to the top replaced the plunging neckline; thick glasses hid the eyes, suggesting the intellectual concentration and social awkwardness of the "brain worker." In short, the nervous new wave musician was defined by a noticeable lack of the physical and sexual prowess that had become the signature of the cock rocker. Benjamin Nugent suggests in his book *American Nerd* that new wave musicians like Elvis Costello who cultivated this particular appearance emerged in the late 1970s as a manifestation of a different, yet related, white cultural stereotype, that of the nerd.[28] The portrait of the nerd that Nugent sketches is one distinctly at odds with the openly emotional image of the loosened up 1970s swinger. The nerd harbors a "fear of intimacy" that manifests itself in an obsessive devotion to nonphysical, often technological, activities. Communication for the nerd veers away from the slang and black cultural appropriations of conversational English toward the formal diction of written Standard English. As the linguist Mary Bucholtz has argued, this controlled, intellectualized "hypercorrectness" correlates from a racial standpoint with a perceived "hyperwhiteness."[29] Bleached of black culture, both the nerd and the neurasthenic uphold a certain vision of what it means to be white.

By all accounts, this focus on self-control found its way into new wave rock discos as well, where what the California new wave group Suburban Lawns self-consciously parodied as "Intellectual Rock," refused the eroticized bodily impulses that dance music might otherwise suggest. As Will Straw has observed, the audiences that rock discos attracted differed radically from those that had frequented the glitzy seventies discotheque: "The highly ritualized and couple-oriented nature of most disco dancing in the 1970s gave way, within rock dance clubs, to styles marked by more restrained movements and an unspoken prohibition on physical contact between dancers."[30] New wave rock disco dancing veered toward a form of "disciplined militancy" imbued with "intellectual substance."[31] Or as *Creem* magazine's Richard Riegel put it, a "bouncyllectual, I'm-dancing-as-distanced-as-I-can" style came into fashion.[32] Rigid and regimented bodies filled the dance floors, shunning the libidinal excesses and bodily displays that had ruled the late 1970s.

For the white middle-class patrons who frequented these clubs, the tight, restricted dancing body given over to the anxieties of the new modernity also certainly acted as a novel, if circumscribed, form of class revolt. Through its exaggerated representations, the appearance of the nervous repressed body made visible that which the middle class had tried to absorb and shuttle away as part of its identity. Nervousness, as such, was most of all a *performance,* a persona to assume that could both celebrate and self-parody the whiteness of the middle class. In the following section, I will examine more closely the means through which new wave musicians communicated a nervous quality to their audience. Specifically I will explore the relationship between nervousness as it is perceived socially—through certain audible and visible emotional characteristics—and the nervousness of the new wave, where it was realized through numerous stylized musical techniques.

Performing Nervousness

The white body, as an uneasy site of regimented control and discipline, was a crucial element of the new wave. Next to David Byrne and the Talking Heads, no group played upon the body's awkward nervous tensions with as much creative imagination and bizarre humor as did Devo. Like the Talking Heads, who had formed at the Rhode Island School of Design, Devo was very much an art school band. The group's two main members, Gerald Casale and Mark Mothersbaugh, were graduates of the Kent State University Fine Arts program, and they brought to Devo a deep interest in avantgarde visual arts and experimental filmmaking. By the time that they released their 1978 debut album, *Q: Are We Not Men? A: We are Devo!* the band had developed a highly theatrical multimedia stage show, complete with surreal proto-music videos, props, and conceptual costume changes that contributed heavily to the group's popularity. Devo's five band members appeared in their films and played their concerts frequently dressed in matching yellow factory suits and dark 3-D styled glasses, a collection of five identical automatons (see figure 8). Their live shows were kinetic affairs that featured the band members patrolling the stage in a series of sharp, jerky motions and deliberately stiff dance steps, a paradoxical assault of "precision spastic robotics" that highlighted the conflicts of their performing bodies.[33]

The majority of reviews and interviews with Devo centered on the same theme: the novelty of the band's appeal lay in their dehumanized, robotic approach to the music. Whether it was their robotic vocals, their "suburban-robot image," or the way in which they had sacrificed disco's "hip humping" dancing for "the choreography of synchronized robots," the comparison was inescapable.[34] The band's main spokesmen, Casale and Mothersbaugh, happily used these descriptions to their advantage, and in their interviews fed the steady stream of curious journalists with a variety

Figure 8. Devo strikes a robotic pose while filming the video for "Satisfaction" at the Akron Civic Theatre, 1978. Photograph by Janet Macoska.

of explanations that ranged from the utterly preposterous to the entirely plausible. The band's name, they claimed, was short for "de-evolution," a deliberately vague theory that posited that society was not evolving but regressing, and becoming *less* human and more robotic in the process.[35] They also observed, more astutely, that American consumer society had become enslaved to some falsely idealized sense of the "good life" that supposedly could only be attained through a stringent, mechanized work ethic and the conspicuous consumption of material products and goods.[36] In this context, Devo's matching outfits, assembly line appearance, and robotic demeanor symbolized the loss of individuality that had accompanied this turn toward a modern "corporate feudal society."[37]

One can reasonably trace Devo's evocation of uniformed robotic, mechanical bodies back to the early twentieth century, when the robot was quite clearly understood to be a metaphorical representation of the worker in the new Taylorist and Fordist assembly line factory economy.[38] This type of manufacturing industry called for an efficiency of physical motion, and

was dependent upon workers who were wholly dedicated to their functioning tasks and oblivious to the distractions of human emotions. As Antonio Gramsci famously wrote in his 1929–30 essay "Americanism and
Fordism," the success of a worker in this system essentially required that he
act like a machine, that he sublimate his sexual urges so as "not to squan-
der his nervous energies in the disorderly and stimulating pursuit of occasional sexual satisfaction."[39] Should these primitive sexual instincts be left
unregulated, the worker would malfunction and break down. Seen in this
light, Devo's "spastic robotics" serves as a striking visualization of the white
male man-machine torn between discipline and the urges of the flesh.
When the robotic body is no longer able to maintain its tight repressive
control, neuroses spill over, manifesting themselves in nervous tics and
spastic gyrations.

Devo's "Uncontrollable Urge," the lead track off *Q: Are We Not Men? A:
We are Devo!* deals directly with these issues of self-denial and self-conscious control, mandated from within or without, and the body's need for
release and subsequent breakdown. Lyrically the song seems straightfor-
ward. Mark Mothersbaugh sings in general terms of a pent-up, uncontrollable urge, a need to "scream and shout" and release his emotions. The
lyrics never state directly that these urges are sexual in nature, but when
Mothersbaugh sings that he wants "to purge" them, one is reminded of the
shame of sexual release associated with the white middle class's bodily impulses. The music matches his excited state of anticipation with a fast
tempo and crisp, clean staccato rhythms. The verses are built around a
quasi call and response structure that reinforces the sense of urgency expressed in the lyrics. In the "call" section, Mothersbaugh sings a two-bar
phrase while the rhythm section vamps underneath on a driving eighth-
note power chord on A. In the "response" section Mothersbaugh drops out
and the rhythm section answers for two bars with two repetitions of a descending A mixolydian power chord riff (I–VII–V). Taken as a whole, the
churning rhythms, sharp accents, and clearly framed cadential harmony of
the descending riffs emphasize a powerful and purposeful, directed motion. They exhort the body to move.

There are numerous ways in which Mothersbaugh mirrors the music's
concentrated burst of energy, communicating a sense of nervous excitement through his vocals. He precedes each of the verse sections by singing

"yeah, yeah, yeah . . ." as a rising chromatic line that moves from a quarter note to a double-time eighth-note pulse, giving the impression of his urges creeping up and bubbling over the top. During the verses he crams together the phrasing of the words, as if he is speaking in a hurried, excited manner. His tone—aggressive, high in the register—contributes as well to the song's nervous edge. All of these "uncontrolled" gestures fight against the band's highly controlled sound. From the tight eighth notes on the closed high-hat and the muted staccato lines of the rhythm guitars to the phrasing, which falls squarely on the beat, the band's arrangement is marked by a tense, controlled disciplined sound. To be sure, it is energetic, but it is also rigidly ordered.

For all these familiar rock conventions, it is most of all the ways in which Mothersbaugh frames this nervousness as a sense of difference and disorder that places the song squarely within the new wave aesthetic. This is most apparent at the endings of the two-bar vocal lines in the verse, where he sings of being "out of control" or "losing control." A phrase ending, as such, is a pronounced, exposed spot, and generally offers an opportunity for a smooth closure, usually in the form of a melodically conjunct line that falls within the basic chordal accompaniment. Mothersbaugh's phrase endings, however, are deliberately jagged, highlighting a dissonance through melodic and rhythmic tension. He begins subtly on the first couplet, accenting "out of control" by leaping up to the 7th (g) over the A chord. With the second couplet he turns to more obvious word painting, singing "losing control" as a sharp, syncopated descending line that teeters on the edge of a 3:2 polyrhythm. In the second verse (which reuses the lyrics from the first), Mothersbaugh exaggerates his loss of control to an even greater degree. This time he sings the entire first phrase—"got an urge, got a surge and it's out of control"—volleying back and forth between b and g, which land directly outside the A power chord underneath. From a melodic standpoint, he is deliberately "out."[40] The second time through when Mothersbaugh sings "losing control," he now voices it as a descending line with a pronounced legato slur (again hinting at, but not quite achieving, a 3:2 polyrhythm) that throws it outside the song's persistent pulse.

Beyond these moments of strategic text painting, it is the overall tone of Mothersbaugh's voice, as much as the specific words, that communicates a nervous emotional quality. One hears this most clearly at the close of each verse, where Mothersbaugh threatens to break loose and "scream and shout it." In each instance, Mothersbaugh sings with an abnormally wide vibrato that suggests a wavering and an inability to control the pitch, one of the most readily identifiable signs of nervousness in real social situations. This is amplified by the contour of the phrase itself, which Mothersbaugh sings sliding into an open fourth alternating between a and e. This is an unusual choice of notes, one that goes against the single conjunct melodic motion of the conventional phrase ending. The exposed alternating open fourth resembles more the type of repetitive interval one might hear from an ambulance siren, a mechanistic warning cry. Taken as a whole, these examples convey a nervous energy that is not simply an outpouring, but a manifestation of the singer's desperate, failed attempts to exact a measure of bodily self-control. From a physiological standpoint, the strained battle to control his urges is made audible through his very vocal technique. Mothersbaugh sings with an excessive amount of air pressure (what a voice teacher might call subglottal pressure) that makes his voice sound tight and compressed.[41] We hear in a very literal sense the mounting pressure, bottled up and trapped inside the overly disciplined body.

In considering Mothersbaugh's vocals, it is helpful to place them within the larger context of rock and popular music singing. In his survey of rock singing, musicologist Richard Middleton identifies a "triangulating intersection of traditions" that regulates the vast majority of rock vocal approaches.[42] The two most common are what he calls a *"natural"* expression—rooted in the direct, emotive speech song of African American blues, gospel, folk, and country—and a contrasting bel canto style, which unlike the dirty timbres of the "natural," is marked by its purity of tone and refined technique. Each of these has accrued an aura of authenticity in rock music: the former for its "emotional integrity" and the latter for its "aesthetic integrity of technique." It is the third category, however, that which Middleton labels *stylization,* into which Mothersbaugh and other nervous new wave singers fall. Unlike the presumed authenticity of the first two categories, the stylized singer noticeably adopts a role or persona. A stylized singer like Mothersbaugh approaches the text and the melody through exaggerations and idiosyncratic quirks that draw attention to the performance behind the voice. Such tactics could provide new wave's vocalists, many of whom admitted to having little confidence in their singing voices, with a certain comfort and security. Stylization could turn a potential weakness into a strength.[43]

The distinction between Middleton's "natural" and "stylized" voices, of course, is not airtight. One could well argue, for example, that stylized singing has itself become so prominent and commonplace within rock music over the past two decades that it has come to denote an authenticity all its own, where the mannered or experimental voice is simply taken for granted as an accepted genre convention. The question remains, though: if Mothersbaugh's voice connotes a stylized nervousness and "uncontrollable" disorder, what is the *basis* for this vocal performance? On what communicative reality is it grounded? *Why* should we hear his voice as a nervous one, or the voice of someone incapable of functioning properly? Studies on the nervous or anxious voice have shown that it is associated with a variety of speech dysfluencies, including increased pauses and most noticeably wavering pitches or "jitters."[44] One could relate the effects that we hear in Mothersbaugh's performance further still to a variety of communication disorders.[45] The rapid, compressed phrasing resembles the communicative speech disorder of "cluttering." The unexpected melodic and registral leaps are similar to the type of aberrant gestural fluctuations associated with autism. Even the repeated "yeah, yeah . . ." refrain plays on one of the most common of these adult communication disorders: stuttering. None of this is to suggest that the vocal traits in "Uncontrollable Urge" *replicate* these disorders. Someone with cluttered speech would not speak with Mothersbaugh's degree of fluency and articulation. Likewise, stutterers struggle with the sounds and rhythms of words so that they are forced to slow down, not accelerate, their speech. Mothersbaugh's rapid stuttering thus is not an accurate representation, but a form of stylized imitation.

While physiologists and neurologists have demonstrated that communication disorders like the ones listed above are of a physical and cognitive nature, it remains a common cultural (mis)perception that a speech disfluency like stuttering is a "nervous disorder" and a symptom of "psychological problems."[46] For that reason, new wave vocalists like Mothersbaugh were heard as symbolic of a heightened neurotic state, as embodiments of a nervous persona. Other vocalists added an array of exaggerations and twitches to this general new wave profile. Singers routinely used sharp hiccups, excessive vibrato and trills, and registral leaps and dissonances to ornament their vocal lines. On these grounds, those who identified with the type of new wave voice heard in Devo did so in a way that cut against the "natural" or bel canto styles that were so formative to rock style. It is important to reiterate, though, that the main reason that a singer like Mothersbaugh sounded so strange in the late 1970s was because he addressed an audience that was conversant in the accepted vocal conventions of rock star singers. Devo was above all a rock band, and hearing Mothersbaugh's stylized mannerisms and exaggerations in a rock context led audiences to question the assumed naturalness of rock singing in general.

While I have focused primarily on the relationship between the voice and the body in Devo's "Uncontrollable Urge," new wave's nervousness extended to its basic instrumental qualities and song structures as well. Critics constantly referred to new wave's "herky jerky" style, an unsettling effect that arose from such elements as uneven phrasing, wandering chord progressions, and busy textures with abrupt, sharp accents. Devo was well aware of the ways in which their use of jerky rhythms could act directly on the body, encouraging a rigid, robotic, and discomforting reaction in their audiences. One of the ways they achieved this effect was through the use of odd meters like 7/8, which appears in one of the band's earliest singles, "Jocko Homo." Queried about this in an interview from early 1978, the band responded at length:

> Those kind of timings actually make you feel rigid right away. They give you that stiff, non-gut feeling to make you get into it on a whole different level than you would on a normal 4/4 beat that people just take for granted. Three-fourths of our songs you can count out in 4/4 time, but there's still that other element in there because it adds, like, a *disharmony* there that's kind of nice, especially if you keep the beat strong enough that it just pulls you into it over a longer time span. ANY rhythm—when you take an objective viewpoint and pull yourself out of it, can still become a BODY rhythm that you can count by any number you want, but people are so incredibly microcosmic about the way they relate to the music, they *need* 4/4 time.[47]

Devo's comments draw our attention to the centrality of the body in popular music, specifically as it relates to dance and its cultural contexts. To bands like Devo such maneuvers were important precisely for the ways in which they deflected and defused certain attitudes about the body and sexuality that in the 1970s rock experience had become virtually doctrinaire. Whereas a song like Led Zeppelin's "Whole Lotta Love" conveyed the orgasm as an element of dynamic eruptive (musical) pleasure, bands like Devo conceived of sexual release not as a type of ecstasy, but as an interloper in the fight for discipline and control. In the end, new wave's nervousness—both vocal and instrumental—offered an alternative conception of male sexuality and rock music.

The Genre with Perpetual Nervousness

Everywhere one turned in the new wave genre, the theme of nervousness was pervasive. It appeared in band names (The Nerves, Nervous Eaters, Nervous Gender, Nervus Rex) and song titles (The Feelies' "The Boy with the Perpetual Nervousness"), and became a common critical descriptor for the tremulous, twitchy vocal quirks of male singers like David Byrne, Mark Mothersbaugh, Roddy Frantz of the Urban Verbs, Danny Elfman of Oingo Boingo, and Tim Finn of Split Enz. As I have pointed out in this chapter, however, nervousness was more than just a vocal quality. New wave's nervous male singers projected a persona, one that extended to dress, mannerisms, and gestures, all of which made clear that their nervousness was a performance. This makes sense given that so many of new wave's singers came out of art school backgrounds or engaged in deliberately theatrical stage shows. None of this is to suggest, however, that these late 1970s new wave musicians consciously tapped into the specific cultural history of nervousness as a marker of the early twentieth-century modernity and whiteness that I have sketched in this chapter. Rather, it is clear that the persona of the nervous singer provided them with an unusual and novel vocal and stage presence, one that provided a safe distance from other rock identities, whether it be the lingering memory of self-indulgent late 1960s hippie psychedelia or rock's prevailing 1970s trend toward overbearing male bravado.

All told, new wave's nervousness could serve a number of functions. New wave musicians could invoke nervousness as a critique or commentary on the physical tensions of white middle-class society, specifically its obsessive focus on bodily control and emotional discipline. They could invoke nervousness as a signifier of modern life. Nervousness could signify their own arty, intellectual substance, or it could come across as a more bouncy and novel version of punk's frenzied, hysteric energy. In all of these cases nervousness signified a socially acknowledged, and self-conscious, form of white, middle-class difference. No matter what its desired effect, recognizing the history behind nervousness can help us to understand the formation of a nervous identity in new wave, and can help illuminate the genre's status as a modern, intellectualized pop style.

From a cultural standpoint, the musical depiction of nervousness helped reinforce new wave's rejection of a specific authenticity connected with the expressive history of the blues and other African American styles. The tight, nervous constriction of the new wave beat defused any attempt to assimilate the presumed "naturalness" of the black body. Instead, one could say that the aesthetic of new wave's nervous bands was written across the challenges of white cultural duality and the mind/body split. With the arrival of new wave and the popularity of the rock disco, there now emerged a new idealized social context, where fans apparently did not have to loosen up and lose themselves to the bodily allure of the dance floor. As rock critics at the time were quick to point out, the novel appeal of groups like the Talking Heads and Devo was precisely that they made "music to which you can dance and think, think and dance, dance and think, ad infinitum."[48] Through this basic recognition, new wave accepted and even celebrated the cultural contradictions and awkwardness of its own whiteness.

FOUR

Camp! Kitsch! Trash!
New Wave and the Politics of Irony

Fun is a void they drift through like asteroids in a vast expanse littered with cultural artifacts they keep bumping into: Gilligan's Island, Star Trek, *Petula Clark, Lesley Gore, the Mashed Potato, the Supremes,* Beach Blanket Bingo. *The way the B-52's handle these collisions is what makes them wild. They're connoisseurs of trash in a world full of it.*

—*Rolling Stone* review of the B-52's 1980 album *Wild Planet*[1]

In his remarks on *Wild Planet* music critic Frank Rose deploys a tactic common to nearly every B-52's review: he grounds the group's aesthetic in their recycling of pop culture's distant past, a dizzying parade of 1960s television reruns, forgotten female pop singers, novelty dances, and teenage *Beach Party* movies. From the moment the Athens, Georgia, quintet descended in late 1977 upon New York City, where they became "the darlings of the local club circuit," the B-52's attracted the adoring attention of critics who singled out the band's absurdist renderings of the ubiquitous mainstream pop culture of the late 1950s and early 1960s.[2] The band's two female singers, Kate Pierson and Cindy Wilson, appeared dressed in the throwaway fashion of "dime-store wigs and suburban-housewife garb," while their male counterpart, Fred Schneider, in his "Hawaiian shirt and dapper slacks," played the part of a "Key West lounge lizard."[3] The B-52's live performances were frenetic affairs in which the band pasted together B movie "sci-fi" keyboard sounds and surf riffs with invented dance fads like the Shy Tuna and Aqua-Velva, while rattling off odd lyrical puns ("Pass the tanning butter / Here comes a sting ray / There goes a Man Ray / Here comes a dogfish / Chased by a catfish"), which, as one critic observed, bore an uncanny resemblance

Figure 9. The B-52's dressed in secondhand fashion with 1960s Farfisa organ, performing at Max's Kansas City in New York City on May 27, 1978. © Ebet Roberts.

to Gertrude Stein's nonsensical verse.[4] Interviews with the band often bled into a discussion of their wide-ranging influences, where the B-52's rattled off lists of names ranging from singer Yma Sumac and actress Annette Funicello to such cinematic and television fare as *The Crawling Eye* and *The Little Rascals*. Even the band name itself, which they claimed was southern slang for Pierson's and Wilson's ridiculously oversized bouffant wigs, underscored the group's fascination with the ephemera of pop culture.[5]

What exactly is one to make of this eccentric and eclectic dabbling in the detritus of pop culture's past? Many would argue that a group such as the B-52's stands as a prime example of new wave's strong tendency toward irony.[6] That is, one cannot simply read their many allusions as faithful or authentic, but rather as intentionally distanced acts designed to highlight the *strangeness* of the past as it is being playfully jerked into the present. An ironic stance, as such, says one thing while simultaneously allowing the possibility of other more critical readings. It is this "superimposition or rubbing together" of meanings that, in the words of critical theorist Linda

Hutcheon, "makes irony happen."[7] The new wave was flush with various examples of such ironic formations that ranged from the subtle (Debbie Harry's deliberately shoddy dye job, revealing the knowing artifice behind her tribute to the 1950s bleached blonde bombshell) to the glaringly comic situational irony of the Suburban Lawns' "Gidget Goes to Hell." New wave's irony is perhaps most obviously on display in the numerous irreverent cover versions that surfaced, such as The Flying Lizards' "Money," a dismantling of the early 1960s Motown/Beatles R&B standard arranged for passionless deadpan female voice, electronics, and toy instruments. Or the stripped-back amateurism of the B-52's take on Petula Clark's 1964 hit "Downtown," a ramshackle mess of plodding drums, trebly Farfisa organ, and Cindy Wilson's exaggerated mock British accent. It was new wave's humorous ironic mode that punctured and deflated the seriousness that had overtaken the rock scene and turned musicians into contemplative "artists" rather than entertainers.

Irony can be a tricky matter, however, and this was particularly evident in the critical reception that arose around the B-52's and the band's subsequent attempts to defend and define its stance. Faced with the group's flood of go-go boots, wigs, miniskirts, bongos, beach movies, and extraterrestrials, critics clamored to make sense of this potentially messy mélange and dug deep for layered meanings. By resurrecting these pop artifacts, were the B-52's making a cultural and class commentary on an "American trash aesthetic"? Were they enacting a 1960s "revivalist kitsch"?[8] Did their costumes and "flamboyant" mannerisms signal a campy aesthetic?[9] By invoking trash, kitsch, and camp, critics suggested that the B-52's had forged a distanced, critical relationship with the frivolities and trivialities of the lower rungs of the cultural hierarchy. On the surface, the label of trash seemed rather unambiguous, a recognition of pop culture's leftover, discarded remnants that were now completely without value. Kitsch, which derived from the German *verkitschen* ("to make cheap" or "to cheapen"), was used to designate an aesthetic of bad taste and impoverished quality. The label of camp was closely related to kitsch, but implied a more knowing and theatrical inversion of pop's extravagance, artifice, and inevitable obsolescence, and one that was often coded to be read by an appreciative, queer audience.

Faced with the barrage of these labels, the B-52's repeatedly and vigorously denied any such intentions, and refused to cast aspersions on their sources of inspiration. In an interview with Britain's *New Musical Express,* Kate Pierson bristled at the notion that they were reveling in trash: "I mean, we don't use that term and the supposed 'trash' that we're interested in is good trash!"[10] The B-52's, of course, were not the first band, nor would they be the last, to shy away from the rock press's categorical descriptions and analytical readings. Few artists want to be pigeonholed. But in the case of the B-52's, there was an added dimension to such labeling. The band's three male members were all gay, but they kept their homosexuality private and silent from the press, where it went unacknowledged (and would remain so until much later following the tragic AIDS-related death of guitarist Ricky Wilson in 1985). At the time, only a handful of gay musicians—most notably the British punk rocker Tom Robinson, famed for his 1978 single "Sing If You're Glad to Be Gay"—had gone public with their homosexuality.[11] But they had subsequently been received and typecast almost entirely in terms of their sexual orientation rather than their broader artistic and musical merits.[12] As such, embracing a camp identity was a risky proposition for the B-52's, for it might ultimately encourage the critics to brand the group narrowly in terms of the politics of queer performance. It was much safer for the band to insist that they simply liked to dress up and play fun dance music, nothing more nothing less.

My focus in this chapter will rest largely with the B-52's and the complications that arise in understanding how irony figured into new wave's aesthetic, specifically vis-à-vis its relationship to trash, kitsch, and camp. While the group may have denied the appropriateness of all these labels, I believe they merit closer examination. As I will argue, the histories and laden value judgments of trash and kitsch may indeed be problematic, but the subtleties of camp allow for an interpretive framework that makes much more sense applied to the group's performances and recordings. Most of all, I am interested in how all these labels reflected in different ways the B-52's attraction to a specific period of American popular and musical culture, that of the late 1950s and early 1960s. This transitory historical period—what one might consider the tail end of the "Long 1950s" or the prelude of the "Long 1960s"—held a particular fascination for those at the turn of the 1980s who found in its modern "space race" fixations and utopian suburban depictions a humorously naive vision of the future as it had been imagined in the past. Kate Pierson, for example, recalled "being told in school how those jet packs you wear on your back would be a reality when we grew up, and everybody would be using them to just whiz around to work."[13] As art and design historian Elizabeth Guffey points out in her book *Retro: The Culture of Revival,* the fantastical lure of "yesterday's tomorrows," of recently departed modernities, has long fueled the impulse behind retro's ironic nostalgia. Guffey's analysis concentrates largely on visual evocations of the past. But how does this extend to the musical styles associated with this period that are so central to understanding groups like the B-52's? I will explore the intersections of these different domains in the sections that follow.

All the Great Modern Things[14]

You can look at a K-mart Shopping Centre as a modern cultural museum and learn something from what's there and what that means.
—Kate Pierson of the B-52's, 1981[15]

Writing about the B-52's in 1980, *Rolling Stone*'s Anthony DeCurtis compared their pillaging of the past to "a cleverly designed junk-mobile."[16] This analogy, drawn from the visual arts, depicted the band almost as if they were an accumulation of found objects, not unlike the early 1960s pop art of Tom Wesselmann's mixed media collages or James Rosenquist's paintings, which took as their subjects the commingled everyday advertising imagery of automobile parts, canned foods, and female desire. Like Rosenquist, Wesselmann, and other pop artists such as Andy Warhol, the B-52's found in the consumer culture of the late 1950s and early 1960s an exaggerated emphasis on style and design that translated well to the world of art and performance. Also, like the pop artists before them, the B-52's approached their materials ironically, which made it difficult to determine whether they were celebrating or critiquing these remnants of consumer gratification from the past. Regardless of the intended effect, it was impossible to engage pop art or new wave without acknowledging the integral role that consumer goods had come to play in contemporary society.

Many art historians have addressed the historical period that prompted the pop art explosion and, in particular, its relationship to a modern consumer lifestyle. As Christin J. Mamiya shows in her incisive study, *Pop Art and Consumer Culture,* the movement occurred during a period in American history when the idealized pursuit of the "good life" came to be associated, almost exclusively, with the acquisition of an endless stream of new consumer products.[17] A confluence of factors contributed to this situation: a large accumulation of post–World War II capital, the unprecedented expansion of multinational corporations, and, with the Kennedy administration, the full governmental institution of a Keynesian economic policy that sought to stimulate growth not through the traditional means of production, but rather through consumption. To consume was to attain the American dream, which came to be embodied in two overlapping models of social prosperity. One was the rise of the suburbs, where families settling into new housing developments were encouraged to purchase the latest advancements in domestic products. Another arose out of the national "space race" drive, which suddenly made possible the imagined fantasy of a new paradise: family life in outer space. The resultant marketing of a variety of earthly "space age home" products conflated the suburbs and outer space into a tidy consumer package dream.[18]

Part of what separated this new modern consumer era from previous ones was the degree to which technology, science, and innovative design were placed in the foreground. As the famous 1950s Du Pont manufacturing slogan claimed: "Better Things, for Better Living—Through Chemistry." Synthetic fibers ranging from nylon and polyester to acetate and acrylic (and later PVC, polyvinyl chloride) flooded the fashion market with promises of stylish drip-dry and wrinkle-free convenience, threatening to overtake the wool, silk, and cotton industries.[19] Sleek, streamlined plastic Tupperware containers, fashioned out of polyethylene ("The Material of the Future"), offered a variety of new hosting and entertaining options for the suburban housewife.[20] Processed and fast foods experienced a massive rise in popularity as well, as their standardized contents promised a dining experience free of labor-intensive preparation and potential kitchen disasters. Even a product like the automobile, which was already defined by its advanced mechanical ingenuity, entered into a further realm of technological associations as Cadillacs now began to sport decorative tail fins that evoked the design, and by implication, speed and propulsion of jet fighters and rocketships.[21]

Most of all, what had shifted was the role that technology played in the marketing and advertising of consumer goods. As Michael L. Smith has explained, in the eras prior to the 1950s and 1960s, advertisers would often present technology as a property tied to the specific choices and techniques that went into making products.[22] With the rise of the new post–World War II consumerism, though, technology was presented as some mysterious, magical property with which the products themselves were imbued that would provide individual consumers with greater personal and social benefits. Smith describes three "patterns of technological display" that figured prominently in this new era of advertising success: unveiling, transitivity, and the helmsman. By *unveiling*, products were introduced to the public through dramatic means. Advertisements for automobiles, for example, might entice the viewers by revealing to them secretive glimpses of only a dashboard or a tail fin. Advertisers used the technique of *transitivity* to transfer the illusion of the product's ostensible attributes directly to the consumer. Most commonly they would use the transitive power of utterly superfluous jargon, such as "Level-Flite Torsion-Aire" or "Three dimensional driving—ride control, road control, load control," to initiate this transfer and convince customers that they were somehow privy to an insider's knowledge.[23] Ultimately, though, as Smith points out, it was humans who sold products; smiling, winking, gratified humans who by their mere presence in the advertisement provided the proof that the new product would improve the consumer's life. Of these human figures, the *helmsman*, an assured leader such as the "Marlboro Man" or "the astronaut," served as a powerful role model whose mastery of the environment and technology positioned him as a figure to whom consumers could aspire.

Much as the 1960s pop artists before them, new wave bands parodied the language and imagery of this advertising era, repeating with ironic distance the very same patterns of technological display outlined above. One can see this especially in the visual designs and appropriations of Devo, a group that critics frequently lumped together with the B-52's, praising them both for their stabs at the ludicrous nature of American consumer culture. The 1980 catalog for Devo's fan club "Club Devo" (in itself a parody of 1970s stadium rock fan clubs like the "Kiss Army"), complete with descriptions and an order form for such Devo merchandise as T-shirts, flicker buttons, and 3-D glasses, is a particularly good example. The catalog is conceived in a manner imitative of a 1950s black-and-white advertisement, and acts as a parody of product transitivity and consumer helmsmanship (figure 10 reproduces just the catalog images, and not the order form). Devo's 3-D glasses will add "a new dimension to your 2-D life!" the catalog exclaims, mimicking the empty appeal of transitive techno-jargon. The catalog is also dotted with random images of what Smith calls "commodity scientism." Lab technicians hover over tubes and beakers, a doctor examines an x-ray, atomic-like particles hover about the page; the function of all these is purely to transfer a symbolic aura of unspecified technological authority to Devo's merchandise. These floating snapshots of "technology at work" serve most of all to assure the viewer that Devo's products are sufficiently advanced. Juxtaposed with these images, the catalog includes illustrations of customers (helmsmen) modeling the band's merchandise, and most importantly smiling, disembodied faces, whose glamour and collective cool has been achieved, we are to assume, only through their consumption of Devo's products.

Part of the irony in Devo's catalog relates to the very nature of their merchandise—flicker buttons and 3-D glasses—which mimics the disposability of so many supposedly "modern" products of the late 1950s and early 1960s. This disposability was a key component of the era's marketing and promotional tactics, which were based around a strategy of planned obsolescence. In this industrial model, manufacturers attempted to accelerate spending habits by introducing increasingly newer and more stylishly novel goods that were seen to render the previous round of products obsolete. In this way a product's function was less important than its novelty and newness, those qualities that would make it immediately desirable to consumers. Such products were doomed, of course, no matter how successful, to become outdated themselves, and it is this aspect of the consumer culture that most attracted the pop artists. As art historian Sara Doris points out, pop art's irony was inherent in the choice of its subject matter: products whose stylishness and newness had expired, and were now seen as "cultural phenomena that were not-quite-new rather than up-to-the-minute; things which were palpably dated in a culture obsessed with nov-

Figure 10. The catalog for the 1980 "Club Devo" fan club (originally issued with Devo's *Freedom of Choice* LP), parodying the "commodity scientism" of the 1950s advertising world.

elty."[24] Frozen in their formerly modern shell, these consumer goods were now reduced to the surfaces upon which their marketability had been predicated, and the flatness of their exaggerated style, garish packaging, and hyperbolic appearance became the essence of their materiality.

The acceleration of new products in this model of planned obsolescence had an inevitable side effect, one that would heavily influence the new wave. As goods were continually replaced and thrown out at a rapid rate, the old (or once new) soon came to far outweigh the brand new. The result was "great heaps of cultural rubbish—goods not worn out, but discarded simply because they were no longer stylish."[25] It was from the midst of this rubbish heap, for example, that new wave groups like Blondie and the B-52's pulled the combo organs that would provide one of the movement's signature sounds. Vox Continental and Farfisa combo organs had exploded in the early 1960s because they were relatively cheap and portable, but also because they had a sleek, modern design suited to the performing stage. The "thin, reedy" sound of the Vox Continental and the "deeper, more flute-like" sound of the Farfisa both presented a percussive chordal attack and piercing melodic lines that fit perfectly with the loud, fast-paced big-beat style of the emerging British Invasion movement.[26] At its peak of popularity the combo organ figured prominently with such bands as the Dave Clark Five, Paul Revere and the Raiders, Manfred Mann, the Beatles, the Monkees, and most famously on songs like ? and the Mysterians' "96 Tears" (1966), which featured the Vox, and the Strawberry Alarm Clock's "Incense and Peppermints" (1967), which featured the Farfisa. The combo organ's influence began to wane in the late 1960s as many progressive rock bands turned to the more lush, romantic tones of the Hammond organ. Production of the Vox Continental was halted in 1972, and by the late 1970s the combo organ had filtered into the secondary market of pawnshops and thrift stores. It was here where many new wave bands went hunting for these organs, and soon the distinct sound of this "residual media" had reentered the keyboard lexicon.[27]

Likewise, and of particular importance to the B-52's, by the mid-1970s the burgeoning secondhand market also housed a seemingly endless graveyard of once modern clothes, awaiting all manner of serendipitous discovery, and odd mix-and-match fashion combinations. As *New Yorker* fashion critic Kennedy Fraser observed in 1975, a new ironic "flea-marketry" style had emerged among a young generation of artists in search of nostalgia and novelty.[28] There were practical reasons that struggling musicians and artists flocked to these stores as well. Their merchandise presented affordable shopping options. As Fred Schneider of the B-52's explained, "You pay a quarter for a Goodwill shirt, wear it ten times, and throw it away. It's kind of recycling."[29] In this respect, the disposability of the late 1950s and the 1960s was rewritten in the 1970s. Whereas these formerly modern fashions had become disposable once they were no longer new, they now engendered a disposability equated with cheapness. In this manner the B-52's acquired dynamic stage props that required little care or monetary investment.

As these commodities completed the migration from their former domestic environments into the secondhand market and then finally onto the B-52's stage, they now appeared in an array of unusual stylistic assemblages: go-go boots matched with bouffant wigs and sci-fi sound effects. The result was what one might call a bricolage, a combination of appropriated commodities whose connotations were now thrown into question, and who potentially acted as objects of subverted, rather than straight, meaning. Sociologists working in the 1970s at the Birmingham Centre of Contemporary Culture, most notably Dick Hebdige, borrowed the concept of bricolage from the anthropologist Claude Lévi-Strauss as a way to explain the travel of cultural commodities in late capitalist British society.[30] In Lévi-Strauss's original formulation, the concept of bricolage stemmed from the bricoleur, a French "handyman" who set about his tasks by applying in heterogeneous ways his collected resources of odds and ends to the task at hand.[31] For Hebdige, the bricoleur was recast as a member of various youth subcultures. The bricoleur became the mod who claims the conformist suits, collars, and ties of the business world as rebellious sartorial motifs. Another example was the punk who patched together torn clothing with safety pins and brandished bondage gear and the Nazi insignia.[32] Bricolage thus described the potentially powerful array of amalgamated signs, and how this might enable us to see the familiar objects of our world in new and startling ways.

Part of the significance of the new wave was that its focus on pop and style, rather than on the aggressive violence of punk, allowed a window for more women to enter into this semiotic bricolage. As such, fashion styles emerged that drifted away from the male-dominated discourse of mod and the unisex fashions of punk and more into the realm of both conventional and unconventional feminine attire. The two female members of the B-52's represented only the tip of the iceberg. Following on their heels, the all-female Los Angeles quintet the Go-Go's routinely attracted attention for their constant swirl of retro fashions. Writing in *Sounds* magazine, Sylvie Simmons saw their eclectic clothing statements as a strike against the male-dominated music business's usual sexist tendencies:

> Their look onstage—very much the same as off—is as changeable as it is fascinating. From Biba-pixie to day-glo pin-up, surfing shirts, spandex, sweatshirts, baby-dolls, schoolgirls, glossy wet-dream K-Tel punkettes, or maybe just jeans and tees. They're cute, no question, but they wear it well—no coy, low cut frill-thrills or butch-dyke leathers. Sex, the way the male end of the music business packages it, hardly touches up the picture.[33]

Simmons deliberately positions the Go-Go's as girls rather than women, a strategy that accentuates their connection with the early 1960s, when the ascendance of both the girl groups and the Beatles saw the teen female audience and their tastes and fashions come virtually to stand in for popular music as a whole. At the other end of the spectrum, singer Dale Bozzio of Missing Persons played upon the synthetic fibers and disposable commodity fetishism of modern fashion in a decidedly more sexualized and adult manner. On stage and in photos, Bozzio, a former *Playboy* playmate, would appear clad variously in an industrial plexiglass brassiere, transparent jackets constructed out of bubblewrap, and a miniskirt pieced together out of old seven-inch vinyl singles. By the time that Cyndi Lauper exploded into popularity in 1984, attired in a vibrant ragmarket ensemble, the connection between female new wave fashion and thrift store ingenuity was firmly cemented.

As they cloaked themselves in the refuse of the secondhand market, brandishing clothes whose ephemeral novelty and exaggerated style had doomed them to the scrap heap of unwanted goods, it was perhaps to be expected that groups like the B-52's would attract the label of "trash." But the designation was more complex than it might initially appear, evoking associations that were both celebratory and potentially problematic. On the one hand, the recognition of a trash aesthetic linked new wave as a whole with punk, which critics had been heralding in the late 1970s for rupturing and mocking rock's staid adult conformity and pretensions to high culture with trashy juvenile depictions of "glue sniffing" and cartoonish violence, and seedy portraits of urban street life. On the other hand, the trash aesthetic hinted at a social inequality, one that amplified the trashy appearances and culture of the lower classes. It is telling, for example that critics commonly imagined Cindy Wilson's and Kate Pierson's costumes as some part of a working-class parody, describing them as "manicurists" and "waitresses."[34] The implication then was not just that Wilson and Pierson were wading in trash, but that this band from the college town of Athens, Georgia, was having fun with a specific southern *white trash* fashion and appearance, and trafficking in what sociologist Karen Bettez Halnon has referred to as a recreational "poor chic."[35] Of the many ways that white trash inflects, one of the strongest is through an excess that is written on the body, especially through the wearing of exaggerated, cheap fashions.[36] Garish, gaudy, and tacky—the white trash look and manner is marked by an unaffected obliviousness (or one could say supreme confidence) in which bodily display is celebrated.

While few critics referred to the B-52's explicitly as a humorous parody of white trash, it was not hard to see this subtext lingering within their appraisals of the band's supposed dalliance with a trash aesthetic. And it is equally clear why the band would have discouraged such associations. The B-52's did not see their thrift store escapades as acts of cultural and class slumming, especially since many of the band members themselves had eked out jobs as waiters and waitresses and were more connected with Athens's local working class than its transient collegiate culture. Still, it would be foolish to dismiss the alluring exoticism that their southern thrift store pageantry held for the northern East Coast critics and audiences who emerged as the B-52's most vocal and influential supporters. In the end, the aura of trash hovered persistently around the B-52's, threatening to spill over into specific aesthetic, social and class judgments, but kept uneasily at bay by the band's insistence that it was simply having fun.

The Dimensions of Kitsch

The B-52's went through many changes over the course of the seven albums that they released between 1979 and 1992, embracing synthesizers and drum machines on 1983's *Whammy!* and a fuller, more groove-based sound on 1989's *Cosmic Thing*. Regardless of these stylistic developments, the band consistently found itself stuck with the label of kitsch.[37] The release of the B-52's self-titled debut in 1979, and the ceaseless discussions of kitsch that ensued, largely set the tone for the band's critical reception for the rest of its career and can act as a representative window into understanding the B-52's relationship with the pop culture of the late 1950s and early 1960s. As we have seen, much of what fell under this kitsch label stemmed from the group's outdated, outlandish fashion costumes and wigs. But how exactly did the music itself evoke the past, and to what extent did this contribute to perceptions that the group was dabbling in kitsch?

"Planet Claire," the opening track from the debut album, provides a convenient composite of the group's range of musical influences, many of which intersect with the worlds of television and cinema scoring. The song opens with morse code sound effects and ambient background noise that sets an eerie sci-fi context. It is soon joined by a staccato E minor guitar riff borrowed directly from Henry Mancini's theme to the television show *Peter Gunn* (1958–61) and a bongo accompaniment on the backbeat that further cements a Latin-styled "crime jazz" or "jazz exotica" setting favored by so many urban detective movies of the 1950s.[38] The guitar riff is eventually joined by a descending, chromatically wandering legato line played on the Farfisa organ and doubled by Kate Pierson's wordless falsetto vocals. The song's coauthor, drummer Keith Strickland, has claimed that this melody was inspired by Nino Rota's score to Federico Fellini's 1965 film, *Juliet of the Spirits*, which features a similar haunting organ line.[39] But it is easy to hear other, even more obvious referents here as well. For example, the combination of high-register instrument(s) and falsetto female voice was commonly used throughout the 1960s to signify the ethereal mysteries of outer space, appearing everywhere from the Ventures' 1963 album *Ventures in Space* (which guitarist Ricky Wilson claimed as a particularly important influence on his sound) to the television theme music to *Star Trek* (1966–69).

By the time Fred Schneider enters after two and a half minutes with the song's lyrics, the setting is firmly in place for his absurdist descriptions of an enchanting extraterrestrial female from Planet Claire, who drives a "Plymouth Satellite faster than the speed of light," a deft automotive reference to the golden age of modern American space-themed commodities.[40]

Schneider provides only a thin sketch of the woman from Planet Claire, but the song's stylistic sonic cues allow us to fill in the blanks in various ways. Perhaps she is one of the mysterious and lethal femme fatales typical of the film noir and spy movie genres. Or maybe she resembles the woman on the cover of exotica composer Esquivel's 1958 album *Other Worlds, Other Sounds,* cloaked in a leotard and silky cape on the surface of some distant, barren planet. Then again she could easily have sprung straight from some low-budget 1950s science fiction film like *Cat-Women of the Moon* (1953) that commonly conflated the exotic unknown of the female body with the unexplored mysteries of outer space. Regardless of how one reads "Planet Claire," it is difficult to miss its evocations, intentional or not, of the past.

The album's most famous track, "Rock Lobster," extends these references into a different realm of late 1950s and early 1960s B movies, and does so in a much more oblique manner. The song takes place at a party on the beach, and in this respect is an obvious nod to the overwhelmingly popular (and critically maligned) American International Pictures (AIP) *Beach Party* movie series starring Annette Funicello and Frankie Avalon that ran between 1963 and 1965. While Schneider tosses off random allusions to lifeguards, beach towels, surfboards, and the requisite early 1960s dance imagery of people "fruggin'" and "twistin'" on the beach, "Rock Lobster" ostensibly shares very little else with the fluffy romance and teenage shenanigans of the *Beach Party* movies. Instead, as *All Music Guide* critic Rick Anderson notes in his discussion of the song, "There is a thread of darkness weaving through it" that becomes especially apparent in the lengthy two-minute climax, where the band settles into a single, repetitive riff.[41] At this point, Schneider's vocals become increasingly tense and agitated and Wilson and Pierson accent his disconnected imagery of stingrays, piranhas, and narwhales with a variety of bizarre imitative vocal cries. The threatening tone of this section turns the typically romantic beach scenario into one of menacing terror and chaos, a reminder that many horror films of the era—and not just obviously jokey titles like *The Horror of Party Beach* (1964) and *The Beach Girls and the Monster* (1965), but also serious science fiction and horror films like *Creature from the Black Lagoon* (1954) and *It Came from Beneath the Sea* (1955)—portrayed the water and beach as sites and scenes of potential danger.

The musical style of "Rock Lobster," much like its cinematic references, emerges from the same general time period. The song's opening ascending guitar riff in C minor, with its clean, resonant timbre and driving eighth-note rhythm, immediately sets the context of early 1960s surf rock. Ricky Wilson's distinctive thick, almost basslike tone hearkens back to instrumental and surf guitarists like Duane Eddy and Dick Dale who typically played their melodies on the lower bass strings of the guitar, and used heavy gauge strings, thick picks, and downstrokes to create a deep, powerful rhythmic quality.[42] Wilson pushes the instrument's rhythmic and percussive capabilities even further by removing the middle two strings from the guitar, giving him more room to "whack away" at the remaining strings and let them resonate.[43] At the chorus, the song expands Wilson's opening guitar riff to an ascending chord progression (i–III–iv–V) reminiscent of the Marketts' 1964 surf standard "Out of Limits," a song that took its name from the television show *The Outer Limits* and its hypnotic chromatic riff from the main theme of *The Twilight Zone*.[44] Here, as with "Planet Claire," the B-52's evoke the world of television and sci-fi music scoring.

Beyond these instrumental touches, the supporting vocals from Wilson and Pierson draw on yet another range of past influences. They open the song with a nonsense vocalization ("scadoodebop—ooo") that for all its dissonance openly hearkens back to the doo-wop vocal harmonies of the early 1960s girl group, an association that becomes more clear as the song progresses and their vocals are repeatedly heard in a call and response arrangement with Schneider's lead line. The wild vocal gyrations that dominate the extended ending section introduce yet another strand, one that the band claimed stemmed from 1950s Peruvian exotica singer Yma Sumac. One can also hear echoes of the wailing experimental vocal improvisations of Yoko Ono's early 1970s avant-garde recordings, a comparison that John Lennon himself mentioned in an interview with *Rolling Stone:*

> I was at a dance club one night in Bermuda . . . upstairs, they were playing disco, and downstairs, I suddenly heard "Rock Lobster" by the B-52's for the first time. Do you know it? It sounds just like Yoko's music, so I said to myself, "It's time to get out the old axe and wake the wife up!"[45]

Whether it was Sumac or Ono that one heard in Wilson and, particularly, Pierson's vocals, it was clear that the band had built a bridge that ventured into female vocal styles that lay well outside the traditional realm of mainstream rock and pop.

On the surface it is not terribly difficult to see why the late 1950s and early 1960s exotica, television theme music, film soundtracks, B movies, surf instrumentals, and music of the girl groups that fueled songs like "Planet Claire" and "Rock Lobster" might have attracted the label of kitsch. To many these were ephemeral pop culture referents, fully in line with the type of cheapened kitsch lamented by New York intellectual and art critic Clement Greenberg in his seminal 1939 essay "Avant-Garde and Kitsch."[46] As Greenberg argued, kitsch was most of all a by-product of the industrial revolution, one that revealed a severe societal split along two distinctly different cultural routes. The elite culture stood as the eternal patron of good taste, high art, and refined aesthetic sensibilities, while the emergence of a working class had given subsequent rise to a variety of mechanized, mass produced, commercial products that aspired to the status of art and culture. Where high culture looked to art for contemplation and a depth of experience, the culture of the working class was marked by its formulaic trappings and emotional transparency, an exaggerated emphasis on watered-down surface effects borrowed from the language of high art. To the avant-garde of the elites belonged Pablo Picasso and T. S. Eliot; to the masses belonged the kitsch of Norman Rockwell magazine covers and Tin Pan Alley songs. In short, literally *anything* within the domain of "popular culture" fell under the umbrella of kitsch.

Many cultural critics took up Greenberg's arguments in the following decades, none more vigorously than Dwight MacDonald, whose identification in the late 1950s of a debased "masscult and midcult" echoed the concerns over kitsch. To MacDonald, masscult and midcult (a "bastardized" form of masscult that more seamlessly borrowed from the avant-garde) represented a serious threat to overtake high culture completely. As he saw it, the lure of masscult—represented by television, rock and roll, *Life* magazine, movie stars, Boca Raton, and other assorted abominations—lay in its obvious "built-in reactions" and "predigested" effects that emphasized pleasure and distraction over actual engagement. While MacDonald wrote sparingly about music, directing more of his wrath at the literary and visual fields, what little he had to say is instructive. The mass audiences, he argued, would deem a provincial wedding standby like "I Love You Truly" to be more "romantic" than any of Schubert's songs "because its wallowing, yearning tremolos and glissandos make it clear to the most unmusical listener that something very tender indeed is going on."[47] Similarly, Liberace would be judged as more "musical" than the concert pianist Rudolf Serkin, "whose piano is not adorned with antique candelabra and whose stance at it is as businesslike as Liberace's is 'artistic.'"[48] In MacDonald's view, masscult and kitsch thrived on exaggeration and emotional exploitation, effects that instantly gratified and reassured its consuming audience.

These, of course, are precisely the types of effects that populated the world of exotica albums, movie soundtracks, and television music favored by the B-52's. They were all types of functional "mood music," whose main purpose by design was to suggest as explicitly and dynamically as possible specific settings and emotional states. Like the commercial products that provided the subjects for the pop artists' canvases and collages, they were also unashamedly marked by the hyperbole and packaging of modern marketing. Television and film music recordings were by nature promotional, intended to help further the popularity of a specific series or movie. Exotica albums as well, with their deliberately striking orchestrations and bizarre stereo effects, often doubled as hi-fi demonstration recordings that helped promote the sale of new, modern stereo equipment. They were, in effect, little different from the B movies with which they were often equated, where outrageous papier mâché monsters and overwrought acting replaced any hints of subtlety and nuance.

By the end of the 1960s, a definitive portrait of kitsch had emerged, documented most notably in the Italian artist and aesthetician Gillo Dorfles's 1969 edited anthology *Kitsch: The World of Bad Taste*.[49] Dorfles's book identified as kitsch everything from Donald Duck garden gnomes and *Mona Lisa* bath towels to religious "souvenirs" for tourists and modern steel-tubed furniture. Kitsch was that which pretended toward some artistic relevance and aesthetic experience, but in its failed aspirations exposed rather than concealed the chasm between low and high culture. As tempting as it is to fit the B-52's points of inspiration within this kitsch criteria, however, it does not entirely represent the context in which the band was received. After all, the canon against which their musical sources were being judged was *not* that of Greenberg's, MacDonald's, or Dorfles's beloved avant-garde arts and high culture. The B-52's were being critiqued by rock critics, not by artists, art critics, or the New York intelligentsia. What is more relevant, from a historical standpoint, is to consider why rock critics of the late 1970s would have seen the band's musical styles—exotica, television and film music, surf and girl groups—and attendant pop culture as kitsch, and how that might have affected the B-52's aversion to this labeling.

The 1970s was a crucial time in the establishment and writing of rock history, a period when the majority of values that we often now assume unquestioningly to be an essential part of rock's identity came to be formed. As the musicologist Mark Mazullo has shown in his insightful historiography of rock criticism in the early and middle 1970s, critics who were largely dissatisfied with the trajectory that rock was taking in that decade built their own history of rock as a way of cementing their beliefs and reiterating the promises of the countercultural social revolution.[50] Mazullo focuses part of his analysis on the *Rolling Stone Illustrated History of Rock & Roll* anthology, which, upon its appearance in 1976, stood as one of the first attempts to provide a comprehensive narrative history of the music.[51] By stressing what they took to be rock music's uniquely American essence— resonant in its folklike community, working-class rebellion, African American roots, and strong antiestablishment social politics—the contributors to the *Rolling Stone* history identified standards of excellence for the music of *their* era, the late 1960s, and set a template by which future performers might be judged and thrust into the narrative fold. As these modes of valuation fell into place, the *Rolling Stone* critics portrayed the period from the late 1950s through the early 1960s leading up to the British Invasion as a desolate void when the excitement of rock and roll momentarily vanished. It was, in their estimation, a period marked most of all by reincorporation, when the major labels tamed and absorbed the rebellious codes of mid-1950s rock and roll and proceeded to soften and reproduce them across a range of inoffensive teen idols, girl groups, instrumental novelty hits, and sanitized dance fads. As a result, an entire era of music making that only a few years earlier had been deemed a lively, unpredictable "expansion of the rock style" in Carl Belz's 1969 book *The Story of Rock* had suddenly been recast in *Rolling Stone*'s history as a "fallow" period, one that had threatened (unsuccessfully) to suffocate rock's vitality.[52]

The B-52's thus were drawing from a period that by the late 1970s had been roundly discounted and vilified as the antithesis of "good" rock. In this new light, exotica, television music, and girl groups were all portrayed as examples of music as commodity. Not only were they pocked by the stigma of professional session players, contracted songwriters, and orches-tral arrangers, they also exhibited little or none of the African American "folk" roots deemed so crucial to rock's authenticity. Instead, styles like ex-otica and surf—with their clean timbres, unswinging rhythms, and evoca-tions of a fantastical *orientalist* Pacific exoticism and West Coast oceanic utopia—were notable most of all for their exaggerated whiteness. They were styles divorced from the images of smoky clubs, teenage street rebel-lion, and urban danger that ranked as rock's most potent signifiers. They connoted, instead, the privileges and pleasure of leisure, whether it be the adult hi-fi den and bachelor pad or the casual flirtations of the beach party. Furthermore, there was an anonymous quality to the generally wordless music that ensured it would not meet with the lyrical criteria that had be-come one of rock's strongest points of evaluation following in the wake of Bob Dylan, John Lennon, and 1960s protest music. In sum, from the view-point of this new canonical rock hierarchy of values, the musical allusions of the B-52's were kitsch inasmuch as they were *too* commercial, *too* white, *too* feminized, *too* safe. They stood as a reminder of a presumably laughable and lamentable pre-Beatles era, when rock and roll had been reduced to a superficial commodity, something as disposable and obsolescent as the subjects of the pop art movement. To acknowledge that this music was kitsch, then, was an act that simultaneously helped sustain the myth of "good" rock's timelessness and authenticity.

For Greenberg, kitsch was a "static" phenomenon, one that required no translation and that failed to progress art and culture as a whole. But for groups like the B-52's, these supposed musical and cultural kitsch items served as loci for new, creative ideas. The band members entered into an engagement with this material not out of ironic mockery or nostalgia, but out of a decided connoisseurship that entailed a breadth of knowledge and detail in their chosen idioms. Much like the dedicated record collectors who in recent years have overseen exotica's resurrection from obscure cu-riosity to aesthetic object, they found the music to be fresh and inventive in a way that the contemporary rock of the 1970s was not. Undoubtedly their attraction to the music was inseparable from the thrills of their thrift store discoveries, from their delights in rummaging and rescuing the artifacts of the past from the shadowy corners of pop culture's neglected garbage heap. But it was also deeply tied to their own personal histories, whether it was Fred Schneider's genuine love for female vocal groups (especially Martha and the Vandellas) or Ricky Wilson's modified Mosrite that he considered to be an homage to one of his favorite groups, the Ventures, who had briefly popularized the guitar line back in the early 1960s. In short, the B-52's found in their musical relationships not the outdated exaggerations of "bad taste," but an unfettered, and often delightfully bizarre, musical world unburdened by rock's pretensions and its continuing concern with concealing its commodity status.

The Dimensions of Camp

As with kitsch, one of the keys to understanding camp relates back to the circulation of commodities in a consumer culture. In his 1969 essay "An Anatomy of Rubbish," the British anthropologist Michael Thompson proposed a context for camp that broke down the value of commodity objects into three discrete stages. A manufactured good begins with an established marketplace value. Over time, it enters into a *transient* stage, where its value decreases as it becomes more dilapidated and ultimately obsolescent. At some point it becomes *rubbish,* an object of no value that lies neglected or finds its way into the secondhand market. Eventually, though, the object is rediscovered, at which point it proves to be a *durable* collectible item, and its value subsequently increases. As Thompson goes on to argue, "The essential feature of 'camp' taste is that things are lifted out of the rubbish category 'before their time.'"[53] Camp rescues items from the scrap heap of commodities, goods, and objects, and invests them with new, often *ironic* meaning.

It is this active, subjective process that distinguishes camp from kitsch. Admittedly, the two terms are closely related, as they both ostensibly refer to categories of bad, degraded, or awful taste and value. But the differences between the two are crucial. Kitsch is generally taken to be a quality that resides in objects, a pretension to artistic legitimacy that reflects the class aspirations of a low- or middlebrow audience. Camp, on the other hand, is more slippery. An object can only be camp, or become "campy," if it is knowingly recognized as such by the producer or the audience. The irony in the process of camp is thus more explicit and suggestive of a critical distance that has often been attractive to connoisseurs and those with informed tastes. The cultural theorist Andrew Ross has summarized the differences as such:

> The producer or consumer of kitsch is likely to be unaware of the extent to which his or her intentions or pretensions are reified and alienated in the kitsch object itself. Camp, on the other hand, involves a celebration, on the part of cognoscenti, of the alienation, distance, and incongruity reflected in the very process by which hitherto unexpected value can be located in some obscure or exorbitant object.[54]

In the 1960s, when camp exploded into the mainstream consciousness, largely thanks to the popularity of Susan Sontag's 1964 essay "Notes on Camp," it was widely recognized that the cognoscenti of which Ross writes consisted primarily of an urban homosexual audience.[55] Camp was attractive to gays because of the nature of the objects that were chosen. As Sontag pointed out, those who entered into camp were attracted to superficiality, artifice, exaggeration—qualities that emerged especially through the passage of time when styles became outmoded and their surface affectations now offered a space for imitation and parody. There was a practical reasoning behind this. As the queer studies scholar Richard Dyer argued in his 1976 essay, "It's Being So Camp As Keeps Us Going," gays had "developed an eye and ear for surfaces, appearances, forms—style" because by necessity they had become adapt at role playing, at learning how to hide their gayness and "pass" in straight society.[56] Queer camp derived its power then from a semiotic *doubleness,* a "transformation of the sign" whereby gays took exaggerated gender representations—Dyer mentions the queer fascination with the passé masculine virility of John Wayne—and exposed the construction and artifice behind them.[57] In the 1960s and 1970s, this encompassed most noticeably the repertory of drag queens, whose re-creation of faded and ill-fated formerly glamorous Hollywood stars like Marlene Dietrich and Marilyn Monroe revealed the intense stylization behind society's construction of idealized womanhood. While camp, as such, was theatrical and humorous, it also emphasized the tragedy of alienation and the sad, fleeting temporality and ephemera of fame. Camp in this regard was intimately tied to obsolescence, the passing of style that opened space for new meanings.

It is against this contextual and interpretive backdrop that I would like to read the B-52's, and "Rock Lobster" in particular with its beach party setting, as camp. By the late 1970s it was difficult to imagine a more obsolete film genre than the early 1960s *Beach Party* series. The fun, frolic, romance, and impromptu singing and dancing on the beach had given way in the 1970s to movies like *Jaws* (1975), *The Deep* (1977), and *Orca* (1977) that emphasized the entirely plausible and realistic potential dangers that lurked beneath the ocean's watery surface. The *Beach Party* movies, which now seemed goofily quaint and innocent by comparison, thus easily allowed for camp's ironic dance with the past. Given camp's inherently playful doubleness and semiotic confusion, it is entirely fitting that the beach should provide the location for the B-52's inspired glance toward the past. As various scholars have noted, the beach functions as a liminal zone, pitched as an ambiguous threshold halfway between "nature" (the water) and "culture" (developed land).[58] As such it was an aptly symbolic setting for the late 1950s/early 1960s beach-themed movies that took as their subject the liminal status of the teenagers themselves, about to leave adolescence and poised on the precipice of adulthood. Here, in this fluctuating, searching state, the beach perfectly captured the uncertainties and thrills of dating, romance, and heterosexual partnering that acted as a prelude to the inevitable pairings that would come with marriage and the entrance into traditional societal roles.

The lyrics of "Rock Lobster," with their nonsensical wordplay and imagistic flow, take the carnivalesque setting of the beach as an opportunity to highlight the potential for gender drag and role inversion. This comes across most obviously when Schneider sings of "boys in bikinis" and "girls in surfboards." Such inversions had been common in the group's early stage routines, when the band's male members would routinely don wigs, dresses, and skirts.[59] This extended to the female singers as well, who at the band's 1977 New York City debut were mistaken by the audience for drag queens.[60] In "Rock Lobster," however, a host of more subtle inversions and doubleness occurs, for example, when Schneider puns on the image of "mussels" or "muscles" flexing. From Santa Monica's famed Muscle Beach that provided the inspiration for 1964's *Muscle Beach Party* to the Venice Beach bodybuilding competitions of today, the beach has long been associated with the display of sculpted bodily physiques. "When 10,000 biceps go around 5,000 bikinis . . . you *know* what's gonna happen!" screamed the movie posters for *Muscle Beach Party*. For all the heterosexual titillation that the advertising tagline promised, however, the site of the well-oiled beefcakes invading the beach equally raised the specter of homosexuality with which bodybuilding "pinup" and "physique" magazines had been associated throughout the 1950s.[61] This link between bodybuilding and queer subculture had only grown stronger by the late 1970s, as witnessed in the 1978 promotional video for the Village People's camp classic, "Macho Man," which interspersed shots of the disco band dancing and lip-synching in their full costume regalia with clips of an anonymous muscular man pumping iron and posing in a gym.

As important as all these visual signifiers and queer subtexts are to understanding the B-52's as camp, the linchpin of this interpretation is Schneider's voice. It is not difficult to discern why Schneider was heard as a campy singer. His diction—a mixture of hyperarticulated vowels, extended *s* sibilants, and heightened pitch variability (swooping up into the falsetto, for example)—is a veritable catalog of what linguists have pointed to as culturally perceived gay male speech patterns.[62] More importantly, Schneider's vocal approach deftly sidesteps the typical musical phrasings and contours of blues-based rock and melodic pop singing for a delivery that falls more within the realm of dramatic speech-song. It is almost as if he is imitating the act of singing. As *Rolling Stone*'s Anthony DeCurtis aptly described, Schneider approached the band's lyrics quizzically, "as if he hoped that by singing them, he might be able to figure out their meaning."[63] DeCurtis reacts here to the doubleness in Schneider's singing; on the one hand we hear the dynamism of his surface affectations, but on the other hand it is difficult to read in his voice any direct emotional underpinning. Like the camp of the drag queen, Schneider's singing comes across as deliberate role-playing. But the question remains, *what* exactly was he camping?

I would argue that Schneider's vocals can be heard most of all as a camp play on male whiteness, and more specifically a symbolic white masculinity of the late 1950s and early 1960s. Schneider's tone is best described as deadpan, an emotionally blank delivery that sounds chaste and edgeless when compared with the typically aggressive rock voice.[64] As such, it seems more at place in the world of the sanitized post-rock and roll "clean teen" *Beach Party* movies, whose white, leisurely, good-natured teenagers were miles removed from the juvenile delinquents that had populated the sensationalistic mid-1950s youth crime films.[65] As the B-52's developed their live show, Schneider began cultivating a visual correlate to this aural association, cutting his hair short and dressing in a "white sports shirt with rolled-up sleeves and tan Sta-Prest pants" that made him look like "Mr. Collegiate U.S.A. circa 1962."[66] Schneider's deliberately heightened delivery—*too* precise, *too* clear in its pronunciation—underscored the artifice behind this démodé male whiteness. It served as a reminder that this male ideal rested predominantly on a pre–civil rights hegemonic order where women, blacks, gays, and "others" still occupied the lower rungs on the social ladder. While Schneider's deadpan revealed the lie behind this masculine construction, its naive innocence also afforded him a unique marginal position from which to operate, one that circumvented the overworked codes of raw rebellion and sensitive vulnerability that had provided a durable twin axis of expression for male rock singers up through the 1970s.

At the same time, part of the allure of the beach was precisely the sense of the exotic and forbidden that shared the same space with the white middle-class "clean teens." Film historian R. L. Rutsky has convincingly argued that the *Beach Party* movies were not simply affirmations of white middle-class morality and sexless romance.[67] They in fact both celebrated and humorously parodied the beach as a site where all manner of outsider groups could cohabit, whether it be nonconformist surfers, beatnik dropouts, live rock and roll bands, overaged bike gangs, or exhibitionist bodybuilders. And this exoticism extended well beyond these social stereotypes, articulated in the probing shots of bikini-clad temptresses and white teenaged bodies perversely tanning themselves to attain a darker, more attractive hue, closer in color to the Hawaiian and Pacific female bodies so frequently exoticized as objects of white male desire. Ultimately, the beach offered an open, liminal space that was inviting to a host of "others," queers included.

Over the course of its nearly seven minutes, "Rock Lobster" introduces various musical representations that suggest a semiotic slippage between the exotic as typified by the *Beach Party* movies and the exotic rendered from a queer standpoint. This emerges most strikingly in the song's harmonic identity. While "Rock Lobster" begins unambiguously in C minor, at the instrumental outro of the chorus sections Kate Pierson adds a descending counterpoint line in the Farfisa organ that employs a diminished fifth interval (g♭). Played on the nasal, reedy tone of the organ, the melody acquires a distinct "Middle Eastern" flavor that evokes images of snake charmers and pungi flutes.[68] More specifically, it also draws the song further into the world of surf and *Beach Party* movies, where "exotic" modal scales commonly appeared in hits like Dick Dale's Arabic derived "Misirlou" (1962). The g♭ would seem to serve a largely decorative and ornamental purpose in "Rock Lobster," but there are two crucial moments where it reappears in a strategic position that supports a queer reading. These both occur at what is most properly called the bridge section, where the rhythm section halts, and Schneider implores the rock lobster to go "down, down." This bridge is highlighted by a methodical melodic descent that starts on f and heads downward chromatically, eventually landing on the g♭, where it stops to linger without ever resolving and completing the octave. This near-octave descent became one of the song's most notorious moments, as audiences and dancers routinely sank to the ground, waiting in joyous anticipation for the band to resume the beat. But there was another way to read it as well. In his poignant essay on the B-52's debut album, and its significance to his fumbling discovery of his sexual orientation, the gay author Clifford Chase suggests that Schneider's invocation to head "down" could be heard as an act of fellatio.[69] Here the emphasis on the g♭ serves as a reminder that musical *othering* can serve a variety of purposes and meanings.

Chase's interpretation reminds us that "Rock Lobster," through its ironic mode, speaks in many different ways. On the one hand, in the vein of the classic surf songs from which it knowingly draws, it comes across as a propulsive, energizing dance number. Schneider's delivery throughout the majority of the song may be camp, but when he shouts "Let's rock" near the beginning of the extended concluding section, it is hard to hear his declamation as anything but an impassioned and genuine cry of communal empowerment. On the other hand, the song's power derives in part from its implications of passive societal alienation that dwell beneath the surface. By definition, a rock lobster differs from a "normal" lobster in its lack of pincers. It has a shell for defense against predators, but no means of reciprocating or initiating an attack. In his book *Reflections of a Rock Lobster,*

Aaron Fricke chooses the metaphor of the rock lobster and the B-52's song to describe his experience growing up as a gay teenager in a late 1970s high school, and it is clear that the "rock lobster" for him stands as an outsider in this social alignment.[70]

Dig beneath the surface of the beach movies and one finds a similar emphasis on the outsider even *within* the supposed white middle-class normalcy of its main stars. The first teenage beach movie, 1959's *Gidget,* played upon this experience explicitly in its depiction of the diminutive title character, a "girl-midget" yearning to move beyond the liminality of her adolescent girlhood and experience a sense of romantic fulfillment and belonging. The *Beach Party* movies were more subtle, however, as here the outsider was not a role written into the script, but rather to be found in the rather unusual sight of two dark-haired East Coast Italian American entertainers—Annette Funicello and Frankie Avalon—trying to pass as typical California teenagers amid a bevy of blonde beachcombers and bikini models.[71] In numerous interviews throughout the late 1970s Fred Schneider expressed his fondness for Annette Funicello. While it is tempting to see her as just one more appealing remnant of a kitschy, obsolete past, one wonders if Schneider saw in Funicello something different, someone perhaps passing in a world utterly foreign to her own experiences and identity.

Kitsch and Camp, a Slight Return

In the end, the discourse of kitsch and camp that swirled around the B-52's and other ironic new wave bands was fraught with tension because it created a confusion of categories. To be sure, a large part of this confusion stemmed from the blurry line separating camp's homosexual subtext from its circulation in mainstream, "straight" culture, and the attendant anxieties over such muddled mixing. Much of the concern over camp, however, related back to issues of taste. As camp, issued from above, focused its gaze on obsolescent objects from popular culture's past, it threatened to destroy the boundaries of aesthetic categories. Was it now an act of good taste to celebrate something that was of demeaned value? Did this now make the object of bad taste suddenly *good*? Did camp essentially make it safe for bad taste to recirculate and accrue new value? The B-52's balked at the labeling of kitsch and camp because it forced on their chosen objects a hierarchy of taste, one that assumed that B movies, exotica, surf, girl groups, and television and film music resided somewhere far below the newly established countercultural rock canon. They refused to accept that they were investing these objects from the past with some new, elevated, ironic meaning. Rather, their evasiveness implied that the objects themselves were to be enjoyed for their own inherent worth and value.

Ultimately, camp in new wave figured most powerfully as a marker for rock critics because it reinforced the notion of their own elevated status amid the rock cognoscenti. It is little surprise that the B-52's found their most important initial critical approval in New York City, for their theatrical approach easily fit with the avant-garde and performance art that was then the rage of the downtown arts scene. As with the camp of the 1960s, the band's choice of marginalized, forgotten, grossly excessive and hopelessly outdated sources appealed to a smart, intellectual audience who now had an acknowledged and approved way to revel in "bad taste." The B-52's offered their fans an exciting alternative to the bland social conformity of the middle class, a form of ironic play that was layered and rich in its meanings. They engaged ironically with the lapsed modernities of the past, and in doing so, created a music that moved many to label the B-52's among the most modern of bands at the turn of the 1980s.

FIVE

"(I Wish It Could Be) 1965 Again": Power Pop and the Mining of Rock's Modern Past

In the summer of 1979, as *Billboard* magazine declared that the new wave was finally having a "significant impact on the U.S. market," no recording signified the genre's newfound success as dramatically as the Knack's "My Sharona."[1] The Los Angeles quartet's debut single emerged seemingly from out of nowhere to land atop the *Billboard* Hot 100 chart for six straight weeks, eventually becoming the top selling song of the year. While *Billboard* ceaselessly hailed the new wave as "progressive," it noted paradoxically in the same breath that groups like the Knack sounded so fresh because they echoed so clearly the familiar sounds of rock and pop from the mid-1960s. As a reviewer for *Trouser Press* magazine noted, the main hook of "My Sharona," a propulsive eighth-note bass and guitar melody that bounces back and forth between an octave, was essentially "an inversion of the signature riff" from the Spencer Davis Group's 1967 hit "Gimme Some Lovin'."[2] And as the Knack's front man and songwriter Doug Fieger admitted, the song's driving tom-tom drum rhythm was simply "just a re-write" of Smokey Robinson and the Miracles' Motown single "Going To a Go Go" from 1965.[3] Another main hook, a recurring stuttering vocal effect—"Muh-muh-muh-my Sharona"—brought to mind, if somewhat indirectly, such famous staggered syncopations as the Who's "My Generation." Even the song's stripped-back production—"crisp, clean, and clear"—hearkened back to the energetic sound of the early 1960s British Invasion.[4] Recorded in less than two weeks for just eighteen thousand dollars, the album on which "My Sharona" appeared, *Get the Knack,* reflected more the spirit of independent new wave production than the profligate recording budgets of most major label acts.

The Knack's connections with the 1960s extended beyond the aural and into the visual as well, specifically the artwork for their debut album. The back cover (see figure 11) shows the group's four members dressed in the British Invasion era fashion of matching suit pants, white dress shirts, and skinny black ties, playing their instruments against the stripped-down, glaring white backdrop and probing cameras of a re-created 1960s television studio set. From the stark black-and-white setting and distinct period fashion to the sense that one has wandered into the middle of a media pop event, the photo is a letter-perfect allusion to similar imagery of the Beatles circa 1964's *A Hard Day's Night.* The parallels with the Beatles do not stop there. As some argued, the album's black-and-white front cover, a medium close-up shot of the Knack against a plain backdrop, mirrored the tightly framed shots that had adorned such early Beatles albums as *Meet the Beatles* and *Beatles for Sale.* Even the imperative album title itself, *Get the Knack,* seemed to mimic the similarly titled command of *Meet the Beatles.* Capitol Records, home to both bands, no doubt had such connections in mind when it happily announced that "My Sharona" had become the fastest debut single to achieve gold sales since the Beatles' "I Want to Hold Your Hand," fifteen years earlier.[5] The Knack even requested that Capitol press copies of *Get the Knack* using the famous colored swirl label that had been on the Beatles' recordings in the 1960s, and had since been retired in the 1970s in favor of a nondescript solid orange and gray label. By reviving the swirl label, the Knack thus ensured themselves an even stronger identification with the Beatles.

Get the Knack was but one symptom of a larger nostalgia for the music and culture of the mid-1960s that was well in place by 1979. The musical *Beatlemania,* wherein look-alike musicians re-created the career of the Beatles against a backdrop collage of 1960s slides, had been running on Broadway since 1977. In England, new wave groups like the Jam had deliberately resurrected a mid-1960s mod sensibility, and coupled with the 1979 release of the mod nostalgia movie *Quadrophenia,* would help spark a full-fledged mod revival. At the dawn of the 1980s, the nostalgia for a mid-1960s gen-

Figure 11. The Knack strike a characteristic Beatles pose, from the back cover of their 1979 debut album *Get the Knack*.

eration stood most of all as a longing glance back at what had been a distinctly modern period marked by an accent on youth, optimism, leisure, experimentation, and the transformation of popular culture into objects of art. The narrow, cuffed Italian styled suits of the mod subculture, sporty Vespa and Lambretta scooters, Mary Quant miniskirts, the sleek ironic manufactured designs of pop art: such symbols captured the instantaneity and speed of a newly affluent postwar British society, of modernists and futurists in motion. At the center stood the Beatles, a group whose "new sound," young audience, and irreverent humor and charm, memorably displayed through the experimental *nouvelle vague* cinematic techniques of their 1964 debut film *A Hard Day's Night*, placed them at the vanguard of modern pop groups.[6] Crucially, the invocation of these mid-1960s touchstones in the music of groups like the Knack diverged sharply from the retro allusions of the B-52's and Devo described in chapter 4. Whereas their depictions of a faded past modernity were rendered with a discernible parodic distance, the Knack appeared to be utterly without irony. Their borrowings seemed based more on notions of authenticity and a devotional rereading of the past. As harmless as such an act might appear, however, it ultimately triggered a storm of controversy that hounded the group mercilessly throughout its brief run at the charts.

Much of the debate surrounding the Knack related to the group's place of privilege in the Los Angeles club scene, where it had easy access to the major labels.[7] Capitol had signed the Knack only after winning an intense bidding war, one that saw them pay the band what was the largest signing sum in the label's history at that time.[8] From the very beginning, then, many viewed the Knack as an overly calculated attempt to usurp the memories of the Beatles' musical "art" for their own selfish commercial gains. In this way the band was seen to violate one of rock's long-standing myths, which asserts that art and commerce are in some way incommensurable.[9] What seemed to anger the music press most of all, though, was that "My Sharona" and Get the Knack were selling particularly well to a young teenage audience. If the Knack's Beatlesque imagery and nostalgic big-beat sound was popular among teenagers, it could only be, they reasoned, because that audience was unfamiliar with the original British Invasion. Get the Knack was popular, as one reviewer assumed, primarily among "kids who thought of Paul McCartney as the bass player in Wings."[10] The great irony, of course, is that the Knack had simply attracted the same type of "teenyboppers" that had initially helped launch the Beatles to international fame. Just as the majority of the Beatles' young female audience had little knowledge or appreciation for the four mop-tops' American R&B source materials, the Knack's primary audience showed little concern over the recycling of an era that was not their own.

Doug Fieger acknowledged the band's relationship with its audience in countless interviews, unashamedly claiming that his intention was to present the Knack's fans with a replica of the 1960s British Invasion. Fieger painted a picture of a young 1970s audience deprived both of the riches of AM radio and the music of the Beatles and the Who that had informed his own adolescence. When accused by the critics of plagiarizing the Beatles, Fieger turned to the Knack's audience as his defense, claiming, "They haven't seen it before. They don't know. So are you going to deny them the privilege of seeing rock'n'roll."[11] But the critics objected that the Knack were imposing their own (inadequate) memories of the 1960s upon an audience "too young to know what they're buying."[12] In this respect, then, the discourse surrounding the Knack became a struggle over the power of memory and the musical education of a young audience. Critics resented that they were not in a position of power comparable to that of the Knack's: one where they could steer the young audience to a more "correct" memory of the 1960s and have them listen to the Beatles instead of a cheap new wave imitation.

The more albums that the Knack sold, the more critical abuse was heaped upon them. By the time it had accumulated six million album sales worldwide, the group was meeting with hostility not only from critics but from other similar sounding bands in the Los Angeles scene as well, who felt that the intense marketing behind the Knack had invalidated the integrity of their own efforts to evoke a similarly nostalgic mid-1960s sound. One band, the Plimsouls, even had a photograph of itself taken with machine guns, under the heading of "Get the Knack," adding an entirely new dimension to the album's title.[13] The backlash reached its venomous height when a group of protestors in Los Angeles led a vigorous anti-Knack campaign that centered around the memorable slogan "Nuke the Knack," a phrase that drew on the threat of nuclear war haunting the early 1980s political headlines.

While many of the harsh criticisms that the Knack drew related to its status as a new band encroaching on familiar territory, in many respects it was also the unfortunate recipient of a critical mass that had been gathering around a nostalgic new wave genre, that of "power pop." The label had appeared in the music press two years before the Knack's debut, assigned to groups such as the Jam, the Romantics, Shoes, the Flamin' Groovies, and Cheap Trick, all of whom were seen as reviving in some form or another both the intricate vocal harmonies and melodic arrangements of the British Invasion groups and the ragged, distorted guitar sound of mid-1960s underground American garage bands. By combining the power of a driving rock beat and guitar sound with the sophisticated arrangements of pop, 1970s power pop bands fashioned updated versions of the type of hit singles that had dominated mid-1960s radio.

Those power pop groups who modeled themselves after mid-1960s groups, particularly those of the British Invasion, were trying to re-create what they saw as a utopian form of commercial songwriting, or as some have called it a "poptopia."[14] For many of these power pop groups, the mid-1960s represented a classic, timeless period, and by writing and playing within the standards of that era they believed they were learning and replicating a form of "art."[15] Power pop groups invoked the rhetorical power of "art" to signify a level of craftsmanship that provided instant justification for their endeavors, a maneuver that distanced them from the irreverence, cynicism, and irony that attended so much of the rest of the new wave. And had their audience been comprised solely of musicologists like Wilfrid Mellers, who in the early 1970s had already analyzed the Beatles' albums as if they consisted of Romantic art songs, then such comparisons might likely have fallen on sympathetic ears.[16] But such was not the case. Once power pop's stab at authenticity entered the American mainstream via new wave's popularity, it came under the scrutiny of numerous music critics who subsequently discounted the genre as a hollow and derivative enterprise. The discussion surrounding power pop thus became a tense conflict between value judgments of art and pastiche. Such judgments demonstrate that the past, far from being a fixed object, can be mobilized in the present to suit the meanings and purposes of different ideological positions.

In the sections that follow, I trace the emergence of power pop as an integral and heavily contested part of the new wave. The arguments that swirled around power pop reveal tensions not only about the evocation of the past, but also an aesthetic conflict over the very meanings of its two components: "power" (read *rock*) and "pop." What did it mean for new wave groups to look back with reverence upon a past popular music modernity as an art or craft, something that could be replicated through musical conventions that would signify a certain style? On the one hand, the equation of popular music with a set of rules or formulas would seem to echo Adorno's notorious disparaging view of the mechanization and repetition at the heart of popular music. On the other hand, this must be balanced against an appreciation of power pop not as a commodity or object, but as a performance practice and a specific lived experience for its practitioners. This discussion will ultimately return at the chapter's end to the Knack to consider further how it brought to a boiling point the powerful feelings that the revival of the modern 1960s past evoked among audiences at the turn of the 1980s.

Welcome to Poptopia

I believe pop music should be like the TV—something you can turn on or off and shouldn't disturb the mind. Eventually these people are going to go too far and leave the rest of the world behind. It's very hard to like "Strawberry Fields" for simply what it is. Some artists are becoming musically unapproachable.
  —Pete Townshend of the Who, 1967[17]

While the "power pop" label first came into prominence with the new wave, it did not originate in the late 1970s. Guitarist Pete Townshend of the Who is generally credited with coining the phrase during a 1967 interview with *Hit Parader* magazine.[18] Townshend used "power pop" to describe the mix of powerful rock and roll beats and melodic vocal harmonies that his band was playing at that time, exemplified by short energetic songs like "Substitute" and "I Can't Explain." Townshend positioned power pop strategically as a style that was more accessible than the experimental directions that groups like the Beatles had begun to take with "Strawberry Fields Forever." From the very beginning, then, power pop was assumed to be more pure in nature, more immediate and less cluttered, than the trend toward art rock that was beginning to take hold in the late 1960s. In this respect, the Beatles' ambitious 1967 concept album *Sergeant Pepper's Lonely Heart's Club Band* serves as a convenient axis around which one can define power pop. The Beatles' power pop of the past to which groups like the Knack turned was grounded in the hand claps, ringing guitars, harmony vocals, and direct romantic lyrics of songs like "I Want to Hold Your Hand," and *not* the comparatively thick orchestration, complex form, and obtuse poetic lyrics of a song like "A Day in the Life."

As the 1960s turned into the 1970s, the sounds of "I Want to Hold Your Hand" became more and more a distant memory of a past musical style. To the extent that a Beatles influence continued to hold sway, it was predominantly the music from their later art rock years that could be found resonating in progressive rock groups like the Electric Light Orchestra. The fragmenting of the rock scene into a plurality of new styles, ranging from glam and acid rock to singer-songwriters, Philly soul, funk, and disco rendered the sounds of the mid-1960s British Invasion virtually obsolete. As such, the few early 1970s bands, like the Raspberries, who *did* claim the early Beatles and Who as their models stood out as glaring exceptions. As the Raspberries' front man, Eric Carmen, recalled, "There were a lot of people in 1972 who were not ready yet for any band that even remotely resembled the Beatles. It seemed like our audience was teeny boppers and rock critics. The great mass of album-buying, trend-setting 17–21 year-olds didn't want any part of us."[19]

While early 1970s groups like the Raspberries and Badfinger have since been positioned as part of a power pop continuum leading up to new wave's late 1970s renaissance, the recognition and formulation of this genre was by no means organic. It developed specifically through the conscious efforts of rock critics who offered a carefully assembled and annotated history of the genre, resurrecting the label from the ashes of the 1960s. Chief among them was Greg Shaw, editor of the independent music magazine *Bomp!* In the magazine's March 1978 issue Shaw, with the help of regular contributors Gary Sperrazza! [*sic*] and Ken Barnes, attempted for the first time to map out the historical narrative of power pop (which was conflated to a single word, *powerpop*), identifying canonical figures old and new and providing coverage of the genre's key geographical scenes in such cities as Los Angeles and Chicago. At nearly forty pages in length, Shaw's power pop coverage was extensive in its scope, a shining example of new wave's distinct connoisseurist underpinnings. The now famous cover illustration (see figure 12), provided by art director William Stout, captures the main thrust of the magazine's contents.[20] The striking pop art-styled graphics immediately roots the power pop genre within a familiar 1960s milieu. The rendering of the mod-suited guitarist as a cartoon superhero works on another level as well, connecting *Bomp!* with the world of science fiction fanzines that heavily influenced Shaw and many other rock critics who first got their start in the 1960s. As the cover's capsule headlines make clear, the magazine's focus is primarily historical (pronouncing the greatness of long-deceased 1960s groups like the Easybeats and Creation), with a clear dismissal of present musical trends ("No Disco!").

Inside the magazine Shaw positioned the power pop phenomenon as part of a "dialectical theory of rock history," one that saw rock music's temporal trajectory as swinging back and forth on a pendulum between moments of hard rock and light pop domination.[21] Within this theory, Shaw viewed power pop as an idealized combination, the realization of pop's as-

Figure 12. *Bomp!* magazine's March 1978 "Power Pop" special issue. Cover illustration by William Stout. Courtesy of *Bomp!* www.bomp.com.

cendant late 1970s moment, flavored with the hard power of punk rock. This was not the first time that readers of *Bomp!* (and its previous incarnation, *Who Put the Bomp*) had encountered Shaw's gonzo musicological appropriation of Hegel's familiar thesis/antithesis/synthesis construct. Throughout the early and mid-1970s Shaw had repeatedly preached the crucial role of "rock theory." For Shaw, such theorizing was important because he believed that the post-1967 music scene had fallen into desperate times, with the rise of free-form progressive rock forcing the "memorable hooks & melodies" of pop to its margins.[22] Only by analyzing the ebb and flow of rock's various historical patterns, phases, and cycles, he argued, could one predict the next "pop revival" and rock and pop's subsequent reunion.[23] As part of this theory, Shaw believed that the periodical renewal would occur by returning to rock's roots, specifically to the "high mark of the previous peak era," which would be least familiar, and thus most fresh, to rock and pop's core teenage audience.[24] Just as the Beatles had revived 1950s rock and roll for a new, young 1960s audience, so it stood to reason that whatever revolutionary music would triumph in the 1970s would do so by mining the riches of the mid-1960s.

In prescribing the formula for a power pop genre, Shaw was in many respects following a path similar to the one that he and other renegade rock critics like Lester Bangs had trod earlier in the 1970s, when they theorized a punk aesthetic stemming from such underappreciated, forgotten mid-1960s American garage bands as the Count Five, the Seeds, and the Troggs. As Bernard Gendron shows in his book *Between Montmartre and the Mudd Club,* such theorizing provided an influential discourse that predated the emergence of the New York CBGB's scene and the 1976 British punk explosion by several years.[25] By the time that groups like the Ramones and Sex Pistols seized the attention of the mainstream music press in the mid-1970s, rock critics had already firmly established punk's connection with a specific 1960s aesthetic. In fact by that point punk's frame of reference had extended well beyond Bangs's rather circumscribed coterie of garage bands. Seymour Stein of Sire Records, for example, repeatedly claimed that the Ramones reminded him most of all of the early Beach Boys. Similarly Legs McNeil, one of the cofounders of the influential mid-1970s fanzine *Punk,* heard echoes of the early Beatles in the Ramones. To him, the Ramones sounded like "what was played on the radio in the '60s. . . . I thought they were the most commercial band in the world. I was kind of shocked when everybody said 'No.'"[26] Punk's link to the past thus proved to be fundamental to the genre's very definition.

In recognizing both punk's and power pop's roots in the musical past, it is telling that the genres' advocates turned to the sounds of the most recent musical generation rather than the rock and roll of the 1950s. As Gendron points out, this was partly motivated by practical considerations, as there already existed a sizable number of "oldies magazines" devoted to music of the 1950s, with whom Shaw had no desire to compete.[27] In addition, for rock critics like Shaw and Bangs, who were intent on instigating a revolutionary musical change, the ubiquity of a conservative 1950s rock and roll nostalgia throughout the 1970s likely tainted that particular source material even further. From popular "Rock-and-Roll Revival" shows, featuring such 1950s luminaries as Fats Domino and Bill Haley and the faux stylings of groups like Sha Na Na to the 1972 debut of *Grease,* the 1973 theatrical release of *American Graffiti,* and the appearance of the television show *Happy Days* in 1974, the decade was suffused with the fifties' warm nostalgic glow.[28] Buoyed by a dramatic rise in antique collecting and flea market sales, and sanctioned through colorful *Life* magazine photo spreads of 1950s fashions and fads, the fifties revival that swept the early 1970s amounted to what sociologist Fred Davis aptly described as a "nostalgia orgy."[29] By championing the uncharted territory of the mid-1960s, Shaw and Bangs sidestepped the pop culture mainstream and in doing so positioned themselves as radical rock historians.

For all the links with the past that created a shared bond between punk and power pop, however, the aesthetic discourse surrounding the two diverged sharply. Bangs praised punk specifically for its "assaultiveness, minimalism, rank amateurism"—an appreciation that railed against rock music's artistic pretensions while embracing the shock tactics of the avant-garde art world.[30] There was little room for the comparative polish of the British Invasion bands in this aesthetic, a point that was dramatically underscored when the Sex Pistols booted bassist and main songwriter Glen Matlock from the band, reputedly (and most likely apocryphally) because he was a fan of the Beatles. In appraising the punk aesthetic, Shaw acknowledged the significance of its "calculated offensiveness," which had served to jostle the 1970s rock industry out of its complacency.[31] At the same time, he felt that punk had a "built-in obsolescence" and that its primitivism was incapable of sustaining the movement beyond its initial triumphant blast.[32] The power pop that Shaw envisioned, on the other hand, would merge rock's raw power, as well as the best elements of punk, with an undeniable polish and melodicism, achieving the "pop revival" for which he had argued tirelessly since the early 1970s. Shaw imagined that power pop's accessibility would ensure a slew of hit singles and thus work to revitalize the music scene in ways that had been impossible for punk in the United States.

Shaw was not alone in this regard. The March 1978 *Bomp!* power pop issue was followed one month later by *Trouser Press*'s similarly framed six-page "Power Pop Primer" special assembled by the magazine's editor, Ira Robbins.[33] Like Shaw, Robbins had embraced the American and British punk explosions of 1976–77 with open arms, and his magazine had become largely associated with the new wave movement. But by early 1978, both magazines had recognized and declared that the new music had reached a point of crisis. Robbins had already declared the new wave "dead" in an October 1977 *Trouser Press* cover feature, and Shaw believed the music was on its last legs as well.[34] Both argued that power pop was the one genre most capable of salvaging the new wave movement from the general malaise and media stigma that had come to claim punk. Crucially, power pop for them provided the first evidence of a genre from *within* the new wave movement that could force a decisive evolution away from the primitivism of punk. Power pop was thus heralded as a savior. In the introduction to his "Power Pop Primer," Robbins made clear the contrast with the punk aesthetic that power pop would provide for the new wave:

> If one may hazard an absurd guess based on no real information, it will probably be around November [1978] when some smart punk rocker will wake up and realize that a change has occurred since the inception of the new wave. In place of similar sounding four-piece noise machines, groups that used to be called punk are replacing hoarse shouts with melody, and volume with a sense of dynamics. Not that groups have abandoned their instruments or ideals, just that a new influence has been taken on. At that point, the renaissance of power pop will have officially occurred.[35]

As Robbins observes, with power pop's arrival, the new wave would undertake a more sophisticated, and ultimately commercial, direction that once and for all would render punk's nihilistic musical aesthetic obsolete. Thus it can be argued that it is with power pop specifically that new wave in the United States began to become identified with "hit music," an association that would become one of its most defining characteristics.

As if to emphasize power pop's break from underground and DIY politics, both Shaw and Robbins presented the genre as one not simply represented by obscure indie acts and voices of the past, but also open to contemporary pop and rock trends of the 1970s. Shaw's list of "All-Time Power Pop Records," for example, goes beyond such obvious 1960s touchstones as the Who, the Kinks, and the Creation to include such mainstream mid-1970s acts as the Bay City Rollers and Abba. Likewise, in Robbins's power pop primer obvious new wave choices like Blondie, the Jam, Nick Lowe, and Shoes rub shoulders with arena and stadium rock outfits like Kiss (who, as Robbins notes, had covered the Dave Clark Five's "Any Way You Want It"), Bachman Turner Overdrive, and Boston. In this light, it is important to remember that while both Shaw and Robbins were known as Anglophile rock critics who held most American AOR in disdain, they were first and foremost collectors, archivists, and fans who through their publications sought to document rock and pop history for a knowledgeable, enlightened readership that could appreciate good music, "regardless of fashion styles or the posturing of performers."[36] Their power pop canons thus provide a window onto their version of an idealized musical style, one that they hoped could transcend the often too rigid boundaries and ideological biases of conventional genre formations.

In considering their interest in power pop and their reverence for the music of their personal past, it is tempting to view Shaw and Robbins not just as rock critics, but as individuals particularly susceptible to the pull of nostalgia. Both Shaw (who was born in 1949) and Robbins (who was born in 1954) were members of a generation of Americans whose adolescent and teenage years spanned nearly the entirety of the 1960s, but who found themselves, as they moved into social roles of adult independence in the 1970s, in a transitional stage of their lives. As Fred Davis points out in his book *Yearning for Yesterday*, it is during such periods of turbulence in the life cycle that we are most susceptible to nostalgia.[37] Overwhelmingly, as sociological studies have shown, through nostalgia we tend to privilege our formative years as idealized reference points by which we can compare and critique the meanings of other historical periods.[38] As other studies have noted, we feed our nostalgic impulses through the gathering and maintaining of collections.[39] For rock critics like Shaw and Robbins, whose magazines offered numerous historical narratives and discographies, their accumulation of recordings, while vital to their publications, also served as a visible manifestation of their attachment to the past. It was perhaps to be expected, then, that in finding fault with the direction of rock in the 1970s, these critics should turn to the mid-1960s music of their past. Such actions offered them not only a certain safe, grounded reality, but also a chance through their discovery of unknown bands from the past to reimagine and reinvent the persons they once were.

The genesis of power pop was one that emerged out of a small group of rock critics whose hope for an idealized rock and pop aesthetic drove them to define a new genre. But how exactly did power pop balance this rock-pop merger? What were the terms of this union, and how did the bands who found themselves lumped in with this new power pop genre adopt the conventions of the past as part of their music-making practices in the present? The next section looks more closely at power pop as a style and new wave's rereading of a mid-1960s golden age.

Power Pop and the Rock/Pop Dialectic: The Politics of Nostalgia as Style

I am proud to be a pop guy even though at times it's been like walking around with a "kick me" sign.
   —Mitch Easter[40]

While Shaw's power pop genre was forged from the merger of rock and pop, it was clear from the very beginning that its center was located on the rock side. After all, power pop was music played almost exclusively by *rock bands*, by white male musicians who were following the group model that had emerged in the wake of the Beatles and the British Invasion, and who consequently saw themselves as autonomous artists. As such, it is the identification of the pop element in power pop that deserves the most attention, not the least because the word *pop* is so loaded. *Pop* has a complex lineage that dates back many decades, but its utter ubiquity and familiarity has rendered it as a strongly coded word whose meaning is attainable only through the specific context in which it appears. To one person, pop might signify a star performer like Britney Spears or Justin Timberlake, and a whole host of assumptions concerning mass radio and television markets, puppeteering songwriters or producers and the privileging of style and spectacle over substance and depth. To another person, though, pop might connote a special gift for memorable melodies or hooks and the strong vocal quality of a recent "indie pop" outfit like the Shins. The divergences here indicate the wide range of pop's associations as a musical style and mode of production, and its connection to different audience formations. Add to this that since the 1960s pop music has also been linked with pop art and avant-garde notions of style, color, media, and ironic intent, and the whole notion of pop becomes increasingly unwieldy.

These difficulties notwithstanding, various popular music scholars—most notably Simon Frith—have tackled the problem of pop, often choosing to draw its distinctions through a comparison with rock.[41] As we have already seen through the example of the Beatles, the key moment in the rock/pop dichotomy dates back to the mid-1960s. This split engendered not just stylistic changes, but a symbolic shifting in the dissemination of the music as well. The release of *Sergeant Pepper's Lonely Heart's Club Band* in 1967 was a major event that signaled the eventual privileging of the full-length rock album over the seven-inch pop single and the possibility of longer and longer songs. In hand with this new development, the opening of the FM airwaves to "progressive" rock stations introduced free-form programming and a medium much more amenable to lengthy album cuts than the tight confines of the AM hit single playlist. As such, FM became synonymous with rock music, while AM retained an antiquated association with pop.

For the power pop bands of the new wave era, it was clear on which side of the 1967 rock/pop wall they fell. There was an obligation to confine one's musical expressions to the limit of the "three minute" AM radio pop single, a challenge to work within the framework of a restricted form.[42] One group even incorporated this pop lineage into its very name, adopting the moniker Two Minutes 50. Many power pop bands also expressed a direct nostalgia for AM radio, explaining that for them it was "a great education," because it exposed them not only to the music of the British Invasion, but other pop sounds as well. Recalling his adolescence of the late 1960s, Paul Collins of the Beat remembered "many nights falling asleep with WABC on the radio listening to all the hits from the '60s—everything from The Monkees to The Buckinghams to the Supremes to The Who to The Beach Boys to The Stones."[43] By the late 1970s the AM stations that had dominated the previous decade had been in rapid decline for many years, with FM rock radio's graduation to the popular AOR format rendering the once popular AM stations all but obsolete. As Tommy Dunbar of the Rubinoos complained to *Rolling Stone:* "Top Forty AM—songs with melody and stuff that strikes a romantic chord—is dead. . . . But there's gotta be *someone* out there who still wants to listen to pop music."[44]

It may have seemed that the Top 40 AM's "melody and stuff," as Dunbar put it, had disappeared, but as the power pop groups found, these elements could be retrieved through specific musical stylistic references that gazed back upon the music of the early to middle 1960s. Whether it was their song forms, vocal arrangements, chord progressions, rhythmic patterns, instrumentation or overall sound, power pop groups developed a musical practice rooted in the pop of the past that sat at the core of this emergent genre. Sometimes the borrowings were specific. Both the Jam's "Start!" (1980) and the Bangles' "I'm in Line" (1982) are built around syncopated bass riffs that recall Paul McCartney's famed melodic bass line from the Beatles' "Taxman," a connection that each group further reinforces by mimicking John Lennon's rhythmic guitar strokes on the backbeat. Nearly every power pop band employed smooth harmony backing vocals that recalled the signature style of the British Invasion as well. In the Spongetones' "She Goes Out with Everybody" (1982), for example, the two main vocalists employ a "clothesline harmony"—where one vocalist sings a descending melodic line that is left, "hung out to dry," under the other vocalist's stationary one-note line—directly imitative of the famous vocal arrangement in the verse of the Beatles' "Please Please Me" (which they themselves had borrowed from the Everly Brothers' 1960 hit "Cathy's Clown"). Other American groups like 20/20 evoked the British Invasion simply by adopting a distinct British accent in their vocals, a result of immersing themselves in the style of their mid-1960s favorites.[45]

Many power pop bands connected to the music's past through their conscious choice of instrumental gear, specifically their guitars, basses, and amplifiers. Groups such as the Jam, Romantics, Plimsouls, Bangles, and the Church turned to the Rickenbacker guitar (the Records and the Knack used Rickenbacker basses), not only for its clean, trebly tones but for its specific role in defining a mid-1960s style.[46] Both John Lennon and George Harrison played Rickenbacker guitars in the Beatles' early incarnations, with Harrison employing a twelve-string Rickenbacker on many of the group's recordings from 1964 and 1965. Roger McGuinn of the Byrds would follow Harrison's lead in the mid-1960s, arriving at a distinctive arpeggiated style on the twelve-string Rickenbacker that would bear a great influence not only on the late 1970s power pop movement, but also guitarists like Peter Buck of R.E.M. and Johnny Marr of the Smiths who followed soon after in the early 1980s. Whether they chose the Rickenbacker, the more standard Fender Stratocaster (Buddy Holly's guitar of choice), or in Elvis Costello's case a vintage mid-1950s White Falcon hollow body Gretsch, power pop and new wave guitarists sought a bright, cutting tone that departed significantly from the prevailing trends of the 1970s. Their choices were, in the words of Cars guitarist Elliot Easton, "a reaction to years of Marshall heaviness," and the thick, fat sound of guitars like the Gibson Les Paul that had contributed mightily to the forging of a hard rock and heavy metal style.[47] Heard against this backdrop, the power pop guitar stood out for its nostalgic sound.

Other musical ties to the 1960s were more subtle. A number of power pop songs, for example, such as Blondie's "One Way or Another" and "Sunday Girl" (1978), Kirsty MacColl's "They Don't Know" (1979; covered by Tracey Ullman in 1983), the Go-Go's' "Our Lips Are Sealed" (1981), and Marshall Crenshaw's "Cynical Girl" and "There She Goes Again" (both 1982), returned to the AABA song form that had dominated nearly every popular music style of the early 1960s ranging from girl groups to surf instrumentals, but had all but disappeared by the 1970s. Many of the Beatles' early singles—songs such as "Love Me Do," "I Want to Hold Your Hand," "Can't Buy Me Love," and "A Hard Day's Night"—were cast in the AABA mold. The basic outline of the AABA is similar in some respects to the verse–chorus–bridge form that came to replace it as the standard for rock songwriting, but the differences are important. Both forms begin with two repetitions (AA or verse–chorus and verse–chorus) that are followed by a bridge and then a return to the main section(s). The AABA, however, is a more compact form, especially suited to the limits of the three-minute single. The A sections generally consist of a verse and a brief refrain (often containing the song's title), that taken together act as a single self-contained unit. A typical AABA song like Crenshaw's "Cynical Girl"—with its eight-bar A sections, and nine-bar B sections (reminiscent of the Beatles' "Middle Eight" bridges with a one-bar extension)—allows for a great deal of repetition. "Cynical Girl" cycles through an entire AABA sequence and then runs through a truncated ABA return that fades out on the A section. The typical verse–chorus form, on the other hand, features verses and the choruses that are distinctly separate units, each of them often eight bars or more in length, and distinguished by noticeable changes in lyrics, melodies, chord progressions, and textural arrangements. By the 1970s, as rock songs had grown in length and slowed in tempo, the verse–chorus form expanded as well to include a prechorus that enabled bands to exploit more fully the verse's build toward a dramatic, emotional chorus. Boston's "More Than a Feeling" (1976) is a particularly good example of the expansive verse–pre-chorus–chorus rock song at its peak.

Power pop's musical connection to the past extended beyond its melodies, instrumentation, and song forms and into its very rhythmic foundations as well. Critics repeatedly compared drummers like Clem Burke of Blondie and Bruce Gary of the Knack to the Who's Keith Moon. Like Moon, both Burke and Gary had developed an active or "busy" style that incorporated multiple fills within, and sometimes as part of, the song's basic drum beat. Other rhythmic allusions to the past were more nuanced but no less important to defining a power pop style. One that was particularly ubiquitous, and deserving of some extended historical explanation, is a drum pattern sometimes referred to as the "Mersey Beat"—because of its strong association with the early Beatles—but which I will call the "double backbeat."[48] As the name suggests, this rhythmic trope is essentially a variation on the most common of rock music's syncopated accent patterns: the backbeat. A regular snare drum backbeat normally accents, with single quarter notes, the second and fourth beats of a four-beat measure. The double backbeat modifies this basic pattern as the drummer "doubles up" on the snare and plays two eighth notes on one (normally the first) of the two backbeat accents. Example 1 notates one measure of the double backbeat.

Example 1: The double backbeat

This drum pattern appears in various power pop singles, such as the Romantics' "Tell it to Carrie" (1978), Blondie's "Sunday Girl" and "Hanging on the Telephone" (1978), the Knack's "Good Girls Don't" (1979), and the Spongetones' "She Goes Out with Everybody" (1982). The double backbeat was one of popular music's most pervasive signature rhythms of the early 1960s, appearing in songs like Del Shannon's "Runaway" (1961) as well as numerous girl group singles ranging from the Shirelles' "Will You Love Me Tomorrow" (1961) to the famous hand-clap beat that opens the Angels' "My Boyfriend's Back" (1963). It was a prominent rhythm among surf bands as well, as any of the myriad early 1960s versions of such standards as "Penetration" or "Walk, Don't Run" testify. And naturally it is featured in numerous early Beatles songs such as "Please Please Me" (1963) and "I Want to Hold Your Hand" (1964).

The double backbeat can be traced back to a variety of lineage points. As Jacqueline Warwick has suggested in her study of 1960s girl group music, the rhythmic patterns has roots both in the clapping and stomping practices found in Pentecostal churches as well as the handclapping and body-slapping of girls' games. Another potential link can be found with Latin American styles such as the habanera and bossa nova.[49] As scholars like John Storm Roberts and Ned Sublette have illustrated, throughout the first half of the twentieth century the syncopated rhythmic patterns of these and other Latin American styles worked their way seamlessly, through various processes of dissemination and transformation, into American popular music's basic stylistic language.[50] By the mid-1950s, the syncopated pattern of the habanera had become, as Roy Brewer points out, a "standard rhythm" in rockabilly and rock and roll songs like Elvis Presley's version of "Hound Dog."[51] The appeal of such a pattern was its syncopated accent shape. The accents of the habanera and bossa nova divide a 4/4 measure into a 3 + 3 + 2 pattern, as notated in example 2.

Example 2: Habanera and bossa nova pattern

Rockabilly players normally played the pattern in example 2 with a swinging triplet feel. By the end of the 1950s, however, such swinging syncopations were in decline within rock and roll and had given way to songs that employed the straight eighth-note subdivision feel endemic to so many Latin American styles. While rockabilly's popularity diminished, the Latin American patterns continued to flourish, and easily matched the shape of new eighth-note subdivision patterns like the double backbeat. Example 3 shows how the habanera's 3 + 3 + 2 accent pattern is mapped out within the double backbeat.

Example 3: Double backbeat and habanera pattern

As Brewer points out, very few 1950s rockabilly musicians associated the syncopated rhythmic pattern of example 2 specifically with the habanera or with Latin American styles. But with the pioneering efforts of Latin jazz composer Antonio Carlos Jobim in the late 1950s, and the subsequent craze for bossa nova styles in the early 1960s, many listeners likely heard the double backbeat of example 3 within a very different context. For them, the double backbeat probably bore a striking resemblance to the rhythm of the bossa nova, an association that Petula Clark makes explicit in her 1964 hit "Downtown," where she sings "listen to the rhythm of the gentle bossa nova" while the drummer is playing the double backbeat in the background.

Aside from whatever grounding the double backbeat might have had in girls' games, Pentecostal church practices, or Latin American music styles, there are practical reasons why this rhythmic trope surfaced in rock and roll and pop music of the late 1950s and early 1960s, why it reappeared in the late 1970s power pop, and why one finds scarcely any hint of its presence between these two eras. These reasons reveal the logistics behind playing such a rhythmic beat. First, as I have mentioned, the double backbeat emerged most forcefully at the point where popular music began to move away from the swing and shuffle feel of the 1950s to more even eighth-note subdivisions. Second, and equally important, the double backbeat is a pattern most suited to a fast or medium-paced tempo. Its heightened accent serves to push the beat forward and provides the song with momentum. There simply is less inclination to play this pattern in a song with a comparatively slow tempo.[52] Tellingly, in the late 1960s and early 1970s, as the general pulse of rock music began to slacken, the double backbeat became less and less common. Only with the appearance of new wave's faster-paced songs in the late 1970s did drummers again begin employing this beat with any frequency.

The crucial point here is that a rhythmic trope like the double backbeat is a contextual element. Power pop drummers in the 1970s returned to this pattern because it sounded right. That is, they heard, perhaps within a rehearsal or live setting, how the drum pattern fit the riffs that the other band members were playing. They may or may not have set out, in a premeditated fashion, to insert a double backbeat into a particular song. But by the time they arrived at the point, after rehearsing the song, where they knew that the double backbeat provided an ideal fit, they were likely aware that the pattern resonated with the group's stylistic aims, or that it somehow emulated a song or songs that they remembered from the past. Or perhaps they recalled playing that way from when they were younger, when they had first picked up a pair of drumsticks in the 1960s. Nostalgia in this scenario is not a regressive act; it is an active process initiated by a communal activity. As the anthropologist Kathleen Stewart reminds us, nostalgia is always part of a social situation: it is grounded in active cultural production.[53] In a similar way the historian Michael Schudson has emphasized that "the act of remembering is most often social and interactive, occasioned by social situations, prompted by cultural artifacts and social cues that remind, employed for social purposes, even enacted by cooperative activity."[54] These are viewpoints that encourage us to analyze power pop's nostalgia and memory as part of vital, lived experiences.

The various connections that I have thus far drawn—power pop's resurrection of the seven-inch singles medium, a yearning for Top 40 AM radio, and the genre's connection with specific song forms and musical stylistic elements of the early and mid-1960s—all combine to locate power pop
within a specific commercial context. As such they are intimately bound
with what Simon Frith refers to as a pop "aesthetic." Specifically, he sees
pop not as an art, but as a craft. Pop "is not about realizing individual visions or making us see the world in new ways but about providing popular
tunes and clichés in which to express commonplace feelings—love, loss,
jealousy."[55] Pop, in this respect, is functional, a music that implores us to
dance, feel sentimental emotions, or express romantic longing in unambiguous terms. Its very transparency ensures its popular appeal. Many
power pop bands enthusiastically viewed their musical endeavors through
precisely such a lens. Steve Allen of 20/20 talked of writing "the kinds of
songs that kids will call up the station and dedicate to their girlfriends."[56]
John Murphy of Shoes spoke of writing his group's songs for "Joe Average,
who just wants to hear a good song on the radio."[57] While Chris Stamey of
the dB's justified his band's musical aesthetic by explaining that "it's real
easy to sneak into some housewife's mind with voices singing thirds in major scales. . . . Music is functional."[58]

And yet the irony is that because power pop bands wrote their songs
tailored to an imagined pop audience conversant with the sounds of the
1960s, their music did *not* fit within the 1970s AOR mainstream. Their music rarely made it to the radio where it might be available for a teenager's
dedication or where it might fall within earshot of some housewife. The
music's sincere nostalgic 1960s commercial style, promoted and distributed
through the new wave's small, noncommercial network of independent
record labels, virtually ensured that its audience would be limited to a
smattering of fans and connoisseurist rock critics. At the same time, given
their fringe status, lying well outside the mainstream, power pop groups
like Shoes, the dB's, and 20/20 easily adopted rock's resistant pose, and the
belief that their chosen medium was indeed an artistic one that represented
their special individual vision. Their "art," so to speak, was one of convention. If one could master the various tropes and patterns of power pop's
past and combine them in appealing ways with contemporary touches,
then one could succeed in both re-creating and revivifying an established

musical art form. But this conflict between craft and art, between pop and rock, also proved to be power pop's bane. In a popular music landscape where fans and critics typically have embraced the Romantic myth of the rock star as Dionysian rebel or Promethean hero, power pop's vision of "art" as an exercise in formalized commercial aesthetics failed to exude the appropriate menace, politicized content, or sexual danger that would guarantee its success as an "authentic" form of rock expression. By embracing the conventions of pop craft as its yardstick of excellence, power pop was assured a secondary status.

This problem is hardly unique to rock music, of course. The music theorist Robert Gjerdingen, for example, has gone to great lengths to undo the long-standing Romantic critical bias toward eighteenth-century music of the classical period music, which has elevated the "genius" of Mozart and Haydn at the expense of that era's other composers who worked within the realm of convention. As Gjerdingen argues in his book *A Classic Turn of Phrase,* one can gain a fuller appreciation of that period's Galant style by analyzing the subtle craft through which composers pieced together their music out of particular patterns and tropes that became a shared musical language, one in which Mozart and Haydn themselves engaged. Music of the Classic period, he argues, was "written not by geniuses but by musical tailors—men who stitched together and sewed together swatches woven by others."[59] In a way, this is precisely the argument that I have been making for power pop in this chapter. By weaving together the accepted conventions of stacked vocal harmonies, Rickenbacker arpeggios, doubled-up backbeats, and hand claps, power pop musicians were in a sense "musical tailors." In this respect, Gjerdingen's view of the classical period provides an intriguing historical analogue to power pop's own aesthetic parameters.

But in the end Gjerdingen's example is not a perfect analogy, and its differences illuminate a glaring irony in power pop's role within the new wave. Gjerdingen's eighteenth-century composers or musical tailors produced on demand, for the needs of a patron or court. These composers knew who their audience was, and thus they wrote music for specific occasions and purposes. If the music fulfilled its function, then their "art of convention" was a success. Power pop musicians, on the other hand, *imagined* a nonexistent mass audience whose very absence served to underscore the reality of the music's limited circulation. This dynamic would change in 1979, however, when the massive popularity of the Knack altered much of the discourse surrounding power pop in the rock press. What had been an idiosyncratic, idealized genre for critics like Shaw and Robbins became a catchphrase and marketing slogan as the major labels signed a wave of new power pop bands in the hopes of matching the Knack's success. As we have seen, power pop's increased visibility opened the door for a critical backlash, much of which questioned the validity and application of power pop's nostalgic conventions within a late 1970s rock context.

Power Pop and the Problems of Genre

Power pop is the Rodney Dangerfield of rock 'n' roll. It is the direct updating of the most revered artists—the Who, the Beach Boys, the Beatles—yet it gets no respect.
    —Power pop historian Ken Sharp[60]

As a genre that was beholden to its particular influences, power pop was caught in a tricky bind. If power pop bands adhered too closely to their heroes, then rock critics would accuse them of being unoriginal and derivative, of failing to meet the impossibly lofty standards that they had set for themselves. Should they deviate too far from their chosen models, however, then they would be seen as corrupting power pop's rules, of misreading the genre. Beyond this, they faced the challenge of deftly balancing the "power" and "pop" sides of the genre's equations. Were they to veer too far in one direction, they left themselves open to claims that they were either clichéd hard rockers masquerading as pop, or at the other extreme that they were anodyne bubblegum pop musicians that lacked any real bite or passion. Rare indeed was the power pop band that managed to dodge all these land mines and win the critics' unqualified approval.

Creem magazine's review of the Romantics' 1980 debut album provides a litany of the typical complaints that were hurled at power pop. The reviewer, Mitch Cohen, characterizes the group as "pale, mimetic poseurs," crippled by an "artistic timidity that seems almost invisibly quaint and retrograde."[61] While he admits that the Romantics have mastered all the requisite power pop elements ("bouncy guitars," "handclaps," and "pearly, adolescent-toned singing"), Cohen is unable to locate the substance beneath these surface traits. All he can hear is the craft, and not the art. And art, for *Creem*, which marketed itself as "America's only rock'n'roll magazine," resided in the rawness and passion of rock. Cohen thus proceeds to blast the Romantics precisely for falling too far to the pop side of the power pop genre, where their "overriding attitude of manufactured innocence" proved to be their Achilles' heel:

> "Romantic" is not a word to be used lightly, and certainly not as a synonym for the moony love-struck sentimentality of this foursome. Romanticism involves emotional risk; you make the leap over the moat, or the alligators chomp on your ass. The Romantics' notions are undramatic, and unearned; shivers up and down their spine, crushes on the girl next door . . . "I just can't stand the pain," they whimper, and it sounds like a paper cut.[62]

On the other hand, should a band move beyond the typical teenage pop fare of shivers, goose bumps, or "crushes on the girl next door," and carry the power pop genre into more adult territory, the criticism could be equally damning. In his review of Shoes' 1982 album *Boomerang*, for example, Robert Christgau chastised the band for including lyrics (e.g., "Does he keep you amused between the covers?") that exchanged the harmless power pop problems of adolescent "girl trouble" for the tasteless, offensive afflictions of "woman trouble."[63] Such sentiments sat uneasily with power pop's prescribed mode of teenage address.

These protestations paled, however, in comparison to the discomfort that critics felt with the Knack and their attitudes toward the female subjects of their songs. Whereas the Beatles, on the surface, had sung about romantic longing and innocent love, the Knack, with songs like "My Sharona," which the twenty-six-year-old front man Doug Fieger had written as a desirous plea to a teenaged girl, expressed a lustful appetite for younger women that some felt bordered on perversion. Many of the songs, it seemed, glorified Fieger's voracious libido while reducing the females in his lyrics to mindless sex objects. The cover for the seven-inch single of "My Sharona," which featured the real-life Sharona posing braless in a skin-tight, white tank top, clutching her Knack album next to her waist, provided the appropriately sexualized visual complement. The objections multiplied furiously upon the Knack's second album, 1980's . . . *But the Little Girls Under-*

stand, and specifically the first single, "Baby Talks Dirty," which portrayed a girl who implores Fieger to "hurt me" and who "loves a real neat beating." Reviewing the album in *Rolling Stone,* Dave Marsh recoiled at the band's "repulsive misogyny" and found in Fieger a man who was so deluded that next to him, "Rod Stewart is a paragon of sexual humility."[64] Or, as Charles Shaar Murray of *New Musical Express* put it: "When the little girls *do* understand what Fieger thinks of them, The Knack are going to be in a considerable amount of trouble."[65] The critical fallout from . . . *but the little girls understand* proved to be disastrous for the Knack, especially when the album's sales fell far short of what they had achieved with their multiplatinum debut. By the time the group returned with its third album a year and a half later, in 1981, they were largely forgotten. They would break up soon after.

In the decades following the Knack's phenomenal rise and fall, Fieger repeatedly dissected, analyzed, and tried to explain and justify the group's ill-fated relationship to the music of the mid-1960s. Part of the problem that hounded the second album, he argued, was that it was released a mere sixth months after *Get the Knack.* To put out another record so quickly was largely unheard of at that time, but the Knack had set before themselves an aesthetic goal: to replicate the rapid release schedules of the 1960s bands that they admired so much. It was, in Fieger's estimation, a "very stupid" mistake: "We were operating from this place of fantasy that we wanted to bring back those halcyon days where The Beatles, Dylan and The Rolling Stones released three albums a year."[66] In this context, "Baby Talks Dirty," with its syncopated, bouncing octave eighth-note hook cut from the same mold as "My Sharona," sounded most of all as if the band had plagiarized itself. As Fieger explained, "We got a lot of criticism for 'Baby Talks Dirty.' Had that song come out on a fifth album, I think people would have said 'oh, they've gone back to their roots. They take the 'My Sharona' riff another place.' But as it was, people were gunning for us."[67] With the release of its second album, the Knack was competing not only with people's memories of a 1960s past, but with the band's own recent history on record as well.

Part of the problem, as Fieger saw it, was that people took the Knack's allusions to the past too seriously and too literally. This was especially true of the band's Beatles-esque televisual pose from the back cover of *Get the Knack.* Fieger denied that the Knack in this instance was attempting to place itself on an equal plane with the Beatles. On the contrary, he claimed that they had intended the stock British Invasion look, posed directly for the television cameras, as a cynically ironic joke:

> You've got to remember this is 1978/1979 when these ideas and things came out. Everybody in the '70's was talking about what the next big thing was gonna be. It was our comment: "You wanna know what the next big thing is gonna look like? It's gonna look just like the last big thing."[68]

Fieger goes on to suggest that if the band had only sold a few thousand copies instead of six million, then there never would have been any issues raised over their borrowings from the Beatles. Instead, critics would have understood the "joke" of the back album cover and the Knack would have been appreciated for their "artfulness."[69] But in making this claim Fieger misread the ground rules that had accrued around the power pop genre. Power pop bands approached their songwriting as an authentic effort to apply the musical conventions of the past in new and imaginative yet reverential settings. Power pop as such was notable for its virtual *absence* of irony. The Knack may have intended an in-joke reference, but it rubbed against the expectations that fans and critics brought to the genre.

In the end the Knack found themselves in an impossible situation. As we have seen, power pop's strength rested in a band's ability to concoct a short, catchy, well-crafted song that would sound good on the radio: a hit single. In this respect, the art of the power pop style is inherently commercial. Yet when the Knack actually *did* achieve great success with a power pop hit single, the band was branded by its peers—other Los Angeles bands like 20/20 and the Plimsouls—as contrived, commercial plagiarists. They were criticized for having achieved a level of success and recognition that is the implicit, if generally unrealized, end goal of power pop's musical aesthetic.

For all the distress that accompanied the Knack's rise and fall, and complaints that the band had poisoned the power pop genre, dooming those bands that had been signed in its wake, the Knack did not "kill" power pop. The genre survived and has provided a working stylistic model for countless bands since its peak of popularity at the turn of the 1980s. In fact, power pop has maintained a healthy presence for so long now that few associate the genre's historical origins with the rise of new wave anymore. It has achieved a life all its own. Still, no power pop band since the Knack has come even remotely close to approaching the immense popularity that "My Sharona" enjoyed in 1979. Instead, power pop since that time has become a genre upheld by a small and dedicated following of fanzine writers, aficionados, and specialty record labels, and played by an international array of both obscure and modest-selling bands. But part of the pleasure, I would argue, for current power pop's small audience is that its listeners feel privy to an art form that belongs to them, and to them alone. Power pop fans embrace the commercial aesthetic as art precisely because it presents a chance for them to differentiate themselves from a mainstream audience. And as long as power pop bands continue to write hit songs that fail to actually become hits, none of them is likely to be seriously accused, as the Knack was, of having tarnished our memories of the Beatles.

SIX

"Roll Over Guitar Heroes, Synthesizers Are Here . . ."

At the height of new wave's popularity in the early 1980s, no musical instrument symbolized the movement's modern identity more fully than the synthesizer. The synthesizer had first found its way into rock music at the end of the 1960s, and from the very beginning its ability to produce striking timbres and fantastical sound effects ensured that it would be viewed as a futuristic musical technology. As one new wave keyboardist put it, "As soon as synthesizers came along, everyone said 'Oh, wow, outer space!'"[1] The instrument's reputation eventually extended beyond these first impressions, especially when musicians realized that the synthesizer could also be used to create grandiose arrangements and solos that imitated and even surpassed the flexibility and powerful volume of the electric guitar. With its novel sound design and versatility, the synthesizer would become an integral part of the 1970s popular music landscape. For the most part, however, the synthesizer players who held in their hands the "keys to the future" existed as secondary members of the rock band.[2] Not until new wave did a legion of synthesizer players truly usurp the lead role traditionally accorded the guitar player and push the synthesizer's modern associations fully into the foreground.

England's Gary Numan emerged in 1979 as the first fully-fledged synthesizer star of the new wave era, largely on the strength of his international hit single "Cars" and the influential accompanying album *The Pleasure Principle,* which eschewed electric guitars completely in favor of lead synthesizers. He was soon joined in the early 1980s by a whole host of British groups such as Depeche Mode, the Human League, and Orchestral

151

Manoeuvres in the Dark (OMD) who began assigning the majority of the melodic and rhythmic features of the band to synthesizers, sequencers, and drum machines. In recognition of the synthesizer's impact on the new wave, *Trouser Press* ran a feature in the May 1982 issue entitled "Roll Over Guitar Heros [*sic*]: Synthesizers are Here," which explored the reasons behind the instrument's newfound popularity. Partly, the synthesizer's spread could be attributed to significant changes in the keyboard industry. When the Minimoog, the first popular retail synthesizer, appeared in 1971, its list price was $1,500, a daunting investment that for most fledgling and amateur rock groups would have been roughly the equivalent of purchasing a new touring van.[3] But by 1980 the incorporation of more efficient microprocessing designs and ensuing competition among keyboard manufacturers had diversified the industry to the point where one could buy a basic synthesizer for roughly $200.[4] With this new affordability and accessibility came new views about musical expression as well. As Andy McCluskey of OMD explained to *Trouser Press*, "Someone who's been playing synth for 10 minutes can easily sound as good as someone who's been playing for years, provided the ideas are there."[5] Dave Gahan of Depeche Mode likewise emphasized the importance of ideas over skill and instrumental proficiency: "In pop music nowadays you don't need technical ability, you need ideas and the ability to write songs. That's the main thing."[6] What McCluskey and Gahan appeared to be suggesting was nothing less than a seismic paradigm shift, one wherein a whole level of amateur music makers could find their way to pop stardom via the synthesizer's new level playing field.

Given these rather bold projections, it was unsurprising that the *Trouser Press* article would elicit some harsh reactionary criticisms. As one irritated reader complained:

> Regarding the [*Trouser Press*] article on synth Muzak: Why don't these dressed up, elitist closet queens just send their instruments to the gig and not even bother leaving home to perform? Sure, synths are cheap, convenient and easy to play—but whatever happened to love, passion, skill and sweat in the creation of modern music? These white, middle-class, get-rich-quick trendies playing mindless, regurgitated disco licks can kiss my ass.[7]

Such statements serve as a strong reminder that musical genres are intimately bound with cultural values and taste. In the reader's view, these new synthesizer bands appeared as an affront to the time-honored work ethic associated with rock music. In a musical culture where displays of passionate skill and energetic sweat are taken to be commensurate with bodily authenticity, the apparent musical simplicity and preprogrammed, push-button ease of the new synthesizer players failed to meet rock's symbolic standards. The reader casually refers to the synthesizer players as "closet queens," essentially "queering" the musicians and throwing their masculinity into question. By drawing attention to the synthesizer's "regurgitated disco licks," the reader also implicitly invokes the lingering echo of the homophobic "disco sucks" refrains that had haunted disco and dance music throughout the late 1970s. On the whole, there is a sense that the new synthesizer players, through their refusal to work and "sweat," had betrayed the possibilities that rock music offered for one to "perform" their gender.

To understand more clearly the unease that the new "synthpop" created in music fans like the *Trouser Press* reader, this chapter examines how the rise of the synthesizer forced a new consideration of the intertwined connection between rock music, work, and identity at the turn of the 1980s. Rock's relationship with work has long been conflicted. On the one hand, rock musicians have commonly taken a rebellious stance and portrayed work as "a form of dystopia to be escaped from" or "a false utopia whose promises have been broken."[8] In this instance, the pleasures of rock music promise a liberating romanticist release from the drudgery of the workplace. On the other hand, the discourse of rock has long valorized the rigors of autonomous self-discipline, the type of work that elevates the accomplished professional musician from the ranks of the fumbling novices.[9] Through their countless stories of hard work, dues paid, and relentless practice, and their subsequent displays of demonstrable skill and technical mastery, rock musicians have embraced work as a means toward artistic freedom and integrity. It is this latter notion of work that the new wave musicians surveyed in the *Trouser Press* article were most quick to reject as an outmoded myth of rock authenticity. In its place they opted for simple, repetitive melodic and rhythmic patterns and robotic bodily poses that stressed the mechanized work of the synthesizer's machinery rather than the transcendent work of the virtuosic musician.

If we are to make sense of the radical changes that accompanied the synthesizer's ascendance within new wave, we ultimately must explore the ways in which this new generation of keyboard players conceived the relationship between the performing body and the synthesizer. In recent years scholars across the disciplines have turned their attention toward "the body in the music," hoping to understand how the gestures and bodily presence of performers have influenced the sound, reception, and significations of music.[10] In the case of new wave, we could ask what it meant for synthesizer players to renounce the frenetic bodily motions and emotional exuberance that had signified a "hyperbolic" and "self-disciplining" keyboard virtuosity dating back to the appearance of pianists like Franz Liszt in the mid-nineteenth century.[11] Any such investigation of the body, however, should also consider the synthesizer as part of a "practice" of production and consumption where, as media studies scholar Paul Théberge suggests, "the musical, the socio-cultural, and the economic intersect in a variety of concrete ways."[12] It is important, for example, to look at how new wave musicians adopted the synthesizer as part of a preexisting symbolic domain already well established by the keyboard-manufacturing industry. While the synthesizer's design suggested certain practices and technological possibilities that influenced new wave's style, at the same time new wave musicians reconfigured the synthesizer's meanings in ways that suited their specific needs. This chapter traces the circulation of the synthesizer's uses and reception as the instrument came to the foreground of the new wave movement. I begin with an initial discussion of the synthesizer's various meanings in the 1970s, after which I turn to Gary Numan, the artist who more than any other proved pivotal to the new wave's reorientation of the synthesizer as a modern signifier.

The Synthesizer in the Early 1970s

Prior to the emergence of the synthesizer in the early 1970s, the prevailing image of the rock keyboardist was that of someone seated at a piano or hovering over an electric combo organ. During the 1950s and 1960s, when these two keyboard instruments were at their peak, the synthesizer lingered on the periphery of the rock world, associated primarily with academic art music composers like Vladimir Ussachevsky and Milton Babbitt. The synthesizer at that time existed as an unwieldy assemblage of oscillating tones, filters, and patch cords, more coveted by research universities and electronic music studios than performing musicians. In the mid-1960s, however, Bob Moog reshaped the instrument's design, outfitting the synthesizer with a keyboard interface that more closely resembled that of the organ. Soon news of this expensive electronic "toy" began to circulate among high-profile rock groups ranging from the Beatles and the Byrds to the Doors and the Monkees, all of whom sought to include the synthesizer on their latest recordings.[13] The true breakthrough came in 1968 when composer and keyboardist Wendy Carlos released the wildly influential *Switched-On Bach*, a collection of Bach classics arranged for the Moog synthesizer, which signaled the instrument's versatility and musical legitimacy (while also opening the floodgates for such curiosities as *Switched-On Santa* and *Music to Moog By*). Before long the synthesizer had found its way into the hands of classically inspired progressive rock keyboardists like Keith Emerson, who employed the instrument to create orchestral textures of "simulated trumpet fanfares" and long, flowing thematic lines and dazzling solos.[14]

Emerson was soon followed by progressive rock keyboardists like Rick Wakeman and jazz rock keyboardists such as Jan Hammer and Herbie Hancock, all of whom embraced the synthesizer for its capabilities as a lead or solo instrument. It was no accident that the synthesizer should encourage such performance practices. Throughout the first half of the 1970s, the only synthesizers available were monophonic, capable of playing only one note at a time, which made them poor accompaniment instruments. Given this constraint, a certain type of keyboard player evolved: what one musician aptly referred to as "the one-handed piano player."[15] The keyboardist would use the right hand exclusively to play the synthesizer keyboard, while the left hand would be reserved to "play" the instrument's control panel and make pitch adjustments, or to play chords simultaneously on a polyphonic instrument such as the organ or electric piano. These were minor inconveniences, however, considering what the synthesizer offered in return. A popular synthesizer like the Minimoog, for example, featured a wheel with which one could bend the pitch, and the ability to swoop effortlessly between low and high registers, which created an impressive portamento effect. Run through the appropriate amplification, its intensity of timbre, volume, and pitch-altering possibilities could not only match, but in many ways exceed the electric guitar's prowess. It is understandable, then, why rock and jazz keyboardists would happily substitute the chordal palette of the piano and organ for the synthesizer's ability to compete with the powerful, dexterous single-line fluency of such well-established solo instruments as the guitar, saxophone, and trumpet.

As the monophonic synthesizer came to be associated with a specific type of soloing, so it also began to attract certain kinds of musicians, those whose technical proficiency gave them the latitude to play intricate solo lines with one hand. In a 1984 retrospective article entitled "The Power and Glory of the Lead Synthesizer," *Keyboard* magazine painted a portrait of the kind of keyboardists who had helped forge a "mono synth tradition" at the beginning of the 1970s.[16] As the article described, it was clear that in the hands of these skilled performers the synthesizer had attained a strong masculine symbolism:

> One can almost draw a composite sketch of the type conquered by this electronic seductress: young, but already a veteran on the piano; raised by jazz, but intrigued by rock and roll, or vice versa; blessed with quick hands able to scatter rapid runs over the keys, and with ears left restless by the familiarity of this terrain. Most of them had stood outside the gates that separated fixed-pitch players from guitarists, saxophonists, singers—those artists who were unbound by ties to the familiar tones that had been grounded for centuries in the well-tempered scale.[17]

Keyboard's evocation of the synthesizer as an "electronic seductress" likely comes as little surprise, as it is simply a recognition that the majority of 1970s rock musicians (keyboard or otherwise) were male and part of a music scene that was undeniably patriarchal in structure. Inspired by the synthesizer as some sort of bewitching temptress, it follows that these male musicians would embark upon virtuosic solos of "rapid runs" on the keyboard that demonstrated their prodigious masculine powers. Such masculine displays followed in the footsteps of the virtuosic rock guitar solo that had emerged with performers like Jimi Hendrix at the end of the 1960s, but with an important difference. Where the rock guitarist wielded his instrument as a decidedly phallic symbol, the synthesizer player's powerful musical exhortations worked to quash the feminine *and* feminizing associations that had been linked to the keyboard for centuries.[18] Crucially, the depiction of the synthesizer as seductress helped to wipe away the piano's association with parlor rooms and "little old ladies and pigtailed pupils."[19]

There were other more subtle ways, however, beyond the obvious spectacular demonstrations of skill and mastery, in which the synthesizer reinforced a masculine identity. For one, the technology and design of the synthesizer, which was in its nascent stages, often necessitated excessive manual labor. New synthesizer owners often had to assemble, tinker with, and learn how to operate the instrument that they had purchased. In this respect, they fit squarely within the traditionally male electronic hobbyist culture associated with the early development of other twentieth-century consumer technologies such as the radio, hi-fi systems, and personal computers.[20] The majority of early synthesizers also required the player to define the sound through a carefully determined manual manipulation of various knobs, dials, and wheels. In the era before the digital presets of the 1980s, the keyboardist had to negotiate a tangled maze of patch cords in order to move from one sound to another, and even streamlined models like the Minimoog were subject to wild timbral fluctuations depending upon the alignment of its numerous knobs and controls. The synthesizer thus required an active physical stance, one that emphasized the determined effort and work behind its sound production.

Those professional touring keyboardists who succumbed to the synthesizer's novel allure, quickly discovered that its limitations necessitated that they accumulate numerous instruments in order to have a wide range of sounds readily available at their fingertips. On the one hand, they found that the *types* of sound that any one synthesizer model could produce were particular to the individual instrument. As Keith Emerson complained in 1974: "If I could find one instrument that could get the sound of each of them, I would use that. People are working on it, but the synthesizers are still limited."[21] His solution? Emerson surrounded himself with thirteen different keyboards. As excessive as that might seem, it pales next to Rick Wakeman, whose frustration with the synthesizer reputedly compelled him to acquire thirteen separate Minimoogs, "each with its knobs superglued into position to make a different sound."[22] Given these circumstances, early 1970s progressive rock keyboardists like Wakeman soon found their bodies hidden and immobilized on stage, their head peering from behind a towering wall of bulky synthesizers.

Keith Emerson was the first rock keyboardist of note to grapple, quite literally, with the problematic relationship between the performer's body and the stationary design of his instruments. As early as the 1960s when he was playing for the Nice, and his main instrument was the Hammond organ, Emerson developed a reputation for a stage show filled with astonishing physical feats, whereby he asserted his dominance and control over the instrument: He "would use knives to sustain notes on the keyboard, then, while riding the [Hammond] L100 across the stage as if it were a horse, he would bury knives in the speaker cabinets. He would pour lighter fuel over the organ and set fire to it, and play it from behind, inside, or even with it lying on top of him."[23] When Emerson formed the progressive rock trio Emerson, Lake and Palmer in 1970, he approached his new array of keyboards, which included the Moog manual synthesizer, in a way that once again placed his performing body squarely in the foreground. Rather than surrounding himself with keyboards, Emerson separated them into two sides. He would then situate himself between the two keyboard banks so that he could play them simultaneously with his unobstructed body and bare, open shirt torso facing out toward the audience. Emerson's most celebrated gimmick, however, involved the use of the Moog's remote-controlled pitch modification device called the "ribbon controller," which allowed him to *play* the synthesizer while wandering about the stage. The ribbon controller was a slender three-foot-long device that was used most often to create sliding pitch effects, but in Emerson's hands it became a suggestive phallic stage prop. As he stroked the ribbon controller vigorously, and slid it repeatedly between his thighs, he reimagined the keyboardist on a level with the cock rock superstars of the day.

Eventually the keyboardist Edgar Winter took a more reasoned approach to solving the synthesizer's problem of limited mobility and attached a shoulder strap to his ARP synthesizer so that he could move more freely with it around the stage. Keyboard manufacturers were sensitive to these concerns and soon began marketing custom-designed portable models so that synthesizer players could exert a degree of bodily control over their instruments. Inevitably, the genesis of the strap-on synthesizer encouraged the same masculine posturing and array of hip-grinding phallic poses that electric guitarists had been doing with their instruments for years, a connection that was implicit in the generic "keytar" name by which these instruments came to be known. In general, most new wave musicians would come to renounce these excessive and sexualized associations that both the guitar and the keyboard had accrued over the course of the 1970s.[24]

The Synthesizer in the Late 1970s

By the mid-1970s the synthesizer had become an accepted part of the popular music landscape and the keyboard industry had experienced a substantial boom. This growth was reflected in part by the launching in 1975 of *Contemporary Keyboard* (which would eventually change its name to *Keyboard* in 1981), a practicing musician's magazine spanning the worlds of rock, classical, and jazz that featured interviews, expert columns, reviews, and advertisements, all with a focus on the latest keyboard technology. Unsurprisingly, in its early years the magazine routinely featured such storied progressive rock keyboardists as Keith Emerson, Rick Wakeman, and Tony Banks of Genesis. By the late 1970s, the magazine's coverage had expanded to include keyboardists like Kerry Livgren and Steve Walsh of Kansas, Al Greenwood of Foreigner, David Paich and Steve Porcaro of Toto, and Dennis DeYoung of Styx, all of whom were part of a radio-friendly American progressive rock movement that popular music studies scholar Kevin Holm-Hudson has since dubbed as "prog lite."[25] Beginning in 1980, the magazine extended its reach even further as it started to feature interviews with new wave keyboardists ranging from Jimmy Destri of Blondie and Greg Hawkes of the Cars to Mark Mothersbaugh of Devo and Gary Numan, a trend that would continue into the mid-1980s with profiles on Duran Duran's Nick Rhodes, Thomas Dolby, and others.

In 1985, surveying the various musicians who had graced *Keyboard*'s pages during its first ten years, the magazine's assistant editor Bob Doerschuk drew a sharp distinction among the musical movements that they represented. To the generation of late 1970s American progressive rock bands like Kansas and Styx, he affixed the label of "new romantics."[26] As Doerschuk described, like the early 1970s progressive rockers that had preceded them, the "new romantics" had devolved into a "Barnumesque approach to performance, with intricate props and stage designs, breakneck

instrumental cadenzas, immaculately rehearsed arrangements, and pre-
dictable 'Do-you-feel-all-right' raps." The result had been a general malaise,
a "betrayal of the music, a sell-out of spirit for showbiz."[27] As an answer to
this troubling trend, he labeled the new wave keyboard players as a revolutionary group of "new classicists." In their search for an aesthetic based in
simplicity and uncluttered formal melodicism, these new classicists, Doerschuk argued, represented a conscious rejection of the previous generation
of "new romantics."

Doerschuk's polemical designation of the "new romantics" and "new
classicists" draws much of its obvious rhetorical power from its roots in the
study of art music, where the alternating flow between subjective,
grandiose "romantic" statements and a coolly objective "classical" approach has long provided a convenient, if reductive, template for project-
ing the linear flow of style and history. As he points out, new wave's "new
classicists" renounced the virtuoso solos of the progressive rock era in favor
of keyboard parts that were devoid of ornamentation and filigree and could
serve the song in more fundamentally direct ways. Beyond this, Doerschuk
mentions two further "classical" attitudes that proved crucial to the new
wave keyboard style. First, as he explains, new wave keyboard players revolted against the synthesizer's excesses of the 1970s by turning to older,
"classic," electronic keyboards from the 1960s such as the Vox Continental
and Farfisa combo organs that had fallen out of favor in recent years. With
their lean, economical design, and stabbing chords and trebly timbres,
these instruments perfectly suited the new wave's evocation of garage
bands and AM radio hits of the past, and also offered an alternative to the
Hammond organ's soulful, gospel-associated sound, which had become the
dominant rock organ of the 1970s. Second, those new wave musicians who
did embrace the synthesizer vehemently disavowed the overt pitch bending, vibrato, and nuances of tone shading that had made the instrument
seem so "musical" or "expressive" in the hands of progressive rock keyboardists. Instead, they relied on a range of "steely sounds, more obviously
electronic and less orchestral in texture."[28]

Much as the return of the Vox Continental and Farfisa organs was a
reaction against the Hammond, so the new wave keyboardists' turn toward "steely" and "electronic" synthesizer settings marked a departure
from the seemingly warm and expressive synthesizer timbres that had

prevailed throughout the 1970s. In this instance, though, the change resulted less from a difference in keyboard choices than from the ways in which new wave musicians subverted many of the marketing assumptions and practices that had built up around the synthesizer through the course of the decade. As a case in point, consider the ARP line of synthesizers, which along with Moog had dominated the electronic keyboard industry throughout the 1970s. By the latter part of the decade, ARP was increasingly turning toward the production of synthesizer models that featured polyphonic capabilities. One of the first of these, the ARP Omni (and its upgrade, the Omni-2), found its way onto numerous recordings, and figured prominently in the setup of both "new romantics" such as Foreigner's Al Greenwood and "new classicists" like Greg Hawkes of the Cars. Given the monophonic synthesizer's already established role as a lead instrument, manufacturers like ARP naturally assumed that players using a polyphonic synthesizer such as the Omni would want an instrument that improved upon the monophonic's strengths and could also more ably fill the musical texture or provide background accompaniment. ARP thus packaged the synthesizer with violin and viola settings imitative of orchestral instruments, which the company believed would enhance a keyboardist's accompanying needs. ARP accented these "orchestral" aspects in the marketing of the Omni, claiming that its synthesizers possessed a timbral quality equivalent to "real" instruments and a creative flexibility that could accommodate the performer's musical goals. Bolstered by a hyperrealized language of verisimilitude, ARP addressed the Omni-2's potential audience directly: "You want *authentic* strings, horns, and a big sound" (emphasis added). ARP also attempted to soften the musical technology by humanizing the synthesizer's mechanical features. Everywhere in these advertisements one finds crucial keywords—"flexibility," "variety," "creativity," "unlimited expression"—that assure prospective buyers that this is "a synthesizer that plays as good as you do."

New wave musicians found the new range of synthesizers like the ARP Omni captivating, but in ways that the keyboard manufacturers had likely not anticipated while contemplating the instruments' design and marketing. In a 1980 profile for *Contemporary Keyboard*, for example, Hawkes praised the ARP Omni not for its purported "authentic" imitative capabilities, but rather for its glaringly *artificial* string sound, a quality uniquely attuned to his own particular aesthetic:

> Greg relies on his other polyphonic synth, the Omni, for string sounds, which he considers the instrument's strongest feature. When playing them, he generally uses the viola setting. "But I'm not even looking for an accurate string sound," he points out. "Again, I like the fact that it sounds somewhat electronic. To me it sounds like an even more electronic version of the Mellotron sound. If I was looking for an accurate string sound, I would write out string parts and record them that way, using real string players."[29]

Hawkes's comments illustrate the perverse relationship that new wave musicians enjoyed with the keyboard industry, as they gravitated toward an electronic artifice that the manufacturers were attempting to conceal in their marketing campaigns. While ARP and other manufacturers may have wished to emphasize a warmth in their synthesizers akin to the resonance of acoustic instruments, more and more new wave keyboardists began to echo Hawkes's sentiments. As Billy Currie of Ultravox explained, the synthesizer was ideal precisely for its range of "chilly string imitation sounds. . . . [which were] very synthetic and cold."[30] Given these relationships, it becomes apparent that much of what new wave musicians revolutionized in the use of the synthesizer can be explained vis-à-vis their appropriation of a preexisting symbolic domain linking the players and the music industry. Through the ways in which they adopted the synthesizer to their specific attitudes and modes of performance, new wave musicians resituated in dramatic fashion the synthesizer's rhetorical power. Crucially this shift extended beyond the qualities of the synthesizer's sonic features and into the *production* of the sound itself. It is important to remember that when new wave keyboardists jettisoned the bends, slides, and vibrato that a previous generation of rock keyboardists had employed to add some measure of warmth and touch to the synthesizer, they rejected not just a timbral idiom, but the physicality and work required to achieve those particular sounds. In this new context, the synthesizer's cold, icy legato timbres seemed to emanate from outside a bodily context, emphasizing instead the instrument's unadorned machinelike nature.

This is not to say, however, that new wave keyboardists broke completely with all of rock's synthesizer habits. While new wave keyboardists may have held the solos associated with the progressive rock style in suspicion (as Hawkes summarized, "I do get bored by endless soloing . . . in the Minimoog sort of tradition of fake guitar-style playing"), one can nonetheless find a good number of synthesizer and keyboard solo sections in various new wave songs, such as the Cars' "Bye Bye Love" (1978) or Split Enz's "I Got You" (1980).[31] The difference lay in the view of the solo itself. For someone like Devo's Mark Mothersbaugh, for example, the synthesizer allowed the means to explore more abstract musical structures: "When I'm doing a solo on a synthesizer, I opt for more of a sonic Lysol effect than a cake icing effect. I guess my songs are closer to musical erector sets than to musical pastry."[32] Mothersbaugh's statement borders on the absurd, but his point is fairly clear. In general, new wave musicians harbored a basic mistrust of the excess and wanton display that had come to characterize the synthesizer. In some respects they embraced instead a new asceticism, a denial of the keyboard's and synthesizer's accumulated symbolic capital as an instrument of flashy spectacle, on which one was obliged to "perform."

In Doerschuk's view of this stripped-back "new classicist" ethos, the band that best embodied the new wave's musical sensibilities ironically was one that operated on the fringe of the movement itself. Specifically he singled out Kraftwerk, a reclusive German quartet whose thoroughgoing use of synthesizers and electronic percussion instruments, many of them self-built, provided a guiding light for many Anglo-American new wave artists at the turn of the 1980s. In place of the bombastic progressive rock synthesizer solo or the ambient atmospherics of fellow German keyboard artists like Tangerine Dream and Klaus Schulze, Kraftwerk shifted its musical emphasis toward clipped staccato rhythms, simple, repetitive melodic figures, sequencer patterns, and insistent beats. In doing so, the group showed how an exclusively synthesized texture could provide the structural groundwork for a new generation of keyboard musicians.

Equally important, Kraftwerk wedded its minimalist musical vision to lyrical themes and a visual presentation that dealt exclusively with themes of technology and modernity ranging from the German Autobahn and "Trans-Europe Express" to Geiger counters and computers. This was not necessarily a new phenomenon. Composers have for centuries employed music's unique expressive power to imitate the qualities of our technological environment, whether it be the rhythms and timbres of clocks, trains, and factories or some other machinery. It is precisely this connection that led Doerschuk to hear "the cyclic rhythms of the assembly line" and "the soulless wails of shortwave interference" in Kraftwerk's music.[33] But music has also provided a conceptual space in which we can imagine the symbolic representation of technology that is less obviously sonorous or rhythmically repetitive, and it is here where Kraftwerk especially excelled. Utilizing a variety of angular and tonally abstract melodic contours, unwavering rhythms, and accented bursts of processed noise, Kraftwerk suggested the technological "otherness" associated with "The Robots" of 1978's *Man-Machine* or the "Pocket Calculator" of 1981's *Computer World*. To Kraftwerk, such depictions pronounced the welcome fusion between humans and machines. They also, however, reinforced the perception that the technology of a "robot" or "calculator" marked a breach that exceeded the boundaries of certain human capabilities. Machines such as these possess an advanced logic, intelligence, and precision, characteristics that the synthesizer could connote through its seemingly mathematical pitch arrangements, random melodic patterns, and insistent repetition. Such representations proved to be popular with the new wave, and one can hear the synthesizer's abstract sequenced patterns convey everything from playful anxiety on Gary Numan's "Praying to the Aliens" (1979) to the bustling exotic tourism of Wall of Voodoo's "Mexican Radio" (1982).

It is helpful to remember just how different such representations were from the more typical flights of synthesizer fancy favored by Doerschuk's legion of mid-1970s "new romantic" rock keyboardists. Consider, for example Top 10 singles like Gary Wright's "Dream Weaver" (1976), the Steve Miller Band's "Space Intro / Fly Like an Eagle" (1976), and Styx's "Come Sail Away" (1977). All of these foreground the synthesizer as a means of representing majestic space travel and soaring, graceful flight, or as rock historian John Covach has aptly put it—"hippie dreams of fantastic voyages into the bright technological future."[34] Bolstered by reverb and delay, and saturated, washed tones, each song's synthesizer arrangement swoops along on a gliding portamento, and hovers and envelopes the listener with warm timbres. In the true tradition of nineteenth-century romanticism, the synthesizer here tends toward sublime figurations and hints of dreamy reverie. It is a sonic world far removed from that of Kraftwerk.

Kraftwerk's unique visionary output would prove to be a great influence on other new wave musicians, but at the same time we should be cautious of overstating its historical impact. In recent years Kraftwerk's reputation has reached an almost mythical status, as it has assumed a place of hyperbolic prominence in the histories of disco, EDM (electronic dance music), hip-hop, and rock itself. The band's biographer, Tim Barr, asserts that "Kraftwerk's modest output has provoked a paradigm shift in modern music that has been unequalled since The Beatles," a sentiment echoed by *All Music Guide*'s Jason Ankeny, who states that Kraftwerk's "self-described 'robot pop' . . . resonates in virtually every new development to impact the contemporary pop scene of the late-20th century."[35] However, during its period of greatest activity in the late 1970s and early 1980s, Kraftwerk was marginally successful at best in the United States, where it remained a favorite predominantly of critics and select audiences. After the surprise Top 40 breakthrough of its "Autobahn" single in 1975, none of the band's albums managed to crack the Top 100 until 1981's *Computer World,* a six-year period when the band did not tour the United States. Instead, its singles landed primarily in disco clubs and on black radio, where it wielded a significant, yet marginalized influence. For all of its undeniable importance, Kraftwerk would not be the band to propel the synthesizer and its futuristic symbolism into mass awareness as part of the new wave. That honor would fall to someone else.

New Wave's First Synthesizer Star

When I arrived at the studio the previous band had left behind a Mini-Moog synthesizer and so I asked if I could have a go before it was collected by the hire company. I had never seen a real synth before and, to be honest, had never really thought about them very much. Although I liked some electronic music I still associated it mainly with pompous supergroups, like Yes and ELP. To me they conjured up visions of disgusting, self-indulgent solos that went on for half an hour. Pressing that first key changed my life. Luckily for me it had been left on a heavy setting, which produced the most powerful, ground-shaking sound I had ever heard. I realized immediately that this was what I had been looking for.

—Gary Numan, describing his first encounter with a
   synthesizer in July 1978[36]

In 1978 Gary Numan was a member of a fledgling punk-inspired band being courted by a small independent label, Beggars Banquet. As his anecdote reveals, Numan's discovery of the synthesizer at that time was an epiphanic affair. Realizing that the Minimoog offered a new sense of power unattainable through his main instrument, the guitar, Numan switched allegiances and concocted a blend of synthesizer-based rock with imagery and lyrics inspired by science fiction, making him an instant star. By 1979 he had three albums lodged simultaneously in the U.K. Top 20 and two chart-topping singles. One of those, "Cars," would propel him to popularity in the United States, where it entered the Top 10. While that song would stand as his lone American hit, he remained hugely successful in his homeland of England. By the time that Numan decided to retire from touring in 1981, at the age of twenty-three, his stature was such that he could hold a series of mammoth sold-out farewell concerts in Wembley Arena, embellished with an extravagant stage design steeped in new wave's modern and futurist tropes. Complete with "a spectacular spaceship landing" modeled on *Close Encounters,* seventy-two sheets of colored Perspex panels, radio-controlled robots, a radio-controlled car, and a film of Numan flying his own airplane, it was an unabashed technological spectacle. As journalist Myles Palmer observed of the occasion, "Space was no longer science fiction. It had become cabaret for suburban teenagers."[37]

Numan's presence within new wave was unavoidable at the turn of the 1980s, most of all because he successfully arrived at an image and sound that resonated with new wave's modern aesthetic. The reviews and features that accompanied Numan drew constant attention to the ways in which his music captured the tensions surrounding urban life, a direly ineffective British government, and a new technological age filled with both promise and dread. Writing in *Melody Maker,* Ray Coleman claimed that Numan was making "uncomfortable sounds for a neurotic age . . . anthems to mirror our world of computers and calculators and multi-storey car parks, advanced technology, self-service petrol and two million on the dole."[38] Numan also proved to be a polarizing figure, one whose celebrity status, attitude toward the synthesizer, and distinct musical mannerisms inspired a vociferous and often antagonistic critical reception. Numan's influence was substantial, and for that reason, his brief reign as new wave's first synthesizer star is worth examining in some detail.

Like many other new wave performers, Numan first entered the British music scene through the doors initially opened by punk, singing and playing guitar under his given name of Gary Webb in the group Tubeway Army. As Numan has stated, he initially gravitated toward punk primarily because at that time "everybody was signing punk bands."[39] Numan (Webb), however, never truly felt comfortable in his punk skin, first because he found the music's stylistic limitations to be stifling, and second because he wanted a degree of success that seemed at odds with punk's declared distrust of pop stardom. The synthesizer provided a fortuitous means of escape. After his chance encounter with the Minimoog, Webb began to adapt Tubeway Army's new material to the instrument, adopted the futuristic ring of *Numan* as his name, and placed the synthesizer at the heart of the "new and unusual" style of music that he envisioned.[40]

From the beginning Numan downplayed his abilities as a keyboardist, stressing that he had only recently switched to the synthesizer from the guitar. As he casually confided in an interview with *Contemporary Keyboard*, his keyboard technique was severely limited. He was more adept at operating the synthesizer than playing it:

> Well, I'm not really much of a musician anyway. I approach the piano or the keyboard as a guitar player. My brother took piano lessons and he said that all my fingers are wrong. Apparently you have to use certain fingers for certain notes. Well I don't know none of that [*laughs*]. I'm very much limited to a one-finger motion, two at the most. To be honest, I'm not that good a player at all. I can get quite nice sounds [however]. I know what the dials do on a Minimoog. I know what the gadgets are and can work them quite well.[41]

Numan's nonchalant admission of his nonmusicianship predictably rankled the magazine's readership. As one reader summarized in a terse, two-sentence letter: "Gary Numan in the same magazine with Glenn Gould? Come on now!"[42] At one level, the readers were upset by the astonishing stardom that Numan had attained with his seemingly marginal skill, a development that overturned the expectations of work, skill, and professionalism that had been deemed necessary to become a successful keyboard musician. At another, more symbolic level, Numan's statements hint at the drastically different ways in which new wave musicians approached the relationship between the synthesizer and the performer's body. By the turn of the 1980s, readers of *Contemporary Keyboard* had grown accustomed to reading profiles of "one handed" keyboardists whose heroic technical prowess had allowed them to overcome the handicap that the monophonic synthesizer presented. Numan, however, subverted that connotation and took the meaning of the one-hand player to its more literal extreme: that of a physically debilitated player limited to a singular, simplistic hand motion. Because many new wave synthesizer players like Numan initially approached the instruments not as trained pianists but as converted guitarists, nonmusicianship became, just as it had in punk, a politically potent badge. If the punk guitar manifesto had been "This is a chord, this is another, this is a third. . . . now form a band," then the new wave synthesizer equivalent might have been expressed in similar terms: *This is a finger, this is another . . . now write a song.*[43] The composite picture of the new wave synthesizer player that Gary Numan presented was thus someone short on technique, but long on creative curiosity.

Just as Numan presented a radically different portrait of the synthesizer player as a creative musical artist, likewise his accompanying visual image eschewed overtly expressive or emotional bodily displays for a more modern and minimalist demeanor. This was apparent early on from Numan and Tubeway Army's first performances in 1979 on Britain's two premiere televised music shows, *The Old Grey Whistle Test* and *Top of the Pops.* As Numan has explained, he carefully plotted the group's appearances on these programs. He was determined not to repeat the "huge mistake" that one of Britain's first new wave synthesizer bands, Ultravox, had made when performing its single "Hiroshima Mon Amour" on television in 1978, when the lead singer dressed in a decidedly inappropriate Hawaiian short-sleeved shirt.[44] To set the right atmosphere, Numan instructed *Top of the Pops* to replace their familiar flashing multicolored light show with cold, bare white lights in order to create a more stark stage setting. He also gave his band members specific instructions on how to act: "Most of the pop stars in the late '70s smiled all the time and looked sickeningly happy, which I found very naff and resolved to avoid . . . [For the television shows] I had the band dress in black and I told them there was to be no looking at the camera unless it was appropriate, no smiley faces mouthing Hello Mum."[45] The result was a performance that stood in stark contrast to the other musical acts on the television, one that emphasized music making as a job or task rather than an act of direct communication. As Numan describes:

> The night we were on, there was a band of dudies, who looked very clean cut and conservative, and then there was some punk band, jumping up and down and trying to look very outrageous. Suddenly there was us, and we just stood there and stared; it was all very, very cold, just the way we always are. The boys have their machines, and they have [to] stand there and play them, they very rarely look up and they never smile, because they've got to concentrate. They've got an awful lot to do, no time to stand around smiling and carrying on. There are always two or three synthesizers going at once, sometimes four.[46]

Placed at the center of the band, Numan stood out with his rigidly "wooden" mannerisms, an "unnatural" appearance that was partly by design, but also partly because he was unsure of how to maneuver his body performing for the first time without a guitar.[47] Caked in a sheen of ghostly white makeup (applied at the show's behest to hide his acne) and black mascara, Numan presented an emotionally detached, unsmiling visage that would set a striking precedent for his future stage shows.[48] Taken as a whole, the players' stiff postures, black uniforms, and "concentrated" approach to their instruments made them appear as if they were technicians in a work cubicle rather than musical performers. There was no sense of masculine mastery over the synthesizer; rather they undertook their musical roles in a dispassionate, robotic manner. The presumably separate realms of humans and machines had bled over into one another in Tubeway Army's presentation. In many ways the band had left behind rock's normal expressive domain, and was closer in spirit to the performing automata of the eighteenth century or Frederick Winslow Taylor's early twentieth-century conception of "scientific management," which equated industrial human labor with mechanical efficiency.

The combination of Numan's synthesizers and his robotic appearance provided a suitable opening for the music press, which quickly filled it with a host of futuristic references, many of them directly reflecting Numan's expressed interest in science fiction. A review of a Numan live show in *Sounds*

Figure 13. Gary Numan, rigid and unsmiling, on the *Old Grey Whistle Test,* 1979.

magazine, for example, ran under the heading of "Do Sheep Dream of Electric Androids?," a play on Philip K. Dick's science fiction novel *Do Androids Dream of Electric Sheep?,* while a Numan cover feature in *Melody Maker* entitled "The Numan Who Fell to Earth" conjured the specter of David Bowie's cinematic alien in the 1976 film *The Man Who Fell to Earth.*[49] Numan had managed to fill the role of both android and alien, and while obviously there are differences between the two, that mattered very little, as the main significance was that they both represented a sense of "otherness."[50] This came to the fore most strongly in Tubeway Army's 1979 album *Replicas,* a loose concept album that drew its inspiration from the dark dystopian science fiction of J. G. Ballard, William Burroughs, and Philip K. Dick. With *Replicas* Numan presents a scenario set in a futuristic city cohabited by humans and machines. The machines are engaged in a covert project to rid the earth of the error-prone humans, and at their disposal are menacing an-

Figure 14. Tubeway Army keyboardists Chris Payne (*foreground*) and Billy Currie (*background*), both dressed in black, concentrate on their synthesizers, on the *Old Grey Whistle Test,* 1979.

droid "Machmen" who serve as a form of law enforcement. There are other androids available to humans as a service, and these are referred to as "friends." As Numan has explained, "You can call for a Friend to play chess with, or indulge your most obscene sexual fantasies, or anything in between. No one else will know because they all look the same. As anonymous as a brown paper bag."[51]

These "friends" form the subject of "Are 'Friends' Electric?," the song that first catapulted Numan's career in England.[52] The song's lyrics unfold in a desolate and decaying urban landscape, with the singer sitting isolated in a room with paint peeling off the walls. The (presumably human) singer opens the door to find a "friend" that he invites inside. As we learn, the singer's old "friend" has broken down, and now he has no companion to keep him company; he has, as he sings, "no one to love." Numan's lyric approach lends the song a subtle sense of melancholy. At the same time, the rhythm and tempo are propulsive, pushed and prodded during the verses by the familiar motion of an alternating I–VII mixolydian chord progression (C–B♭) and a recurring high-pitched descending tritone riff (b♭–e) in the synthesizer that accents the song's "alien" otherness.[53] Numan twice interrupts the song's main verse sections with an unrelated, more personal, monologue, one that he had originally written as part of a different song, in which he details his feelings of rejection in the midst of an unrequited love. Placed within the framework of "Are 'Friends' Electric?" the juxtaposition with the imagery of the broken-down "friend" deftly adds an air of vulnerability to the protagonist's sense of loss.

Though this dual lyric construction is an anomaly among Numan's songs, its shifting nature hints at one of the main reasons why Numan was able to achieve and maintain his status as a futuristic new wave pop star: in his delivery and overall image he presented himself as a combination of both the human protagonist and the electric "friend." On the one hand, the listener is aware of Numan's subject position as a sensitive musical artist who experiences emotional isolation and alienation, as someone who perhaps suffers in his social relationships.[54] On the other hand, the listener hears Numan's clipped, pinched vocal style and sees his dour, unsmiling visage, and it is easy to position Numan in the role of the android "friend" as well. Contradictions as such are absolutely fundamental to the ways in which celebrities, musical or otherwise, are constructed. The majority of stars possess an ambiguity, a slippage between the intimacy of their "real" selves and the staged complexity of their "public" personas. This contradictory nature allows the media to disseminate and dissect celebrities from a variety of angles, in the process offering their fans a multitude of connections and interpretations.[55] In the case of Numan, his choice of the android as a stage persona ensured that he would be perceived through a basic doubleness. An android, after all, is by definition a robotic machine cast in the image of a human. So it should come as little surprise that Numan's reception in the press often revolved around the singer's apparent contradictory qualities. As the title of *Melody Maker*'s very first feature on Numan declared, he was an alienated pop star, "Alone in a Crowd."[56] A similar headline in the British *Daily Star* tabloid trumpeted "Gary—We Love You! But Numan is So Alone."[57]As Numan's 1982 biography proclaimed, the pop star was "shy, cocky, hard, soft, cruel, kind, infuriating, neurotic, obsessive, introspective . . . and, for all his machine-based sounds, a very human guy."[58]

What is perhaps less obvious is the way in which these dualisms also figured into the very means through which Numan, the synthesizer star, produced his music.[59] The synthesizer of the rock and pop world, it should be remembered, is a hybrid invention, one that combines the familiar keyboard and tonal melodic possibilities of the acoustic piano with the electronic circuitry of sound synthesis. The synthesizer's construction, as such, mirrored the doubleness of Numan's persona. This extended as well into the very design and conception of the synthesizer's range of sounds. As we have seen in the case of Greg Hawkes and his ARP Omni, while manufacturers conceived their synthesizers with settings that reflected the natural acoustic world of strings, brass, and other instruments, musicians themselves often embraced the sounds for their blatant artificial quality. One of Numan's signature synthesizers, the Polymoog, was no exception. It remains a great irony that the one synthesized string sound that would come to most signify the cold, alien artifice of his particular sound world on songs like "Cars" was found under the Polymoog preset label of "Vox Humana." Even Numan's band itself embodied a certain doubleness. While the press focused most of its attention on Numan's synthesizer arrangements and his alien vocal presence, his group also featured a conventional rhythm section with a drummer and bassist, both of whom accented the music's rock orientation with funk and dance rhythms. The combination created an alluring, yet distancing, disjunction for fans like hip-hop legend Afrika Bambaataa, who observed that "the beats were there but the singing was so weird, so gone, so off, people were freaked."[60]

The song that inspired Bambaataa's comments, and the one that in many ways best captures the multiple contradictory levels on which Numan's music operates, is "Cars." Released in 1979 on *The Pleasure Principle*, as its automotive title suggests, "Cars" deals with one of rock music's wellworn tropes. The automobile has long been a popular lyric subject among rock musicians, for it symbolizes the "high living and conspicuous consumption" attached to the rock and roll lifestyle, while also providing a measure of freedom and independence, an "easy escape route" from the restrictions of home and domesticity or the drudgery of the everyday workforce.[61] Numan's "Cars" captures both these dimensions of the automotive experience. On the one hand, the song's repeated refrain, where Numan sings that "the only way to live" is in cars, confirms through its material relationship the status and empowerment that the automobile offers its driver. Its forceful streamlined message reads like a virtual tagline for an automotive marketing campaign. On the other hand, Numan hints that the car may offer a getaway when he confides his thoughts about "leaving tonight." It is thus easy to see how one could interpret Numan's car as a representation of his individualism and identity within an overcrowded modern society.

Musically, the song's propulsive, syncopated bass riffs, layered acoustic/electronic backbeat and thick, loud, multitiered synthesizer textures act as a convincing aural analogue to the automobile's speed, power, and motion. That this connection is so strong can be attributed in large part to the song's unusual form. The first 1:45 of "Cars" is fairly standard, consisting of an introduction that showcases the song's powerful, piercing Polymoog melody followed by an AB form that alternates two lyric verses (A) with a brief instrumental section (B). For the song's remaining two minutes, however, Numan's vocals drop out and with the exception of a momentary return to the B section the band plays a lengthy instrumental extension and variation of the Polymoog introduction. As this climactic closing section swells and expands, one can easily imagine the magnificence and vastness of the unfolding open highway, a powerful effect that lingers as the song fades into the studio mixing board, suggesting the ceaseless motion of an automobile disappearing into the distant horizon. A vessel of leisure and open possibilities, Numan's car promises a voyage without destination, echoing the liberating sentiments of a legion of automotive anthems ranging from the Beach Boys' "I Get Around" and the Who's "Going Mobile" to Steppenwolf's "Born to be Wild" and Judas Priest's "Heading Out to the Highway." It is obvious why the song has achieved an iconic "car song" reputation, featured in everything from the *Grand Theft Auto: Vice City* video game to advertisements for Oldsmobile and Nissan.

If, however, as journalist Gerri Hirshey suggests, the car has traditionally served two symbolic functions within rock music—"as lust wagon and as redemptive chariot"—then it is easy to understand why Numan's song has also been depicted as a striking departure from the grand romanticism of that particular automotive musical canon.[62] As the song's lyrics reveal,

Figure 15. The synthesizer as modern motif. Gary Numan(s) "driving" across the keys of the Polymoog, from the video for "Cars" (1979).

the narrator of "Cars" is not out for a joyride, but rather hidden away inside his car, securely distanced from the outside world. Numan explained his view of the song to *Rolling Stone* magazine in 1980: "I feel very safe in cars. . . . You can lock the doors and they can't get to you. I don't like people gettin' to me. Bein' in a car keeps me safe. It's a cocoon."[63] Numan would elaborate on this theme even further in his 1998 autobiography, as he compared "the modern motor car" to a "personal tank," one that would allow a quick exit "at the first sign of trouble."[64] While Numan potentially complicates this reading in the song when he professes that he welcomes "a visit," at the same time he presents himself as an isolated individual incapable of reciprocating any real communication. Tucked away in his modern mechanical technology, he can "only receive."

The technological dichotomies and contradictions at the heart of "Cars" would ultimately serve as a strong unifying theme for the album on which the song appeared, 1979's *The Pleasure Principle*. While the subjects of the song "Metal," for example, are technologically advanced robotic creations, they yearn to be more human, to be "a man." In the song "Conversation," Numan looks for a point of communication but finds his efforts to be ineffectual, mediated to the point where he may be nothing more than a photograph looking back at a picture of another person. Many of the songs present Numan as a passive subject, as in "Observer," where he stands for hours and days, even a "lifetime" watching and waiting. This technological ambivalence trickled over into the album's reception in the music press. While many critics were quick to praise *The Pleasure Principle*'s musical technology—its "extraterrestrial cascading" and "synthesized buzzes sprinkled like jimmies on an electric sundae"—some also lamented its oddly static and lethargic tone.[65] Writing in *Trouser Press*, Ira Robbins savaged the album, complaining of its "overwhelming tedium."[66] Phil Sutcliffe of *Sounds* likewise lamented a turn in Numan's songwriting style that was particularly on display in songs like the instrumental "Airlane," which he called "the worst of what's happened to Numan's music since he stopped writing on guitar and became infatuated with synthesizers on which he admits to being a primitive one-finger operator."[67]

Sutcliffe's observation is worth considering more closely, for indeed the result of Numan's simple, one-handed (or one-finger) approach was a slowing of the music's harmonic pulse, which emphasized even further the reduced physical effort or work behind his music making. This can best be demonstrated by comparing Numan's approach to songwriting before and after his discovery of the synthesizer. Working within the restrictions of the monophonic Minimoog, and limited as well by his own modest abilities as a keyboardist, Numan was led to write in a certain way. Whereas before, as a guitarist in the early manifestations of his band Tubeway Army, Numan had centered his songs on fairly standard chord progressions, with the switch to the one-finger lines of the synthesizer he made the keyboard's melodic line the song's focus. In the absence of Numan's guitar, which had previously provided an active, driving chordal structure, the new synthesizer songs, led along by Numan's simple keyboard lines, seemed comparatively stationary in their harmonic motion. Numan the synthesizer star had an entirely different conception of phrasing and harmony than Numan the guitarist.

To illustrate the difference between the two styles, consider first an early Tubeway Army guitar song such as "Bombers" (the band's second single from 1978). "Bombers" features a verse with a repetitive chord progression that moves underneath and pushes Numan's vocal melody. Example 4 shows how the progression, which proceeds at a speed of two chords per bar, runs underneath one single vocal phrase. At this pace, the progression moves at two cycles per vocal phrase.

Example 4: "Bombers" verse vocal melody and harmonic progression

With its alternating tonic–dominant construction, from C♯ to G♯ and B to F♯, all of which establishes a strong key area of C♯, "Bombers," like many rock songs, possesses a firm horizontal logic and a cycling harmonic progression that propels the listener along at a brisk clip.

In Numan's synthesizer songs, however, the harmonic motion no longer drives the melody. Rather, the harmony slows to the point where chord changes usually take place only when one complete phrase in the keyboard melody has shifted to the next. Very rarely does the harmony change within, or in anticipation of, a phrase. As a result, the chord progression does not determine the phrase, as in "Bombers." Rather harmony emerges as a distinction of the phrase, and the listener is left with the sensation that the music is moving in large harmonic blocks. This is especially evident in "Airlane" and "Cars," where the synthesizer's melodic phrasing creates formal units that slacken the harmonic motion to a crawl. Examples 5 and 6 show the main synthesizer lines from these two songs and the implied tonal centers that correspond with each song's different sections:

Various details emerge from these two musical examples. First, as one might expect of a player of Numan's abilities, all the synthesizer lines fit very easily within the hand. They are predominantly "white key"

Example 5: "Airlane" three sections

Example 6: "Cars" two sections

melodies—none of the tonal centers are on "black keys"—and when black keys do appear within the melodic lines, they are firmly anchored in the hand, paired next to a direct neighbor white key. Second, the implied harmonies tend to sit in a tonal center often for four measures at a time, which draws attention to the simple figuration of the melodic line rather than the harmonic motion. To compensate for this static horizontal harmonic motion, Numan develops his songs more along vertical textural planes, often by stacking melodies and drones on top of one another to create a layered, at times more contrapuntal, arrangement. This layering effect occurs most famously during the extended coda that closes "Cars," where Numan weaves together at least three synthesizer lines. One of the most prominent of these is a drone that begins on c♯, hovering over the main riff's A major tonality, before shifting to c-natural as the riff changes to G major. Heard on top of the G major harmony, the c-natural drone acts as a dissonant suspended fourth, left hanging in the air. Given the slow procession of the chord changes, the overall effect in the coda is as if we are continually modulating back and forth between A major and G major.

Not all new wave musicians would follow Gary Numan's lead and veer toward such harmonically static settings. But in Numan's case, the end result seems somewhat less like a deliberate aesthetic choice than like an inevitable side-effect of the situation in which he found himself, where the combined limitations of the monophonic synthesizers that had prompted his musical epiphany and his own technical limitations steered him toward a certain way of playing. As a result, he arrived at an idiosyncratic style and the types of songs that a more proficient rock keyboardist likely would have never thought to compose. Numan circumvented the expectations of skill, work, and mastery that had accompanied the reception of rock keyboardists throughout the 1970s and in the end presented a different type of synthesizer musician, one that would wield a great influence over the next wave of British "synthpop" bands in the early 1980s.

Coda: Synthpop after Numan

In April 1981, the month that Gary Numan officially retired from touring with a series of sold-out Wembley Arena shows, the Human League entered the charts with its first Top 40 U.K. hit, "The Sound of the Crowd." As spring turned to summer it was joined by a number of similar new acts—Depeche Mode, Soft Cell, Heaven 17—all of whom had cast guitars and drums completely out of their ensembles in deference to a lineup consisting exclusively of synthesizers and electronic percussion. Whereas Numan had never fully committed to a synthesized sound, always opting for a conventional rock rhythm section and occasionally returning to the guitar in his stage shows, these new groups embraced the new technology completely. Human League records, for example, bore a declaration of purity: "contains synthesizers + vocals only." A new type of pop musician emerged: one versed solely in electronics. As Philip Oakey of the Human League summarized, "We use synthesizers because they're simple. Once you get a grip on them you can do pretty much anything you want. We can't play any other instruments."[68]

As with Numan before them, the new synthesizer players refused to engage with the specific modes of masculine mastery and virtuosic display that had typified the keyboard and synthesizer players of the early 1970s. The members of Orchestral Manoeuvres in the Dark, for example, deliberately wanted a neutral image that blended in with their modern technology, so they cut their hair short, and wore "nondescript clothes . . . ties and white shirts." They ended up looking, in their words, more like "bank clerks" than musicians.[69] Groups with multiple synthesizer players, such as the Human League and Depeche Mode, divided them up into specific functions, so that in live settings one player might be responsible primarily for playing simple, repetitive bass lines. The image of the synthesizer player was transformed into that almost of a wage laborer. As *Musician* magazine described Patrick O'Hearn of Missing Persons, most of the time he was "bent over his keyboards at the back of the stage, looking like a *nouveau punque* auto mechanic fixing a particularly stubborn carburetor."[70] Alternatively, some synthesizer groups simply took to the stage with the vast majority, or even all, of their music prerecorded, refusing to pretend to any authentic representation of work and labor. As Vince Clarke, the sole instrumentalist for the synth/vocal duo Yazoo described his live performances: "All of the actual riffs and bits and pieces are preprogrammed and the sounds presampled. . . . On stage I do very little actually. I might smoke a cigarette, drink a bit. I might clap my hands occasionally."[71] Through his nonchalant attitude, Clarke mocked the seriousness of rock's artistic pretensions and its professionalized work ethic, acquiescing to the mechanization that had become an indelible part of new wave's live synthesized aesthetic.

Clarke's scenario, of course, is extreme. But it gives a good indication of just how much synthesizers had begun to change in the early 1980s. A transition was under way, and the days of the 1970s monophonic synthesizers and simple one-handed motions were being left behind as the production of new digital synthesizers with polyphonic, sequencing, and sampling capabilities entered the marketplace. In this new context, many new wave musicians embraced an energy-conscious push-button attitude toward the synthesizer and remained content simply to stand relatively motionless behind the keyboard, initiating sequencer patterns, hitting noisy effects, and playing rudimentary lines. At the same time, the new sampling technology and polyphonic capabilities encouraged a shift away from the deliberately electronic and "artificial" tones favored by the early new wave synthesizer players toward more "naturalistic" settings. Synthesizers were now increasingly used to imitate not just string backings, but horn hits and choruses, stingers and any number of conventional arranging clichés that had been in the bag of rock and pop tricks since the 1960s and 1970s. While there were still genres such as heavy metal that declared that synthesizers were "gay" and decidedly unmasculine instruments, by the end of the 1980s the synthesizer had become the dominating sound of popular music.[72] As the new digital synthesizers became more versatile, flexible, and reliable, ultimately allowing keyboardists to preside over one or two instruments rather than a forbidding tower of technology, the labor that went along with operating the synthesizer largely vanished. The new wave ushered in a new view of the synthesizer as a modern musical technology and reconceived what it meant to *work* at one's instrument.

SEVEN

Kings of the Wild Frontier

From its very beginnings in the mid-1970s, new wave was characterized by its maddeningly diverse collective identity, a trait that made it difficult to define as a movement. Anyone surveying the new wave landscape at the dawning of the 1980s need not have looked far to find proof of this. Two of the most successful new wave groups at that time, Adam and the Ants and the Talking Heads, seemed to have arisen from entirely different universes. As their unusual name suggests, the British group Adam and the Ants cultivated a cartoonish pop star cult image. The group's leader, Adam Ant, and his band mates dressed in a whirlwind combination of fashions—centered especially on a romantic swashbuckling image—and playfully addressed his large legion of teenage fans as "antpeople." It was, as one music critic described, the most "perfect shallow fantasy pop."[1] The Talking Heads, by comparison, took their name from a sophisticated modern media term used to describe the shots of heads (as opposed to full bodies) that dominated television news and documentary broadcasting. Established within New York City's East Village arts community, they were the quintessential new wave critic's band. Devoid of the types of outlandish costumes and pop extravagance that defined Adam and the Ants, they attracted a more intellectual crowd drawn in by lead singer and songwriter David Byrne's lyrical critiques of human relations and alienation in modern society. The difference between Adam and the Ants and the Talking Heads, in blunt terms, was that which separated new wave's teenybopper from its art rock sides.

For all these differences, the two bands were united in their musical endeavors by a strong Afrocentricism. In the fall of 1980 both released heavily anticipated records, the contents of which, each of them claimed, represented the direct influence and assimilation of African musical sources. As Adam Ant explained to the music press, his band's latest album, *Kings of the Wild Frontier,* had grown partly out of his study of the African tribal drummers of Burundi. Ant's adoption of their rhythmic style, which quickly became labeled as the "Burundi Beat," provided the backbone for the album's first three singles and helped launch *Kings of the Wild Frontier* to the top of the British charts, where it eventually stayed for ten straight weeks in the spring of 1981.[2] Released less than two weeks prior to Ant's album, the Talking Heads' fourth release, *Remain in Light,* displayed an affinity with African music as well. As part of the press kit accompanying the album's release, David Byrne included a two-page letter explaining in detail how *Remain in Light* had been created with "an interest in African rhythms and sensibilities."[3] He concluded the letter with a reading list that included such scholarly titles as John Miller Chernoff's recently published 1979 ethnographic study, *African Rhythm and African Sensibility* and Robert Farris Thompson's *African Art in Motion.* As Byrne would later elaborate, it was a tactic he used so that the critics would "write more interesting reviews."[4] Whether or not that was actually his original motive, its success was undeniable. The music press swallowed Byrne's bait and heralded the band's bold new directions in African-styled music making.

On the face of it, both albums stood as representatives of a new musical globalization, of the travel of musical practices, sound recordings, and aesthetic styles across and between cultures. In this sense one could see them as part of a developing "global modernity," a new connectivity wherein previously isolated societies and their musical arts and entertainments were finally coming into contact with one another.[5] In this context, one can situate Adam and the Ants and the Talking Heads not only within the new wave, but also in relation to two new "global" genres that were emergent at the turn of the 1980s: world music and world beat. The former of these two terms, world music, had actually been circulating in American academic circles since the early 1960s as a shorthand for non-Western music, the subject of study for most ethnomusicologists.[6] By the 1980s, however, world music had entered the mainstream, often attached as a generic marketing category to a variety of non-Western performers ranging from such traditional ensembles as the Royal Drummers of Burundi to the Bulgarian female vocal choir Le Mystère des Voix Bulgares. The latter of the two terms, world beat, first surfaced in the early 1980s as a label used to denote a growing trend in the fusion of Western and non-Western sounds, a polymorphous meeting ground where pop artists could pursue a range of ethnic music traditions and styles.[7] But before long it had become a "fashionable label" for nearly any music that originated in or borrowed from outside of Western musical traditions.[8]

Both world music and world beat would come under attack from critics who blanched at their indiscriminate nature and the ways the terms were used to herd together almost any recording involving some aspect of non-Western music. Such practices reiterated these genres' placement within a powerful Euro-American music industry little concerned with local histories and cultural traditions. Furthermore, as ethnomusicologist Steven Feld argued, this was especially problematic with the politically loaded phrase *world beat,* for the word *beat* emphasized a separation between the West and the outside world:

> Notice the marked word: "beat." That also reminds Westerners that it is "others" who have rhythm, make music of and for the body, music for dance, for bodily pleasure. Tied to a long history of essentializing and racializing other bodies as possessing a "natural" sense of rhythm, the invention of "world beat" reproduces a Western gaze toward the exotic and erotic, often darker-skinned, dancing body. These othered "beats" thus provide the pulse and groove for Western bodies to throw their inhibitions off on the dance floor.[9]

Feld's point—that the West has exoticized "others" who have the beat—is an important one. Adam Ant, for example, crucially proclaimed that his music derived from the Burundi Beat, and *not* the "Burundi Melody" or "Burundi Vocal Chant." Likewise, David Byrne emphasized that the Talking Heads had specifically tapped into the power of African rhythm rather than some other musical elements. Both of their musical enterprises thus revolved around their relationships, as Western musicians, to a group of "other" bodies, possessed of some supposedly natural sense of rhythm.

This chapter explores the deployment of "the other" in the music of both Adam and the Ants and the Talking Heads as a symbol of the increasingly globalized modern musical encounters that became increasingly prevalent in the 1980s. While I will probe how this mixing of Western and non-Western sounds appeared as a catalyzing locus in the junctions between new wave and world beat, it is also important to consider how this development intersected with the mobilization of a different "other" *within* Western popular music itself. Here I am referring to the ways in which white new wave musicians incorporated African American funk and disco and Afro-Caribbean reggae, dub, and ska into their music at a time when most of these styles were seen as lying outside the parameters of mainstream white rock. Crossover relations, as such, historically have drawn heavy criticism, for they are drawn largely along lines of racial power, where white performers have long profited from their assimilations and interpretations of black, Latin American, and Caribbean musical cultures. Popular music studies scholar Reebee Garofalo has described this relationship as one of "black innovation and white popularization," or more memorably, "black roots, white fruits."[10] Because these crossover relations formed an integral part of new wave's definition, they constitute a large backdrop against which new wave's world beat and world music excursions can be read.

New Wave and Crossover in England

From the beginnings of its meteoric rise in 1976 British punk enjoyed a strong connection and crossover with the music of England's large West Indian migrant population. British punks were drawn to many varieties of Jamaican music, such as ska, rock steady, reggae, and dub that had been trickling into England since the 1960s. In particular, they gravitated toward reggae's Rastafarian subculture, an outspoken group committed to the union of the black African diaspora. Both punks and Rastafarians shared in a basic rebellion against societal and political oppression, and thus deliberately positioned themselves as "outsiders." As Paul Simonon of the Clash explained, "Reggae, punk, it's not like most of the stuff you hear on the radio. It's something you can relate to, kids your own age—they've got their battles, we've got ours. Black people are still being suppressed, we are being suppressed, so we've got something in common."[11] Rastafarian DJ Don

Letts helped further the connection when he started spinning reggae records between punk sets at the Roxy Club. In his words, punk was "the first white movement I can relate to as a black man without feeling like I'm doing some kind of black and white minstrel show."[12] Given this symbiotic relationship, the communion between punk and reggae has often been framed as a positive example of racial crossover.[13]

Ironically, this relationship grew stronger in the late 1970s and early 1980s even as punk ruptured and splintered into the messy sprawl of new wave and post-punk. Upon the breakup of the Sex Pistols, for example, singer John Lydon formed the band Public Image Limited, whose sound centered on the reggae and dub bass lines of bassist Jah Wobble. Crossing over from the other side, respected reggae producer Dennis Bovell worked with post-punk artists like the Pop Group and the Slits. Crucially, these post-punk groups did not simply import the sounds of reggae and dub into their music. Rather, they often employed these styles as a deconstructive act, as a means of throwing their riffs and rhythms into convulsive and violent competition with one another. As *New Musical Express*'s Richard Grabel described the Slits: "The rhythm, though reggae based, isn't smooth and seductive like much reggae but angular, jarring and requires you to attune your ears to get a grasp."[14] Similarly, writing in *Rolling Stone*, Greil Marcus described how the Gang of Four used funk and dub to rupture the structure of their music: "Rhythms shifted, stopped, re-formed; violent pauses broke the songs into pieces."[15] The overall effect was one of a fractured, modernist transformation.

Other bands like the Specials, the Selecter, the Beat, and Madness reached back to a more distant style of Jamaican music, mid-1960s ska, whose up-tempo rhythms mixed and matched easily with the energy of punk on the dance floor. All of these groups were associated with the independent label 2 Tone Records, which Specials keyboardist Jerry Dammers had formed in 1979, and nearly all of them were composed of both black and white musicians. In this respect, the 2 Tone label acted as a potent signifier. As Dick Hebdige has pointed out, the phrase "2 Tone" worked as a nostalgic fashion reference to "the shoes the skinheads used to wear back in 1969 on ska nights down at the city-centre clubs with their tonic mohair suits—the 'two tone' suits which changed colour depending on how the light caught them."[16] In addition to these specific connotations, 2 Tone also came to symbolize more generally the biracial lineups featured throughout the record label's roster.

Adam and the Ants and the "Rhythm Thing"

In 1979, at the height of post-punk's avant-garde experimentation and 2 Tone's biracial pop, Adam and the Ants released their debut full-length, *Dirk Wears White Sox*, an album that fit comfortably within neither of these crossover developments. If anything, the group's image and sound were more firmly rooted in punk rock's quickly fading formulaic style. As part of his stage persona Adam Ant employed the leather and rubber S & M fashion so familiar to punk, and like many other punks he flirted with the fascist imagery of swastikas while recording songs like "Deutscher Girls." Likewise, their driving beats and distorted guitars seemed antiquated amid the new adventuresome stylistic explorations. When the album received a flogging in the music press, Adam Ant realized that the group needed a change of direction. Through a series of connections, he met Malcolm McLaren, the Sex Pistols' former manager, and the stage was set for the band's reinvention.

Few figures have a more notorious or infamous reputation in the mythology of rock history than Malcolm McLaren. Because McLaren, a fashion designer turned punk manager, wielded his influence by draping the Sex Pistols in scandalous outfits and encouraging their outrageous behavior, detractors often offer up his name as proof that punk rockers valued depravity and shock effect at the expense of any significant musical content.[17] However dubious the accusations of such arguments might be, they unfortunately have overshadowed McLaren's contributions to the post–Sex Pistols British musical landscape. By 1980 McLaren had moved on from punk, having become convinced that the future of pop music resided elsewhere. His peripatetic wanderings would eventually lead him to a variety of new inspirational sources—ranging from African Burundi drummers and African American rap and break dancing to "primitive" folk singing and dancing—all of which he attempted to appropriate and incorporate either into the music of the acts he was managing or his own solo recordings.

Following the Sex Pistols' dissolution in 1978, McLaren had retreated to Paris, where through a network of acquaintances he gained access to the library of the French label Barclay Records, which housed among its possessions an abundance of African music. Here McLaren encountered a novelty instrumental recording called "Burundi Black" that Barclay had issued in 1971, which featured a rhythm track of Burundi drumming with some dubbed-over piano parts provided by the song's "composer," Mike Steiphenson. He had lifted the material for the single from anthropologist Michel Vuylsteke's 1967 field recordings of Burundi music, originally issued as a full-length album on the Ocora Radio France label entitled *Burundi: Musiques Traditionnelles*. McLaren returned to England in 1979 with Steiphenson's "Burundi Black" in tow. Once in London he met with Adam Ant, and for a modest fee agreed to help the singer overhaul his image and music. Searching for a creative spark, he gave Ant's band a mix tape he had cobbled together, which included the "Burundi Black" track. As Lee Gorman, the Ants' bass player at the time, describes, McLaren wanted the band to emulate the different styles on the tape, to establish a foundation on which to build:

> We were given a tape of about fifteen different songs—from Gary Glitter to Hare Krishna, Turkish music, Hank Williams, Burundi drums, everything— and we had to do our own versions of them. [McLaren] told us to just to pick what we wanted and try and come up with whatever we could.
>
> Well, we did it, and we did it really badly. We just did it like punk rock and it turned out shit. He wanted to sack us. He said, "You're shit, get out of my sight." He was terrible. And we just said, sorry, let's have another go at it. So we had another go with the Burundi Black song and we figured out something. He said, "Hmmmm, you do that one best," so we concentrated on that and built up on it. And suddenly, me and Dave [Barbe, the drummer], we found we had this kind of thing: this rhythm thing.[18]

Out of McLaren's initial crapshoot, the band's interpretation of the Burundi drumming "rhythm thing" emerged as the most promising new direction. At this point, however, the story unfolds like a virtual soap opera. Convinced that Adam Ant was not appropriate star material, McLaren told Ant to concentrate on writing lyrics while he rehearsed the singer's band separately, developing the "Burundi Beat." McLaren then persuaded Ant's band to jettison their singer and join McLaren in his own plans to form a new group. McLaren's project, which he named Bow Wow Wow, stalled at first as he ran into complications trying to assemble the band around fourteen-year-old Burmese vocalist Annabella Lwin. During this time Ant managed to regroup and, using a copy of the rehearsal mix tape that McLaren had unwittingly left behind, concocted his own version of the "Burundi Beat." Both McLaren and Ant were determined to get their version of the "rhythm thing" before the public first. McLaren would win the battle by a hair, as Bow Wow Wow released its first single, "C30, C60, C90 Go" one day before Adam and the Ants' first Burundi-influenced single, "Kings of the Wild Frontier." While Bow Wow Wow would initially enjoy a greater critical reception and a higher chart placing, Ant would eventually win the war as his follow-up singles and full-length album soon outdistanced Bow Wow Wow's success by a wide margin.

Comparing Adam and the Ants' and Bow Wow Wow's songs with Vuylsteke's recordings, it is obvious which basic patterns and ideas the British pop musicians deliberately mimicked in constructing their signature "Burundi Beat." Certainly part of the beat's distinctiveness lay in its timbre, as the drummers moved their main patterns onto the tom-toms and rims of the drums, relegating the snare and kick drum to muted backbeats, and eschewing completely the use of cymbals. Beyond this, the beat was distinguished by two main features: a rumbling shuffle pulse, which sounded like a sped-up version of Gary Glitter's 1972 hit "Rock and Roll Part 2," and a short pickup, roughly equivalent to a five-stroke roll, which marked the division of the beat into discrete musical phrases. In example 7, which shows this basic pattern as it occurs throughout much of "Kings of the Wild Frontier," the pickup roll signals the start of a new phrase every two measures.

Another key component of the "Burundi Beat" was its use of layering. On the Burundi drumming captured on Vuylsteke's recording, the drummers first set in place a stream of unwavering eighths, which sit elastically

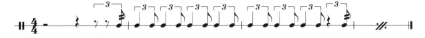

Example 7: "Kings of the Wild Frontier" "Burundi Beat" with pickup roll

between a duple and triplet pulse. On top of this, a second group of drummers accents a series of short phrases and patterns that provides variety to the texture. One can hear this type of layering in the beginning of "Antmusic," shown in example 8. The example consists of three layers, each of which is played on the rims of the drums. The middle voice introduces a truncated version of the pickup roll shuffle, which is then echoed antiphonally in the top voice. A third layer of steady triplets then appears, creating a dense aggregate that gains in volume before slamming together on three strong accents to lead into the song's opening verse. Live, Ant and his band sought to duplicate such effects by dividing the rhythms between two drummers. In the studio, the "Burundi beat" emerged more through prodigious percussive overdubbing, which included everything from maracas and rattles to scratched rhythms on the electric guitar.

Example 8: "Antmusic" three voice rim click layering

One last element featured prominently in the "Burundi Beat" was the use of polyrhythms, which is an identifying characteristic of the music of many African cultures. Ant highlights these polyrhythms in the middle of "Kings of the Wild Frontier," where he strings together a succession of three-beat riffs over a four-beat pulse. This pattern, copied directly from

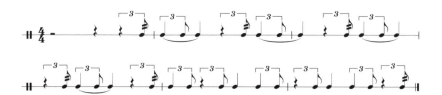

Example 9: "Kings of the Wild Frontier" polyrhythms

Vuylsteke's Burundi recording, serves to create a new accent pulse against the song's regular 4/4 meter. Example 9 shows this polyrhythm, with each three-beat group initially designated by a pickup roll and a slur.

While I have drawn connections between Ant's music and Vuylsteke's original field recordings in these examples to illuminate some general features of Ant's "Burundi Beat," I do not mean to imply that the rhythms heard in the British new wave and those of African drumming are in any way interchangeable or synonymous. These skeletal transcriptions fail to capture accurately the very real differences between the two. For example, as much as Ant promoted the "Burundi Beat" as one that liberated the artist from the strictures of Western popular music, never does he use the beat without the aid of a standard rock backbeat accent. Whether the backbeat is a conspicuous foreground presence, as in "Antmusic," or subtly woven underneath the tom-tom beat, as in "Kings of the Wild Frontier," it is always there. This adds a rigidity to Ant's rhythmic arrangements that is completely foreign to the more loosely pulsed Burundi playing style. On the whole, the Burundi drummers employed many subtleties of pulse, timbre, and phrasing that simply do not fit within rock's repetitive rhythmic structures.

Even though both Adam and the Ants and Bow Wow Wow made the "Burundi Beat" the focus of their initial singles, they also approached it with a certain caution and used it sparingly throughout the rest of their music. Bassist Lee Gorman and drummer Dave Barbe of Bow Wow Wow explained their ambivalence toward the Burundi phenomenon as such: "[Gorman]: The thing about the Burundi beat is it's as versatile as a fucking 4-4 rock beat. you [sic] can write God knows how many numbers on the Burundi beat." "[Barbe]: It all gets a bit boring though."[19] The "Burundi Beat" was novel enough, however, that it soon spread and became a pervasive presence within the British new wave. In early 1981, Rusty Egan of Visage and French producer Jean-Philippe Iliesco issued an updated version of Mike Steiphenson's original "Burundi Black" single, with an added piano track and electronic percussion arrangement that helped it become a minor dance club hit. In 1983 the British synthesizer duo Naked Eyes even used the "Burundi Beat" as the rhythmic basis for their hit cover version of Burt Bacharach and Hal David's late 1960s pop standard "(There's) Always Something There to Remind Me." Over the years the "Burundi Beat" has proven to be a remarkably resilient source of inspiration, popping up everywhere from the heavy metal of Def Leppard's "Rocket" (1987) to the indie rock of the White Rabbits' aptly titled single "Percussion Gun" (2009).

The "Burundi Beat" has become a familiar part of the lexicon of rock rhythms over the past three decades, but at the turn of the 1980s its sense of newness and its direct connection with a recorded ethnomusicological source raised questions of appropriation and cultural imperialism. Writing in the *New York Times,* music critic Robert Palmer complained that "the Burundian drummers who made the original recording are not sharing in the profits. Nobody told them to copyright their traditional music."[20] In their dominant position as Western pop musicians and artists, Ant and McLaren drew the acclaim and rewards for the "Burundi Beat" while the drummers of Burundi received no compensation. On a very basic level, they were the ones with the privileged access to the capital and institutional machinery of the Western music industry, and thus the ones who controlled the flow of the Burundian music and culture. In this respect, rarely has an album title—*Kings of the Wild Frontier*—provided a more barefaced gateway to accusations of musical and cultural exploitation than Ant's. The title brings to mind colonial images of Western explorers taming and ruling over the regions of a dark, uncharted musical continent.[21]

Bound within these larger issues of cultural imperialism are the troubling inequities of copyright protection and financial remuneration that disadvantage those local musicians who reside outside the sphere of the Western music industry. The international copyright system, especially at the time of new wave, functioned as a Byzantine network of blanket agreements, ineffective collecting societies, and profit avenues that channeled disproportionate amounts into the coffers of transnational corporations. As described in Roger Wallis and Krister Malm's classic 1984 study, *Big Sounds from Small Peoples,* songs from little countries were "often picked up and exploited internationally, with the original collector or publisher claiming the copyright on the 'first there, first claim' principle, and with the original *local* composers or 'collectors' getting left out."[22] Ant and McLaren claimed from the Burundi musicians, of course, not a song but rather a "drum piece" whose rhythms and timbres are not the type of material that falls within the more traditional jurisdiction of copyrights, which normally protect lyrics and melodies. In an interview discussing the new sound unveiled on the "Kings of the Wild Frontier" single, Ant was quick to credit the originators: "As for whose sound it is, it belongs to the Burundi tribe."[23] But this can only be read as lip service, for in no way did Ant financially recompense the Burundi, or even Vuylsteke, who had "discovered" the Burundi through his original field recordings. The songs on *Kings of the Wild Frontier* are copyrighted to Ant and the band's lead guitarist, Marco Pirroni.[24]

Following in the wake of the 1980s world beat and world music boom, Steven Feld introduced the concept of "schizophonic mimesis" to address the perpetration of precisely these types of injustices. The Canadian composer R. Murray Schafer had first coined the term *schizophonia* in the late 1960s to refer to the phenomenon of modern recording technology, where we now regularly encounter "the split between an original sound and its electroacoustical transmission or reproduction."[25] By invoking "schizophonic mimesis," Feld wanted to examine the "traffic" that emerged through the "circulation and absorption" of recordings like Vuylsteke's Burundi production. In general, he hesitated to draw many positive conclusions. The majority of appropriations like's Ant's "Burundi Beat," displayed "few if any contextual linkages to the processes, practices, and forms of participation that could give meaning within local communities."[26] Furthermore, in such a scenario a group like the Burundi drummers had no control over the representation of their music and culture. In the context of the Western music industry they were limited to the role of "influences" and "laborers in the production of pop."[27]

At the same time, though, it would be misleading to imagine that the music of the Burundi drummers was simply colonized. After all, the Royal Drummers of Burundi were a renowned touring group, who traveled many times outside their country. By the time that McLaren and Ant lifted their rhythms in 1980, they had been performing internationally at gatherings such as the Festival of Traditional Arts in France for many years, ever since Burundi had been granted independence in 1966. They were not simply some remote tribal group removed from the circulation and commerce of art. In many ways the connection with the British new wave's "Burundi Beat" provided them with a springboard for further exposure. In July 1982 the Master Drummers traveled to Shepton Mallet, England, to participate in the inaugural WOMAD (World of Music and Dance) festival. Organized in part by Peter Gabriel, the festival was planned to showcase an international array of musicians and artists. In addition to their own festival performance, the Burundi drummers joined the post-punk group Echo and the Bunnymen on stage at WOMAD for a version of the band's song "All My Colours."[28] They also furthered their popularity by performing just prior to the festival in concerts at the Brixton Academy and the Commonwealth Institute, and by appearing onstage in London in support of the punk group the Clash.[29] Recordings from the group's visit would eventually appear on the WOMAD festival benefit LP, *Raindrops Pattering on Banana Leaves and Other Tunes,* where the Royal Drummers of Burundi were credited with the rights to their song and performance. Propelled by this exposure, the Burundi drummers undertook more extensive overseas tours in 1983 and 1986.[30] During another visit to England in 1987, the Royal Drummers recorded a live performance at Wiltshire, which appeared for release in America in 1992 under the auspices of Peter Gabriel's Real World label. By that time the ensemble had become among the most popular international representatives of traditional music of any African nation.

Colonial Game Playing

The "Burundi Beat" surely played a large role in the success that Adam and the Ants found. But ultimately what distinguished *Kings of the Wild Frontier* from other new wave records at that time was its alluring, dense mixture of cultural and musical symbols, of which the Burundi rhythms were but one component. Under the guidance of Malcolm McLaren's associate, punk fashion designer Vivienne Westwood, Ant carefully built his image out of a variety of free-floating signifiers that traversed boundaries of historical and geographical space. As the *Washington Post*'s Richard Harrington described, Ant's special look encompassed details ranging from the French revolutionary and Victorian England eras to pirate garb and American Indian warrior paint (see figure 16):

> The fully dressed Adam Ant is a designer's fantasy, starting with the Blackbeard bows and gold braids in his hair, a loose white shirt opened on a hairless chest encased by the 11th Hussar military jacket that David Hemmings wore in "The Charge of the Light Brigade" (rented), a pirate's crossbelt without the sword, the *tricolore* of the French revolution hanging from one side,

a double gold braid hanging from the other, a bright scarf tied Cromwell-style around one arm, black leather trousers whose seams are held together by tiny skulls, fringed boots with found feathers dangling perilously close to the ground.

And in the midst of these flash clothes is the long, curly lock of hair attached near the ear, the eight silver skull-and-crossbone rings, the Apache war stripe meticulously drawn across the bridge of his nose.[31]

This is a whirlwind fashion mélange, one that ably demonstrates Westwood's gift for "keeping something modern while establishing symbolic connections with the past."[32] Ant matched this sartorial experimentation with a musical assemblage that typified the extreme of the new wave's cross-stylistic ventures. Important as the Burundi rhythms were to the group's formula, equally crucial was guitarist Marco Pirroni's twangy, low-string vibrato lines, evocative of Duane Eddy's pioneering late 1950s rock and roll style. Because Eddy's "twang" style had been adopted by countless surf bands, and copied as well by the composer Ennio Morricone for his influential soundtracks to Sergio Leone's 1960s spaghetti westerns, it provided for Ant's music a rich semiotic field.[33] On top of this, Ant and the band punctuated the music with layered vocal parts that, as one music critic described, resembled "yelping that falls somewhere between Indian chants, pirate chanteys and voodoo hysteria."[34] For all the possible chaos such a mixture might encourage, however, Ant emerged with a strong identity.

As British music journalist Dave Rimmer has claimed, Ant had a significant effect on the new wave, because he was "the first artist since the Sex Pistols to sell, not just an unmistakeable 'look' (as he always put it) and an unmistakeable 'sound' (ditto), but also a half-baked set of theories and attitudes that pinned the two together."[35] Infatuated by film and popular culture, Westwood and Ant hung many of the singer's visual ideas on the iconography of a "heroic" thread stretching throughout cinematic history. From the 1968 remake of *Charge of the Light Brigade* he took the military jacket modeled by the actors portraying the British lancers. Much of his pirate imagery Ant credited to the influence of Errol Flynn and his 1930s swashbuckling adventures. He acknowledged his appreciation for the sullen gunfighter ethos made famous through Clint Eastwood's many char-

Figure 16. Adam Ant, live at the Palladium Theater, New York City, April 24, 1981, with Apache war stripe and pirate's crossbelt displaying his "designer's fantasy." © Laurie Paladino.

acters in 1960s and 1970s westerns. Lastly, he claimed an affinity with the heroic warrior tribes of the American Indians. Taken as a whole, one could argue that this amalgamation was an example of the eclectic "overstimulating ensembles" that cultural critic Frederic Jameson labeled as symptomatic of a postmodern crisis in the 1980s.[36] Drawn as we are to accept history through a layering of superficial images, both filmic and photographic, Jameson argued that we had frozen out any real connection with the past. But to make such assertions is to deny the resonant relationships that media constructions have with cultural myths long entrenched as part of a national consciousness. And Ant's creation *does* indeed draw on one such powerful myth, the "frontier" that was evoked in his album title *Kings of the Wild Frontier.*

Few, if any, myths capture the essence of colonial and imperial historical character—of open promise, progress, and development—as forcefully as that of the frontier. So persistent has this myth been in American society, that even though the frontier has generally been accepted as "closed" since the late nineteenth century, it has lived on both as a set of cultural symbols endlessly regenerated through such media genres as the Hollywood western, and in the rhetoric of politicians as a metaphorical justification for military intervention.[37] For all its patriotic trappings, the American frontier that Ant stumbled onto is one tainted by a bloody heritage. The myth of the American frontier hinges on what historian Richard Slotkin has called a "regeneration through violence." As Slotkin iterates, the American settlers and government understood that in order to harvest the riches of the frontier land they would have to remove with force the Indians in residence. In this context American expansion "took the form of a fable of race war, pitting the symbolic opposites of savagery and civilization, primitivism and progress, paganism and Christianity against each other."[38]

In his musical persona, Ant positioned himself squarely within these symbolic binaries, assuming the role of a "savage warrior" fighting against the constraints of "white civilization." As Ant exclaimed in the refrain to "Kings of the Wild Frontier": "I feel beneath the white, there is a red skin suffering from centuries of taming." Ant's stance, however fantastical it may have been, seemed to present genuine pro-Indian sentiments. But there is a snag. Who exactly *are* "the Kings of the Wild Frontier," of which he sings? From the Anglo-perspective, it was the settlers. And ultimately this is where Ant had to situate himself, for it must be remembered that the concept of a "frontier" was one utterly foreign to Native Americans. The myth of the frontier was one solely employed from the perspective of the colonizer. Likewise the American Indians did not recognize the concept of a "savage." Those who marked themselves as civilized evoked the negative image of the savage as a way of legitimizing their moral missions. As the pioneering American historian Roy Harvey Pearce noted, "Civilization had created a savage, so to kill him."[39] By portraying himself as an Indian, Ant took the side of the hunted, but his representation dwelled entirely within the limits of the fantasy land of the hunter.

There should be little surprise, then, that upon his first visit to the United States, Ant met with objections from representatives of the New York City–based American Indian Community House (AICH), who protested the singer's representations of Indians as had been described in a sensationalist feature article in the *New York Daily News*.[40] They presented Ant's record company, CBS, with a letter requesting that he refrain from using the "Geronimo stripe" as part of his facial makeup.[41] Members of American Indian communities have long been rightfully concerned about how portrayals of Indians circulate. As they have seen throughout history, those from outside the American Indian community are all too willing to accept their own constructed stereotyped versions of Indians as accurate cultural representations. These versions then displace and leave no voice for genuine Native traditions. This can have damaging consequences, for as the American Indian poet Wendy Rose explains, "The expectation is that I [the Native American] adopt, and thereby validate, the 'persona' of some mythic 'Indian being' who never was. The requirement is that I act to negate the reality of my—and my people's—existence in favor of a script developed within the fantasies of my oppressors."[42] With this in mind, Ant agreed to meet with the AICH representatives, and was able to allay their fears and concerns. Convinced by "his appreciation and knowledge of Indian lore," the American Indians retracted their complaints.[43] As a member of the AICH explained, "I found nothing offensive as far as my culture is concerned. (Some of the people in my party even liked his music!)."[44]

While Ant was able to persuade the AICH that he was knowledgeable of their customs and history and wore the stripe "as a tribute to their spirit," his appreciation of the American Indians was always interlaced with a distinct tribal rhetoric that he employed in order to prop up his own mythic pop star package.[45] He stressed that he was tapping into a primal, timeless music source that was "unpolluted by commercialism," a connection that reasserted his authenticity as a creative artist untainted by the fickle trends of the marketplace.[46] Repeatedly in his interviews, he idealized tribal warriors for their qualities of integrity, independence, individuality, dignity, and pride. He respected them because in their communities, one had to "earn the right to be called a human being."[47] Tying together all these loose ideas, however, was one overriding "tribal" theme. Ant encouraged his fans to join in his own tribe of sexually liberated "antpeople." As Ant's well-publicized slogan proclaimed, the band was making "Antmusic for Sex People." Ant thus evoked the tribal as a way of bypassing the sexual repression at the core of Western moral values. The tribal for him acted as a gateway into an idealized, uninhibited primal sexual drive.[48] Seen in this light, Ant was a student of Indian culture to the extent that he identified with those aspects—sexual liberation and noble heroism—that squared with his goal of creating a desirous pop star identity. Ant the "researcher" simply used the tribal to give the illusion that his public persona had been founded upon a universal set of values.

One of the reasons that Ant's tribal rhetoric succeeded so dramatically in England was that he attracted a fan base of primarily young teenagers, a relatively disempowered social group often viewed by parents and the mass media alike as if they are a tribe. Adolescence is typically portrayed as a liminal period on the threshold of adulthood, a point where young people must be monitored closely lest their behavior bubble over into primal recklessness. Slang, rituals, and codes, as such, are the "tribal" properties youth have constructed as a means of countering their limited access to real societal power. Sociologists may commonly label the groups of young people they study as "teenagers" or various "subcultures," but they most always work within a framework not far removed from the language ascribed to tribes, a fact recognized by sociologist Andy Bennett, who has suggested that youth formations be considered as "neo-tribes."[49] That Ant was able to tap this vein is a tribute to his recognition that there existed among England's youth the propensity for such a tribal discourse.

On a broader scale it could also be said that Ant's invocation of the savage and the act of dressing up held for his white middle-class audience a certain carnivalesque appeal. Historically in England and Europe the carnival was an arena for ritual play involving classes both high and low.[50] But by the late nineteenth century the middle class had distanced itself almost completely from carnivalesque activities. The middle class undertook a campaign to abolish carnivals, and in the process began to define itself as apart from the carnival's savage and grotesque representations. Through this act, the middle class came to be characterized as a repressed class, locked in self-imposed exile from the carnival's ritual sense of play. In this respect, Adam and the Ants' carnivalesque pop music fantasy world generated excitement among its middle-class audience precisely because it titillated them with visuals and symbols of savage American Indian warriors and African tribes, the likes of which had been deemed impermissible to a middle-class sensibility. He had unleashed the signifying power of a repressed "other."

Once this primitive "other" had been let loose in Ant's swirling pop confection, it was inevitable that its specific sources—American Indians and Burundi drumming among them—would get tossed together in a confusing conglomeration, or what literary scholar Marianna Torgovnick has termed a "grab-bag primitive."[51] Even though, for example, Ant alluded only to American Indian culture and not music specifically, critics located in his Burundi borrowed drums and rhythms the sound of a "warm, rich Apache beat."[52] Critiquing Ant's live show, a writer for *Trouser Press* complained that the band failed to duplicate "whatever that is on record— African jungle drums or American Indian war beats."[53] Even Ant himself fell into primitive generalizations as he compared the drums on the "King of the Wild Frontier" single to the sound of "ten thousand Zulus banging their shields."[54] In the end, for all of Ant's explanations and rhetoric, his music assumed an unspecified, exotic, and savage otherness.

For as much as *Kings of the Wild Frontier* set the tone for Adam and the Ants' identity, like most pop stars Ant was wary of standing still, and by the time the band returned with their follow-up album, 1981's *Prince Charming*, the band had left behind its "Burundi Beat" and American Indian associations. By 1982 Ant had ditched his backing band entirely, save for guitarist Marco Pirroni, in order to concentrate more fully on his role as a swashbuckling, Casanova pop star. During this time England witnessed the rise of the New Romantics and New Pop groups like Duran Duran, Culture Club, and the Thompson Twins who turned to different sources of musical black-ness for their inspiration, such as funk, disco, and reggae. While these bands retreated from the type of tribal exoticism that had driven Ant's sound and image, at the same time their use of black music styles soon turned to a massive, undifferentiated raid reminiscent of the "grab-bag primitive." As *Trouser Press* critic Robert Payes observed of the Thompson Twins in 1982: "Thompson Twins leader Tom Bailey is no fool. Right now, pop success in England hinges on a band's rhythmic constructs, be they hard funk, Caribbean or what have you—any or all of which could be passé in six months' time. Bailey's solution: use 'em *all*. It's what's known as hedging your bets."[55] Musical "blackness" had become the British new wave's most fashionable and malleable songwriting tool.

New Wave and Crossover in the United States

While we have seen that the idea of "crossover" was ingrained in British punk and new wave from the very start, when we turn to the United States we find a much different scenario. If anything, what distinguished so much white mid-1970s American punk from the mainstream rock of the era was the degree to which it distanced itself from the blues mannerisms that had come to signify such an important racial component of America's popular musical identity. Bands like the Ramones expelled many of the black music elements—the blue note singing style of the voice and guitar and the swing of the rhythm—that had become the assumed natural language of rock music expression. Most significantly, punk bands refused to jam and take lengthy solos, a denial of the pervasive influence of the late 1960s psyche-delic and acid rock explosion. By aligning themselves with the strict duple subdivisions, driving rhythms, and diatonic melodies of early 1960s surf and garage bands, American punks placed themselves within what was per-ceived as white musical lineage.

Reggae, the style that formed such an integral part of the British new wave and was so popular among a wide range of British audiences, was a decidedly marginal style in the United States during the 1970s. To be sure, international rock and pop stars from Eric Clapton and Paul McCartney to Paul Simon tapped reggae in the mid-1970s to add some variety to their song repertory, and Island Records relentlessly marketed the Jamaican artist Bob Marley throughout the United States as a future star. But, as Marley's promoter and U.S. label boss Chris Blackwell noted, reggae attracted for the most part a "white, liberal, college-oriented" audience, whose tastes resided outside the normal rock mainstream.[56] It was not until 1979, when the white British new wave band the Police entered the American Top 40 pop charts with the hit single "Roxanne," that a large teenage audience became familiarized with reggae. Other British new wave artists who had some success in the United States, such as Elvis Costello and Joe Jackson, who drew heavily on reggae unveiled a sound that was, for many American rock audiences, something *new*. The Police would go on to a success far in excess of what any traditional reggae artists attained in the United States. For many, their achievement represented a lamentable "cultural dilution" and the epitome of the new wave's "black roots" and "white fruits."[57]

At the same time, it would be incorrect to view these bands solely through the lens of a white audience. Groups like the Police, Blondie, and Devo who branched out into reggae, funk, and disco enjoyed popularity in black discos and on black radio. As black music critic Nelson George described the Police, when the band's third album, *Zenyatta Mondatta*, was released in 1980, a black record promoter told him, "Man, the Police have made a death (meaning *good*) street record. You sure these guys haven't been hanging out in Harlem?"[58] Even with these "reverse crossover" triumphs, though, a significant distance lay between white American new wave groups and the black styles of funk and disco that they were appropriating. American new wave bands such as Blondie and Devo were among the movement's most ironic and detached stylists, and it was clear from their engagements with funk, disco, and rap that they were not part of the black musical culture they were visiting. As one teenage punk fan declared to *New York Rocker*, "When [Blondie's "Rapture"] first came out, I didn't like it because I thought it was just another Sugarhill Gang, and I was sick of that. But then, when I found out it was Blondie, I listened and it occurred to me that it was making fun of 'Rapper's Delight' and I liked it."[59] Blondie's ironic pose thus allowed the punk fan a safe entryway into the vernacular of black musical culture. On the whole, the misunderstandings and confusion surrounding funk's and rap's black social politics and the ugly "disco sucks" attacks of the late 1970s were viruses that ensured that any white American new wave band who embraced these styles without irony or detachment would meet with some resistance.

Ultimately funk and disco entered fully into new wave in the United States along a much more circuitous route: the styles reached the ears of many white teenage Americans through the sounds of the second British Invasion of 1982 and 1983 detailed in chapter 2. In Britain the music of black America does not carry the same stigmas that haunt American society. The music of blacks was, and continues to be, for many British youths, the epitome of a unique American "cool" and a mythologized heroic expression of an oppressed people.[60] British groups like Duran Duran and Spandau Ballet thus delved into funk and disco, uninhibited and undeterred. Much as it had taken the exported efforts of British groups like the Rolling Stones and Cream in the 1960s to introduce a large majority of American fans to the music of American bluesmen Muddy Waters and Robert Johnson, so it was that many American teenagers at the turn of the 1980s were introduced to the style and sound of black artists like James Brown through a new generation of British new wave artists.

The Talking Heads and Eno: From SoHo to Africa

While it may have been the British "new pop" bands of the early 1980s who most fully saturated the American popular music market with the funk-inflected sounds of black America, undoubtedly the new wave band that remains most associated with a funk style is the Talking Heads. But for all the funk elements that dot their music, their association with this style was always of secondary importance to their status as one of the new wave's premiere art rock bands. From the Talking Heads' earliest shows in the mid-1970s they secured their reputation not only by playing at the New York City rock club CBGB's, but also by performing at avant-garde spaces like The Kitchen, located in New York's artistic SoHo community. And while the Talking Heads based their sound around a nervous, tense rhythmic and vocal energy that would become common to many new wave bands (as discussed in chapter 3), their use of delicate, oddly angular minimalist guitar lines and skittish bass riffs fit more within the tone of a reserved chamber ensemble than a rock band. As a result, from virtually their first appearances on the New York city scene, they became mentioned in the same breath as experimental composers and performance artists such as Philip Glass, Steve Reich, Laurie Anderson, and Glenn Branca. It was their involvement, however, with one particular experimentalist figure, Brian Eno, that most of all cemented their status as an art rock band. Much as Malcolm McLaren had transformed Adam and the Ants, so the presence of Brian Eno as a producer and artistic adviser channeled the Talking Heads's funk influences into entirely new directions.

As a respected composer, collaborator, and engineer-producer, Brian Eno has long maintained a unique position halfway between the worlds of popular and art music. Eno's recording career began in the early 1970s as a synthesizer player with the influential British glam, art rock band Roxy Music. In the mid-1970s Eno went on to make a succession of solo records, featuring contributions from members of such groups as Genesis, King Crimson, and Brand X, which established him as an innovative voice on the British progressive rock scene. In the late 1970s he worked closely with David Bowie on his experimental "Berlin trilogy" of records, *Low, Heroes,* and *Lodger.* And in 1978 he latched on to the nascent new wave movement, trying his hand as a producer with Devo, Ultravox, and the Talking Heads. At the same time, in the late 1970s and early 1980s, Eno was the first artist to popularize the term *ambient* as a specific compositional category. Ambient albums such as 1978's *Music For Films* and *Ambient 1: Music For Airports* featured lengthy "non-teleological" pieces that captured Eno's interest in environmental music. On the basis of these influential recordings, Eno's name is commonly placed among the group of 1970s minimalist composers such as Steve Reich, Philip Glass, Terry Riley, and La Monte Young, who set in motion an aesthetic discourse that has wielded perhaps more influence than any other realm of art music composition over the past four decades.

Eno initially was drawn to new wave in the late 1970s because he found that the majority of new wave musicians had "enthusiasm and good ideas, but no or little technical skill," and thus were liberated to experiment with their instruments and explore new possibilities.[61] Eno felt a kinship with the new wave because he always considered himself a "non-musician," and he found with many new wave artists a technical naïveté, like his own, that made them more open to new compositional and production possibilities. It was this interest in the spatial arrangement of the music that led Eno to bands like the Talking Heads, who had flipped the standard rock texture and in a manner reminiscent of funk had pushed the bass melody and rhythm to the foreground while using the guitar mostly as an overlaid coloristic element. Eno joined the Talking Heads in 1978 as the producer for their second album, *More Songs about Buildings and Food* and the band encouraged him to "go mad" and explore and experiment with their songs however he saw fit.[62] Eno's essential contribution, in most cases, was to use his synthesizer to "treat" the band's instruments. "Treating," in Eno's terminology, refers to the process by which he takes a signal from an outside source, such as a guitar, drum, or vocal, and runs it through the synthesizer's settings. By layering these sounds onto the original tracks he creates ethereal and spacious, timbral qualities. This technique results in a signature sound that has kept Eno's production services in constant demand.

Eno enjoyed his closest working relationship in the Talking Heads with David Byrne. Both Eno and Byrne had been fascinated with the music of Africa and other non-Western cultures for many years, and in 1979, following the completion of the third Talking Heads album, *Fear of Music,* they began collaborating on a side project that finally threw their shared interests into a bold conceptual light. For this project, which would result in the album *My Life in the Bush of Ghosts*, Eno and Byrne constructed a group of backing tracks over which they superimposed an array of vocal sources culled from non-Western recordings and radio broadcasts. These ranged from the Lebanese mountain singer Dunya Yusin and the Moving Star Hall Singers of the Georgia Sea Islands to snippets of an "unidentified radio evangelist." The reasons that Eno found such a recording project appealing were twofold. On the one hand, he was drawn, on a purely structural and compositional level, to the disjunctions and cohesions that evolved out of this cultural mixture. Eno constantly referred to his fascination with "musical collage," an act that he believed could "expand the vernacular of Western popular music . . . by melding traditional rock forms with remote cultural modes."[63] On the other hand, he spoke of his responsibilities as an educator, as someone whose creations, "done in sympathy with and with consciousness of music of the rest of the world," could enlighten Western audiences about the "richness" of societies outside their own.[64] Upon its 1981 release, *My Life in the Bush of Ghosts* sparked controversy, as some critics painted Eno and Byrne as rapacious sound sculptors who preached about cultural interchange, yet only had their own creative decisions and recontextualizations on display.[65] Such protestations likely concerned Eno very little, however, who that same year accepted an invitation from Ghana's Ministry of Culture to attend the country's arts festival and record with a group of Ghanian musicians.

The experiences that Byrne and Eno had gone through in constructing *My Life in the Bush of Ghosts* convinced them that a change of direction would benefit the recording of the Talking Heads' fourth album, *Remain in Light.* In the past, the band had, for the most part, begun its recording sessions with a general outline of song structures and arrangements. They would lay down the basic tracks relatively quickly and then add to the detail of the songs through studio manipulations. For *Remain in Light,* Byrne and Eno suggested that the band approach the studio without any fully formed songs. The Talking Heads would instead record improvised grooves, allowing for a spontaneous approach, and the surfacing of Eno's beloved "happy accidents."[66] Eno hoped to prompt interesting ideas by constantly rehearsing the band in new situations, such as having the members switch instruments on a regular basis. Once the band fell into a promising groove, Eno would record two or three minutes of the arrangement and then loop it. With this foundation, Byrne and Eno could then edit and weave together parts that fit into, and on top of, the groove. The finished product was a richly layered recording, filled with pointillistic dots of guitar, keyboard, auxiliary percussion, and vocal lines swirling in a dense contrapuntal mist. The recording process resulted in an obvious sonic overhaul. The Talking Heads, once noted for their twisting chord progressions and inventive harmonies, had arrived at a point where every song revolved around a repetitious one- or two-chord groove. The interest now lay in how the song's surface details intermingled with David Byrne's abstract lyricism.

The album most of all reflected the West African popular music recordings that all the Talking Heads, but Byrne and Eno in particular, had been listening to recently. It is easy to hear on *Remain in Light* a musical language common to the jujú and highlife styles of such countries as Nigeria, Ghana, and the Ivory Coast, and especially the Afrobeat of Fela Kuti. In a 1980 interview with *New Musical Express* journalist Cynthia Rose, Eno spoke ecstatically of Kuti's 1976 album *Zombie* and hoped that he could "make the people of England forsake their new wave records" and rush out and listen to this "beautiful" and "thrilling" music.[67] Like Kuti's music, *Remain in Light* boasts a complex layered surface texture woven together out of multiple cross-rhythms. Eno's principle in constructing grooves for many of his projects was to imagine that he was filling in the points along a continuous sixteenth-note grid, adding as much timbral nuance as possible. With *Remain in Light* he considered the thick web of musical instruments as tactile "interlocking parts" that could be moved in and out of the foreground as necessary. At the helms of the mixing board, he could drop in an instrumental section "aping the way horn sections punctuated a Fela Kuti song" or have the guitars glide in and out in the manner of jújú star King Sunny Adé.[68] Like the majority of West African popular music, *Remain in Light* employs a clean guitar timbre, defined by its plucked and scratched staccato action, which enabled the various textural lines to peek through the thicket of rhythmic melodies. By eschewing the use of distortion, a component vital to most rock music since the 1960s, but highly unusual in African popular music, the Talking Heads completed their stylistic homage.

For all its similarities with the West African pop groove, there is equally much on *Remain in Light* that bears the distinct stamp of Western rock music traditions. First, even with all the rhythmic activity on the surface, every song on the record is grounded by a prominent backbeat accent, a syncopation generally not as central to West African pop music. And while record reviews referred, as a matter of course, to the "swirling polyrhythmic forces at work in all the songs," with the exception of two tracks, "Born Under Punches" and "Seen and Not Seen," there is little on *Remain in Light* that is conspicuously polyrhythmic.[69] Most importantly, as with Adam and the Ants, the rhythmic arrangements, which all fit firmly in a solid duple framework, are not as elastic as the grooves of their chosen points of inspiration. Much West African pop music has a fluidity among the rhythms—often layering triplet and duple patterns—that creates more of a loose and flexible overall rhythmic feel. On the whole *Remain in Light* was, as with the Talking Heads' past music, far more rigid and tense; traits perfectly suited to David Byrne's nervous vocal quality.

While *Remain in Light* undeniably was a hybrid album with elements of both West African and Western musical ideals, it was obvious that David Byrne wanted especially to emphasize the presence of the latter. This much was made clear in the press kit letter that Byrne sent out with the record's promotional copies declaring the band's dedicated interest in African music-making. Byrne's prescriptive Africanist presentation was undoubtedly sincere, but it also had a damaging effect on the Talking Heads that forced serious breaches within the band. As drummer Chris Frantz explained, Byrne's copious allusions to African music-making surfaced only *after* the album had already been recorded and packaged. Byrne had grafted the African discourse onto their album; it was not necessarily integral to the music's creation:

> I was so surprised when *Remain in Light* came out and there was this big brouhaha about African drumming and rhythms and stuff. . . . I found that out *after* the album had been released and I got a press kit. . . . There was even a list of books you were supposed to read to understand the record . . . nothing that I had read and nothing that anybody had told me about during the performance of the record. That really threw me for a loop, and that was when things started getting a little bit tense.
>
> There are African rhythms and sensibilities in American pop music all the time, but I kind of resented not being informed that I was playing African rhythms until after the fact.[70]

Frantz's comments hint at some of the troubled relationships hovering over *Remain in Light.* The presence of Africa raises complex issues that bring into question the relationship between rhetoric, musical practice, and musical production. In this context the invocation and realization of an African aesthetic deserves closer inspection.

Making Africa

David Byrne's deliberate attempts to instigate an Africanist discourse around *Remain in Light* proved to be a successful ploy, as critics and journalists willingly followed his lead. Articles and reviews appeared under headlines such as "Africa Calling," ensuring that the record would be heard in accordance with the dictates of Byrne's prescribed cross-cultural and transnational notions. For most reviewers, though, the symbol of Africa was little more than that: a symbol. Reviews of *Remain in Light* rarely bothered to elaborate on what aspects of African music or culture the Talking

Heads were promoting. Africa emerged in the critic's discourse as more of a romanticized "other." The problem was deep-rooted, running straight to the center of one of Byrne's primary sources, John Miller Chernoff's *African Rhythm and African Sensibility.* As Alan Merriam complained of Chernoff's study in the journal *Ethnomusicology,* his book title encompassed the entire range of a continent and peoples, but its contents drew only upon the author's ethnographic journeys in one primary area: Ghana.[71] It was, as such, a misleading reductionism. For a Western rock audience, however, such details were of little consequence. They were content to accept any part of the African musical continent as a substitute for the whole.

In the months after Byrne had sent out the press kit stressing the Talking Heads' connection to African music-making, this specific relationship came under closer scrutiny in various interviews. As Eno and Byrne both revealed, they realized that their musical creations were not necessarily indicative of any specific African music. As Eno explained, "What we were interested in promoting was this idea of interchange between what we knew of American music and what we *understood* about African music, which we don't claim to be a comprehensive or even accurate understanding."[72] Later, in 1983, after visiting Ghana, Eno would reflect on the musicians he had seen and heard on his trip, and how they had forced him to revise his opinions on the validity of his "African" experiments with the Talking Heads:

> Just seeing how they worked with rhythm made me want to give up right away. All the interactions between players and all the kind of funny things going on with the rhythm. . . . there's a lot of humor in it. And then when I started listening to the stuff that we did with the Talking Heads, it was just so wooden by comparison. I couldn't get very excited by it anymore. I could still get excited about it in other terms, but not in rhythmic terms anymore. It seemed to be really naive.[73]

Likewise, Byrne would echo Eno's evaluation, admitting that "there was a lot less Africanism on *Remain in Light* than we implied . . . but the African ideas were more important to get across than specific rhythms."[74] So, as Byrne would have it, what we are left with in *Remain in Light* are not African rhythms, but African "ideas" or the sensibilities of social interaction so crucial to the making of African music.

Even here, though, it is important to question if the rhetoric of communal music-making on *Remain in Light* was in any way analogous with its
interweaving musical rhythms. Chernoff posits a common viewpoint in
African Rhythm and African Sensibility that describes the importance of social interaction in the *performance* of African music: "Music is essential to
life in Africa because Africans use music to mediate their involvement
within a community, and a good musical performance reveals their orientation toward this crucial concern. . . . music's explicit purpose in the various ways it might be defined by Africans, is, essentially socialization."[75] The
irony here is that Byrne used this same language, descriptive of live musical events, to promote *Remain in Light,* a record that had arisen out of a
complex web of musical parts socially disconnected from one another in
time and space, and patched back together through the controlling dictates
of Byrne, Eno, and the mixing board. One of the necessary illusions of music in the age of mechanical reproduction is that the recorded artifact, the
album, is representative of a unified, real-time event. We imagine that what
we hear is taking (or has taken) place with all the participants playing together. The realities of the modern recording studio, however, prove to us
that nothing could be further from the truth.

When it was released in 1980, *Remain in Light* was both a textbook example, and creative extension, of studio manipulation and production
trickery. When considered as such, it is easy to understand why, from his
perspective as the drummer, Chris Frantz took offense at the idea the record
somehow represented African rhythmic sensibilities. Typically in modern
studio recording techniques, the drums and bass are recorded first and provide a rhythmic backbone over which the engineer can then overlay guitars, keyboards and other auxiliary lines and details. For *Remain in Light*
Eno employed a twenty-four-track recorder, using heavy layering to create
a vast distance between what the rhythm section initially played in a skeletal form and what the song emerged as in the end. Because *Remain in Light's*
songs were essentially composed in the studio, the band had no concrete
notion of what the music would sound like, and thus there was no way for
Frantz and bassist Tina Weymouth, while they were recording their parts,
to imagine the interaction with the other layers. The rhythmic complexities that one hears on *Remain in Light* are not to be found generating from
Frantz's rudimentary backbeat grooves or from Weymouth's bass pops.

They arise more out of the layers selected from Byrne's and Eno's collection of isolated riffs.

Clearly in Byrne's and Eno's mind it was their layering, their studio manipulations, and Byrne's lyrics that had come to constitute the substance of the songs. This was verified when the album's first pressing appeared with songwriting credits attributed exclusively to Byrne and Eno. The Talking Heads' other members loudly protested the maneuver, which had reduced them to the relative status of session musicians, and requested that the second pressing revise the credits to read as "Byrne, Eno, Talking Heads." As Frantz, Weymouth, and guitarist Jerry Harrison had rightly argued, the songs had first emerged only out of collective improvised jamming sessions. Even though Byrne and Eno had then taken those raw materials and built the fragments into real, coherent songs, to claim sole ownership through such actions was to deny and erase their point of origination.[76]

As with Adam Ant, it can be said that Byrne and Eno harbored a sincere interest in non-Western music, but were hesitant or entirely unwilling to share with their sources any of their artistic credit or financial gain. Sequestered as they were in the studio, Byrne and Eno drew on West African sources from an idiocultural standpoint, as an effective means of putting a new explicative twist on musical production techniques that belonged to a tradition of avant-garde Western musical experimentation. The ideas of African rhythm and African sensibilities provided them with a new way of understanding what they could create within the studio. It acted as an interpretive map that they could easily slide, as if it were a transparency, on top of their Western aesthetics.

"You Can Dance to This Music if You Want To . . . But Most People Find Themselves Compelled to Listen"[77]

At the time of *Remain in Light*'s release, reviews indicated that the Talking Heads had scored a critical watershed. As Ken Tucker exclaimed in *Rolling Stone*, the band had managed a unique crossover that worked across entrenched racial boundaries:

Seldom in pop-music history has there been a larger gap between what black and white audiences are listening to than there is right now. While blacks are almost entirely uninterested in the clipped, rigid urgency of the New Wave, it's doubtful that more than a small percentage of *Rolling Stone's* predominantly white readership knows anything at all about the summer's [1980's] only piece of culture-defining music, Kurtis Blow's huge [rap] hit, "The Breaks.". . . None of this has escaped the notice of Talking Heads, however, and *Remain in Light* is their brave, absorbing attempt to locate a common ground in today's often hostile musical community.[78]

Even before the album had been officially released, however, the band had visibly broken racial lines in the summer of 1980 by welcoming five new musicians into their fold, including African American artists Bernie Worrell (keyboards), Nona Hendryx (vocals), and Busta Jones (bass), all of whom would enable the band to reproduce *Remain in Light's* complex arrangements on tour.

At the conclusion of his review, Tucker summarized what, for him, was the band's most significant crossover achievement: the Talking Heads had made music to which one could both "dance and think."[79] The strength of such a seemingly simple statement lies in the conviction that the Talking Heads had been able to bring together two acts that rock music criticism had generally assumed to be incompatible with one another.[80] Other critics noted this accomplishment as well. Mitchell Cohen of *Creem* referred to *Remain in Light* as "cerebral body music," and a "calculatedly hypnotic examination of white rock's burden."[81] "Body music" was, of course, a racially loaded term, one that, as Simon Frith asserted in his 1981 study *Sound Effects,* was equated with "black music." As Frith summarized, "Black music expresses the body, hence sexuality, with a directly physical beat and an intense, emotional sound—the sound and the beat are *felt* rather than interpreted via a set of conventions. . . . Black music as 'body music,' is therefore 'natural,' 'immediate,' 'spontaneous.'"[82] In this respect, the designation of "black music" as "body music" has never been neutral. When imagined in combination with sexually potent black dancing bodies, "body music" has been denounced as a threat to white moralities, and has stirred controversy, whether it be in relation to the "black" syncopated rhythms of early-twentieth-century ragtime or to the "fear of a black planet" articulated in Public Enemy's late 1980s rap music.[83]

The idea, however, that "black music" is somehow synonymous with rhythm, dancing, and the "body" is highly problematic. Such logic could lead one to believe that "white music" is aligned exclusively with the "mind" and its ability to retain narrative and structural complexities, as one might find in European folk traditions of storytelling or the highbrow aesthetics of European art music. The musicologist Philip Tagg has rightly criticized such one-to-one correspondences between race and musical form as exercises in essentialist reductionism.[84] Nevertheless, such stereotypes were absolutely common to rock music in the 1970s. One need only look at the popular genres of that decade. Critics during that time routinely praised the efforts of reflective, artistic white singer-songwriters and fans filled the stadium shows of virtuosic progressive rock bands, while, in contrast, black American music styles like funk and disco were categorized and dismissed as music for dancing and little else. To appreciate the Talking Heads' achievement of collapsing "dancing" and "thinking" at this time, then, is to understand the nature of the imagined boundaries they had transgressed.

Most of all, white new wave bands like the Talking Heads provided a safe entry for white audiences into the black musical appeal of funk. Dancing along to the Talking Heads' funky rhythms was not dancing in the ghettos. It was dancing without the social baggage of black America. And when the Talking Heads invoked the symbolic power of Africa, it presented a distanced, exoticized, and unthreatening version of blackness; one unburdened by the social stigmas of disadvantaged urban Americans. It is undeniable that the Talking Heads' statements about African music and society lent a credibility to *Remain in Light* that likely would not have been accorded them had the band simply chosen to champion the equally important influence of African American music and culture on their music. One journalist posed the position to Byrne in blunt terms: "Don't you think a helluva lot of the critics might have taken [*Remain in Light*] as a plain ole funk album if you hadn't indicated where all this stuff was coming from, including which books on African art?" Byrne's response: "I can't tell if that would have happened. Could be. I wouldn't have been surprised."[85] But then they would have been only dancing, and not thinking.

Postlude

In the spring of 1981, only a few months after *Kings of the Wild Frontier* and *Remain in Light* had been released, Michael Hill of *New York Rocker* undertook a unique journalistic sociological experiment, the goal of which was to explore the extent to which the explosion of new wave crossover acts had truly "crossed over" between white and black audiences. A former resident of Orange, New Jersey, Hill returned to his old high school neighborhood intent on probing the listening habits of its current students. While Hill was denied access to the students of his old school, he did eventually find three white students from Glen Ridge High, a white, affluent school, and three black students from Orange High School, who were willing to participate in his project. Hill explained his experiment:

> What I had proposed was simple: invite three students from the predominantly white school and three students from the largely black school—all of them articulate, interested in music, and a little street-wise—to two separate listening parties. For the white kids, I would choose songs ranging from Prince's pop funk to the Funky Four Plus One's rap. For the black kids, I would choose from a large selection of mostly New York–based cross-over acts, from David Byrne and Brian Eno to the young Bronx band, ESG. I would ask them to relate the music to their own tastes, and to imagine it in their familiar environments. Would the Talking Heads' "Cross-eyed and Painless" go over at a disco dance? Would Dee Dee Sharp Gamble's "Breaking and Entering" make it a rock party?[86]

The results from Hill's project confirmed that there was indeed a gap between the aesthetics of white fans and black fans. It was apparent that very little black music had crossed over into the listening habits of the white fans that Hill interviewed. As one of the white students, who played in a punk band, explained, the black music that he heard seemed to lack the "genuine feeling" that he valued in the music of punk groups like the Sex Pistols and Public Image Limited. All three students agreed that they might dance to disco (their generic term for any type of black music, including rap) at parties, but that they felt no attachment to the music. As one of the students summarized in response to hearing James Brown's "Rapp Payback": "It's good to dance to, but it evokes no emotion in me."[87] Because the music did not make them dance and think at the same time, it had little crossover potential. The split between the body and mind remained intact.

The black students with whom Hill conducted his listening party were all members of a DJ rap crew that performed at school and parties as the Faze Four Rappers. Like the one white student who played in a band, they were especially attuned to the music, judging it in terms of how they might mix it and rap over it. As Hill witnessed, of prime importance to them was the groove and the beat. These were musical qualities that transcended racial and social lines and that allowed a space for white new wave groups like the Police on the turntables of countless black DJs. As for the two "crossover" new wave bands that this chapter has examined, Hill played tracks off of each of their 1980 releases for the Faze Four Rappers, and their responses highlight the disparity between the two. When faced with Adam and the Ants' "Antmusic," the rap crew's response was swift and blunt: "It wouldn't make it at our parties."[88] As their reaction made clear, Adam and the Ants' party soundtrack for the white middle-class carnival simply did not translate and did not groove properly. Its crossover was figurative, not literal, and functioned primarily for its white audience as an imperial playground and fantasyland. When Hill played them the Talking Heads' "Crosseyed and Painless" from *Remain in Light*, however, their reaction was different. To one of them, the beat sounded "old," but to another it showed potential: "If [black] radio played it enough, people would like it."[89] In the final analysis, the Talking Heads, for all the questionable discourse surrounding their music, fashioned a further reaching crossover in the United Sates than Adam and Ants.

As Steven Feld has acknowledged, *Remain in Light* represented a "world beat" watershed, one whose true ramifications would only become apparent in the years immediately following its release. There had, of course, long been a cross-cultural and cross-racial flow of ideas and inspiration among musicians prior to *Remain in Light*. Feld mentions the examples of James Brown, who borrowed complex African polyrhythms for his funk style, and Fela Anikulapo Kuti, who borrowed the scratch guitar technique from James Brown for his own Afrobeat style. In both cases, Feld points out, the economic stakes were insignificant. After *Remain in Light*, however, such transactions and exchanges began to register as more than mere financial tremors. As high-profile world beat releases like Paul Simon's *Graceland* (1986) generated millions of dollars and critical acclaim, no matter how much the white musicians paid tribute to the source of their inspiration, "The gap between the lion's share and the originator's share enlarged, and the critical discourse on race and rip-offs was immediate and heated."[90] In this respect we can view the tremendous financial success of both *Remain in Light* and *Kings of the Wild Frontier* as the beginnings of the artistically fertile, but ultimately inequitable and exploitative, rise of world beat and world music in the 1980s.

Epilogue: The New Wave Revival

Pop cult revivals tend to arrive punctually after roughly 20 years—just long enough for a period to acquire the charm of remoteness . . . At nightspots like Berliniamsburg in the Williamsburg section of Brooklyn, they're adopting new wave fashion, with its asymmetrical haircuts, skinny ties worn over T-shirts, and studded belts and bracelets—and they're doing so in a spirit that curiously mingles irony with admiration.

—Simon Reynolds, 2002[1]

By the early years of the twenty-first century, new wave had lain dormant within pop culture's past for nearly two decades. However, as the music critic Simon Reynolds points out, in the new millennium the 1980s and its new wave style suddenly grew ripe for recycling. Surveying the pop culture landscape in a piece for the *New York Times* entitled "The 70's are so 90's. The 80's are the Thing Now," Reynolds found evidence of an 1980s revival at every turn. Clubgoers at new nightspots like Berliniamsburg in Brooklyn were dancing to 1980s synthpop music from the likes of the Human League and Soft Cell. Radio stations had begun switching over to retro eighties formats. In a nod to the popularity of *That 70's Show*, Fox was now airing a new television sitcom, *That 80's Show*. Meanwhile, over on the VH-1 Classic network, the show *We are the 80's* featured retro music videos from long-forgotten new wave favorites. By the end of 2002, VH-1 would extend this nostalgic reverie even further with a new series, *I Love the 80's*, that featured talking head pop culture celebrities looking back upon the decade with a mix of ironic bemusement and rhapsodic admiration.

While Reynolds's article presented a convincing case for a 1980s revival in 2002, in truth pronouncements of such revivals had been appearing sporadically since the mid-1990s. In 1996 rock critic Gina Arnold had proclaimed the return of new wave on the heels of Rhino Records' fifteen-volume compact disc anthology *Just Can't Get Enough: New Wave Hits of the '80s* and the sounds of new "geek rock" bands like the Presidents of the United States of America that drew liberally from new wave's nerdy white lineage.[2] Over the next two years, a number of Hollywood films such as *Grosse Point Blank* (1997), *Romy and Michelle's High School Reunion* (1997), and the hugely successful *The Wedding Singer* (1998)—all of which looked back toward, or were set in, the 1980s, and featured soundtracks populated by new wave hits from the past—signaled speculation that the lucrative seventies revival that had dominated the 1990s was ready to give way to the "unexploited wilderness" of the eighties.[3] Clearly one could attribute the rise of an eighties revival at the turn of the new millennium to a generational shift, a changing of the guard in the entertainment business that had seen a number of twenty- and thirty-somethings assume positions of creative control within the industry. But it also reflected broader changes within the circulation of rock music itself. Throughout the 1990s, an unending procession of compact disc reissues and box sets, the emergence of glossy rock history magazines like *Mojo* and *Uncut* and the establishment of the Rock and Roll Hall of Fame and Museum in 1995 all pushed an awareness of rock's canonical history into the foreground. In such a climate, it was only a matter of time before such attention would turn toward new wave and the 1980s.

Revivals of this nature, which unearth music and culture from the past to be consumed once again, are central to any understanding of new wave's continuing relevance, but as Reynolds was also quick to note in his 2002 article, equally crucial was the rise of a crop of new artists who swore an allegiance to new wave's influence. For Reynolds, the most intriguing of these were "electro" artists like Adult and Fischerspooner, whose music took its inspiration from the once modern, but now "old fashioned synthesizers and drum machines" of the early 1980s, "when electronic music seemed alien and forbiddingly novel."[4] Reynolds labeled their stance as a "retro-futurist" revolt against the "overproduced" sophistication of contemporary musical technology, and to him it represented the most important musical theme of the eighties revival. Just as the original new wave musicians had turned to the remnants of past modernities as points of inspiration, so this new crop of revivalists viewed new wave's self-consciously modern but also quaintly archaic synthesizers as items of wonder and curious fascination. As retro objects they held "the lure of yesterday's tomorrows."[5]

Reynolds's assessment of the synthesizer's renewed appeal would indeed turn out to be prophetic, as throughout 2003 and 2004, a "technostalgic" revival of new wave synthpop gathered steam.[6] Groups like Ladytron, the Postal Service, Cut Copy, the Bravery, and the Killers featured vintage synthesizer tones and styles in ways that set them boldly apart from the postgrunge and nü metal mainstream of early-millennium guitar rock. The Killers, in particular, garnered significant airplay and exposure as their debut album landed in *Billboard*'s Top 10. In recent years this retro-futurism has expanded even further, most notably in hip-hop, where a number of artists have turned to new wave for their samples, ranging from Mobb Deep's use of Thomas Dolby's 1983 hit "She Blinded Me with Science" on the 2004 single "Got it Twisted" to Rihanna's reworking of Soft Cell's 1981 hit "Tainted Love" on her chart-topping 2006 single, "SOS." Retro-futurism even found its way into Disney, as the company turned heads in 2006 by signing a revamped version of Devo, called Dev2.0, to its record label. As conceived by main Devo member Gerald Casale, the Dev2.0 music and video project consisted of five fresh-faced tween boys and girls dressed in retro black and red Devo outfits singing and miming along on their instruments to updated versions of such synthesized Devo standards as "Whip It" and "Peek A Boo." No doubt Casale reveled in the irony that he was now in cahoots with a company whose past visions of modernity—realized in the utopian "Tomorrowland" of late 1950s Disneyland, with its flying saucer bumper cars and modern domestic appliance exhibits—were precisely the type of retro-futurist kitsch that Devo had lampooned at the turn of the 1980s.

There has been a side effect, however, to the new wave revival's retro-futurist focus. As new wave has increasingly become equated with the nostalgically aged technological modernity of 1980s synthpop, new wave's deeper roots in the late 1970s have become obscured. Groups and artists like the Pretenders, Elvis Costello, Joe Jackson, Squeeze, and the Knack—all of whom essentially launched new wave in the United States—are much more likely to turn up on a classic rock playlist than they are to show up listed as an influence on some new wave revivalist's MySpace page. As we

Figure 17: Lead singer Nicole Stoehr of Dev2.0, from the video for "Beautiful World" (2006).

find new wave increasingly collapsed, for the sake of convenience, into a mélange of synthesizers, MTV videos, and overarching 1980s nostalgia, the earlier new wavers have drifted backward into a closer association with 1970s punk. Consider, for example, Stuart Borthwick and Ron Moy's 2004 study, *Popular Music Genres: An Introduction.*[7] Comprising twelve chapters that explore twelve main genres, the book deals with 1970s new wave as part of its main chapter on punk rock, wherein Blondie, Elvis Costello, and other early new wave artists are covered in the space of one paragraph. Meanwhile, the authors devote an entire twenty-page chapter to the early 1980s synthpop of Gary Numan, the Human League, Orchestral Manoeuvres in the Dark, and Duran Duran—those artists who form the strongest link with the current new wave revival.[8] In the end, the genre of synthpop provides a coherency that new wave's broad stylistic sprawl lacks.

But perhaps it is fitting that the first wave of new wave artists from the

1970s should not be swept up so fully in this current new wave revival. After all, as we have seen, they themselves were essentially engrossed in their own plundering of the past, revisiting the music and popular culture of the late 1950s and early 1960s in numerous ways. That nostalgia occurred along many dimensions, whether it was Elvis Costello's nerdish Buddy Holly glasses or Attractions keyboardist Steve Nieve's use of the 1960s Vox Continental organ, the Knack's brazen pilfering of the Beatles' iconography, or the B-52's ironic rendering of 1960s surf, pop, and garage band culture. As George Lipsitz has argued in his book *Time Passages,* moments such as these should not be seen simply as conservative rehashings but as part of popular music's dialogic stream, a means through which musicians can "rearticulate" or "dis-articulate" a dominant ideology.[9] For new wave's first wave, the rock music of the late 1950s and early 1960s loomed as a potential source of renewal, a presence that invoked styles that seemed to have gone missing with the dawn of the 1970s. Looking back on adolescent memories of AM radio, dance crazes, high school garage bands, and the 1960s mod and art deco revival, new wavers resituated these nostalgic elements as resistant measures against the perceived commercialism and excess of 1970s mainstream rock. The past, in effect, helped them to stage "a revolt into style."[10]

When we examine the recent new wave revival from this dialogic stance, we find many similarities with the original new wave's relationship with the past. Today's revivalists view the 1980s as a golden age, a repository of lost values loosely secured in fading childhood memories. The 1980s also function as a measure of difference against the present. As Brandon Flowers, the front man for the Killers, explained in a 2004 interview with *Spin* magazine, as a kid growing up in the 1990s his interest in the new wave effectively distanced him from the prevailing musical tastes of his peers:

Question: Which bands inspired you to make music rather than just listen to it?

Answer: The Cars. I bought Greatest Hits when I was 12. It was really weird because other kids were buying Tool and Nirvana and I was buying the Cars and Psychedelic Furs. I was pretty alienated as a kid.[11]

It is worth pausing for a moment to unpack Flowers's answer. According to Flowers, in the 1990s—when alternative rock bands like Tool and Nirvana popularized the sounds of societal disaffection and alienation—the only way to be a *truly* alienated kid was to return to the once modern, commercially accessible pop sounds of the Cars and Psychedelic Furs. For Flowers and other revivalists, new wave was appealing precisely because, unlike alternative rock, it did not deem one's personal pain and crises to be markers of authenticity or a validating form of "therapy rock."[12] Rather, new wave's dated technological modernity allowed for a celebration of the "synthetic and artificial," and presented the opportunity to perform one's identity.[13]

This accent on new wave as a musical genre of artifice and performance comes across clearly in the ways that the new wave revivalists have both presented themselves and been received. Consider the three following examples. The first comes from a 2005 band biography of aptly named U.K. artists the Modern; the second from a 2006 review of Black Tie Dynasty's album *Movements;* the third from a 2009 interview with lead singer Elly Jackson of the British electropop duo La Roux.

The Modern bask in a sexier, synthetic and forward-thinking space. Obsessed with glamour, theatricality, synthesizers and style, they're pure pop with brains and balls, electroclash with warmth and tunes, with a sharp New Wave edge . . . we like to follow the rules of theatre, and we like to dress up and put on a show.[14]

Any self-respecting child of the uber-days of new wave, the early 1980s, with its look-into-the-mirror-darkly synth and high drama dance tendencies, will immediately recognize the pitched personas that these Dallas lads inhabit like a second skin.[15]

That whole glamour thing pop had in the Eighties. It used to be a show all the time, with outfits and make-up. I think dressing up and characterisation have been missing from pop. The Nineties will always be known to me as the "casual wear decade": khaki, baggy trousers and vest tops. Fashion is definitely coming back, the glamour and drama is returning.[16]

Drama, dance, theater, performance: it appears that new wave's retro-futurism offers the chance to slip into a persona, "a second skin." Then again, it also offers the chance to slip out of that persona without raising too many eyebrows. Maybe this helps to explain why three of the bands who gained the most press as part of an eighties revival in 2004—the Killers, the Bravery, and the Stills—all deliberately left behind their new wave influences after their debut albums. In each case, they shed their new wave persona, so to speak, to take a turn instead into the sounds of 1970s classic rock.

In the end, new wave has become, like so many other past styles, just one of rock's many accumulated iterations. In our current musical culture, where a seemingly endless choice of easily accessible downloads makes for eclectic and potentially omnivorous listening habits, new wave has become a pit-stop style, a place where one can pause and rest for a moment before moving onto something else equally as intriguing. While its dominance has long since passed, new wave continues to linger as a residual musical modernity ripe for future revivals and reinterpretations.

Notes

Introduction

1. Tim Sommer, "The Sound of the Sinceros," *Trouser Press,* February 1980, 12.

2. Jim Green, "Blondie: Progress Report from the Power Station," *Trouser Press,* September 1979, 14.

3. Joe Gore and Andrew Goodwin, "Your Time Is Gonna Come: Talking about Led Zeppelin," *One Two Three Four* 4 (Winter 1987), 7.

4. Quoted in Robert Elms, "B-52's," *New Styles New Sounds Magazine,* April 1982. Reprinted in *The Third Pyramid: The B-52's Archive,* http://www.btinternet.com/~roc.lobsta/newsounds.html.

5. The average tempo on the B-52's debut 1979 album is 159 BPM. Compare that with two of the 1970s' top-selling studio records: *Led Zeppelin 4* (108 BPM) and Fleetwood Mac *Rumours* (107 BPM). This number is skewed, of course, by the fact that both the Led Zeppelin and Fleetwood Mac albums are populated by numerous songs hovering in the 70–80 BPM range. Nonetheless, between the Led Zeppelin and Fleetwood Mac records there are a total of only three tracks that register a tempo faster than that of the B-52's's *slowest* song (135 BPM).

6. To name just one such station: K-15 AM, Phoenix. See "Hello It's Me," *Trouser Press,* December 1980, 2.

7. For a good overview and critique of the different disciplinary understandings of modern, modernity, and modernism, see Susan Stanford Friedman, "Definitional Excursions: The Meanings of *Modern/Modernity/Modernism,*" *MODERNISM/modernity* 8, no. 3 (2001): 493–513.

8. Ibid., 503–5.

9. Fredric Jameson, "The Politics of Theory: Ideological Positions in the Postmodernism Debate," *New German Critique* 33 (Autumn 1984): 54.

10. Jon Stratton, "Beyond Art: Postmodernism and the Case of Popular Music," *Theory, Culture & Society* 6, no. 1 (1989): 31–57.

11. Andrew Goodwin addresses the many problems that arise from reading postmodernism's aesthetic attributes onto assumed sociological and cultural formations

in "Popular Music and Postmodern Theory," in *The Postmodern Arts: An Introductory Reader*, ed. Nigel Wheale (New York: Routledge, 1995), 80–100.

12. See, for example, Bernard Yack, *The Fetishism of Modernities: Epochal Self-Consciousness in Contemporary Social and Political Thought* (Notre Dame: University of Notre Dame Press, 1997).

13. Horn and the song's cowriter Bruce Wooley have claimed that "Video" was inspired by J. G. Ballard's 1960 short story, "The Sound-Sweep," which describes the rise of inaudible ultrasonic music, and the subsequent passing of a once glorious opera diva. See Ballard, "The Sound-Sweep," in *The Voices of Time* (London: Victor Gollancz, 1985), 41–79.

14. For an analysis and interpretation of the song's production techniques, see Timothy Warner, *Pop Music—Technology and Creativity: Trevor Horn and the Digital Revolution* (Burlington, VT: Ashgate, 2003), 41–49.

15. For more on the influences between disco and new wave, see Charles Kronengold, "Exchange Theories in Disco, New Wave, and Album-Oriented Rock," *Criticism* 50, no. 1 (2008): 43–82.

16. Ira A. Robbins, ed., *The New Trouser Press Record Guide*, 3rd ed. (New York: Collier, 1989), vii.

17. See, for example, Dick Hebdige, *Subculture: The Meaning of Style* (New York: Routledge, 1979); Greil Marcus, *Lipstick Traces: A Secret History of the Twentieth Century* (Cambridge: Harvard University Press, 1989); Neil Nehring, *Flowers in the Dustbin: Culture and Anarchy in Postwar England* (Ann Arbor: University of Michigan Press, 1993); Lauraine Leblanc, *Pretty in Punk: Girls' Gender Resistance in a Boys' Subculture* (New Brunswick, NJ: Rutgers University Press, 1999); Steven Taylor, *False Prophets: Field Notes from the Underground* (Hanover, NH: Wesleyan University Press, 2004); Robert T. Wood, *Straightedge Youth: Complexity and Contradictions of a Subculture* (Syracuse, NY: Syracuse University Press, 2006).

18. See, for example, Andrew Goodwin, *Dancing in the Distraction Factory: Music Television and Popular Culture* (New York: Routledge, 1992); Christina Bodinger-deUriarte, "Opposition to Hegemony in the Music of Devo: A Simple Matter of Remembering," *Journal of Popular Culture* 18, no. 4 (1984–85): 56–71; Gillian Rodger, "Drag, Camp and Gender Subversion in the Music and Videos of Annie Lennox," *Popular Music* 23, no. 1 (2004): 17–29. Two notable exceptions that address the new wave movement directly and in depth are John Covach, "Pangs of History in Late 1970s New-Wave Rock," in *Analyzing Popular Music*, ed. Allan Moore (New York: Cambridge University Press, 2003), 173–95, and Kronengold, "Exchange Theories."

19. Ira A. Robbins, ed., *The Trouser Press Guide to New Wave Records* (New York: Charles Scribner's Sons, 1983).

20. Glenn A. Baker and Stuart Cope, *The New Music* (New York: Harmony Books, 1981).

21. David Bianco, *Who's New Wave in Music: An Illustrated Encyclopedia 1976–1982 (The First Wave)* (Ann Arbor, MI: Pierian Press, 1985).

22. Patricia Romanowski and Holly George-Warren, eds., *The New Rolling Stone Encyclopedia of Rock & Roll* (New York: Fireside, 1995), 709; emphasis added. In all fairness, even a staunch new wave supporter like Robbins considered the genre label to be problematic. He concedes in the preface to the first *Trouser Press Guide to New*

Wave Records (xiii) that "new wave is, admittedly, a pretty *meaningless* term" (emphasis added).

23. "New Wave," *All Music Guide,* http://www.allmusic.com/cg/amg.dll?p=amg&sql=77:381.

24. From the original film soundtrack to *The Decline of Western Civilization,* Slash records, SR-105.

Chapter 1

1. *Random House Unabridged Dictionary,* 2nd ed., s.v. "new wave."

2. Giroud first used the phrase *new wave* in an article entitled "Report on Today's Youth" that appeared in the October 3, 1957, issue of *L'Express.* See Jean Douchet, *French New Wave,* trans. Robert Bonnono (New York: Distributed Art Publishers, 1999), 164.

3. Truffaut was the most vitriolic of the new wave critics. His most famous critique of French national cinema remains an early 1954 article, "Une certain tendance du cinéma français," originally published in *Cahiers du Cinéma.* It is translated as "A Certain Tendency of the French Cinema" in *Movies and Methods: An Anthology,* ed. Bill Nichols (Berkeley: University of California Press, 1976), 224–37.

4. David Fallows credits Johannes Wolf with first using *Ars Nova* as a general periodic designation in his 1904 study *Geschichte der Mensural-Notation von 1250–1460* (Hildesheim: George Olms; Weisbaden: Brietkopf & Härtel, 1965). See Fallows, "Ars Nova," *The New Grove Dictionary of Music and Musicians,* vol. 2, ed. Stanley Sadie (London: Macmillan, 2001), 80–81.

5. As Fred Davis points out in *Fashion, Culture and Identity* (Chicago: University of Chicago Press 1992), 104: "A metaphor often employed for the fashion cycle compares it to waves in the sea. As one wave crests and begins to dissipate, new waves form; these, too, will crest and possibly take over the prior wave." He adds that these cycles are by no means clearly delineated: "As on a roily sea, several different kinds of waves (long/short, large/small, major/minor, etc) overlap at the same moment. Depending on what feature of the fashion repertory one is observing (e.g., silhouette, hem length, fabric, color, decolletage), a different wave pattern is likely to form."

6. Christopher Breward describes the "new look" in *The Culture of Fashion: A New History of Fashionable Dress* (New York: Manchester University Press, 1994), 191. As he explains, it was controversial because it compromised the accepted look of "wartime and post-war austerity" and decidedly objectified women as openly sensuous.

7. Shaw presents his breakdown of two-year cycles, spanning the years 1956 to 1974 in his editorial-essay "'It All Came Back': A Trenchant Analysis of the Pop Revival," *Who Put the Bomp* 12 (Spring 1975): 4, 16.

8. Raymond Williams, *Marxism and Literature* (New York: Oxford University Press, 1977), 121–27.

9. Fields is quoted in Roman Kozak's report on the first National Academy of Recording Arts and Sciences (NARAS) seminar devoted to new wave music, "Punk Music Analyzed, Praised and Blasted at N.Y. Session," *Billboard,* March 25, 1978, 26.

10. Nick Kent, "New York: The Dark Side of Town," *New Musical Express,* May 5,

1973. Reprinted in *Rock's Backpages,* http://www.rocksbackpages.com.article.html?ArticleID=16007. Dave Marsh, "Various: New York New Wave," *Melody Maker,* October 6, 1973. Reprinted in *Rock's Backpages,* http://www.rocksbackpages.com.article.html?ArticleID=9049.

11. Craig Bromberg, *The Wicked Ways of Malcolm McLaren* (New York: Harper & Row, 1989), 65.

12. Ingham is quoted in Jon Savage, *England's Dreaming: Anarchy, Sex Pistols, Punk Rock, and Beyond* (New York: St. Martin's Press, 1992), 159.

13. In the September 28, 1976, issue of *Sniffin' Glue,* Mark Perry refers to punk as a "new wave," wary of the explosion about to occur: "I don't wanna see the Pistols, the Clash etc. turned into more AC/DCs and Doctors of Madness. This 'new-wave' has got to take in everything, including posters, record-covers, stage presentation, the lot! You know, they'll be coming soon, all those big companies out to make more money on the 'new, young bands.' Well, they can piss off." By the next issue, October 1976, "new wave" had gravitated to the fanzine's front page, with the heading *Sniffin' Glue . . . and Other Rock'n'Roll Habits for the New-Wave!* Both fanzines are reprinted in their entirety in Mark Perry, *Sniffin' Glue: The Essential Punk Accessory* (London: Sanctuary House, 2000).

14. On the early usages of "new wave" in *New York Rocker,* see Bernard Gendron, *Between Montmartre and the Mudd Club: Popular Music and the Avant-Garde* (Chicago: University of Chicago Press, 2002), 271–72.

15. Douchet, *French New Wave,* 118. It is worth noting that the French new wave directors were greatly impressed with and influenced by the Italian neorealist films of the late 1940s.

16. Ibid., 187.

17. Ibid., 171.

18. Ira Robbins, "New Wave R.I.P.: Nails in the Coffin," *Trouser Press,* October 1977, 20–22, 32.

19. As Robbins points out, the week that the Stranglers' album (*Rattus Norvegicus*) was number four on the charts, Pink Floyd (*Animals*) was at number five. See Robbins, "New Wave R.I.P.," 21.

20. Hebdige, *Subculture,* 94.

21. Dave Laing, *One Chord Wonders: Power and Meaning in Punk Rock* (Philadelphia: Open University Press, 1985), 32–35.

22. Ibid., 106.

23. Caroline Coon, "Punk Alphabet," *Melody Maker,* November 27, 1976, 33.

24. See, for example, Chas de Whalley, "Jam: Maximum New Wave," *Sounds,* March 5, 1977, in which Jam leader Paul Weller explains that the Jam is not a punk band, but agrees to the new wave label. Reprinted in *Rock's Backpages* http://www.rocksbackpages.com/article.html?ArticleID=8292.

25. See Stein's comments in Roman Kozak, "Punk Rock Grows in N.Y.," *Billboard,* November 20, 1976, 86; and Marty Thau's comments in Clinton Heylin's *From the Velvets to the Voidoids: A Pre-Punk History for a Post-Punk World* (New York: Penguin, 1993), 254.

26. Quoted in Clinton Heylin, *Babylon's Burning: From Punk to Grunge* (New York: Canongate, 2007), 298.

27. Jon Savage, "New Musick," *Sounds,* November 26, 1977; reprinted in *Time Travel: Pop, Media and Sexuality, 1977–96* (London: Chatto & Windus, 1996), 37–38. For a thorough overview of post-punk, see Simon Reynolds, *Rip It Up and Start Again: Postpunk 1978–1984* (London: Faber and Faber, 2005).

28. Quoted in Kevin Eden, *Wire . . . Everybody Loves a History* (Wembley: SAF, 1991), 26–27.

29. Simon Frith, *Sound Effects: Youth, Leisure, and the Politics of Rock'n'Roll* (New York: Pantheon, 1981), 160. While Frith, himself, never refers to the bands in question as part of a "post-punk" movement (he situates them instead as part of a "punk vanguard"), he would become a vocal proponent of this new experimental wave of bands. See, especially, Frith, "The Return of Passion," *New Statesman,* October 2, 1981, 24–25.

30. Greil Marcus, "Wake Up! It's Fab, It's Passionate. It's Wild, It's Intelligent! It's the Hot New Sound of England Today!" *Rolling Stone,* July 24, 1980, 41.

31. Laing, *One Chord Wonders,* 109–13.

32. Caroline Coon, "If the Kids are United . . ." *Sounds,* June 3, 1978. Reprinted in *Rock's Backpages* http://www.rocksbackpages.com/article.html?ArticleID=11035.

33. "The New Wave Coming of Age: A Billboard Spotlight," *Billboard,* January 14, 1978, 47–67.

34. Seymour Stein, "Assault on the Industry!" in "The New Wave Coming of Age: A Billboard Spotlight," *Billboard,* January 14, 1978, 49.

35. Mitch Cohen, "What Price Glory? Ramones Soldier On," *Creem,* June 1980, 25.

36. Billy Altman, "Review of *The Cars,*" *Creem,* September 1978, 61.

37. Covach, "Pangs of History."

38. Kronengold, "Exchange Theories."

39. For more on the song's harmonic analysis, see Covach, "Pangs of History," 191–93.

40. Bill Flanagan, "Cookin' With Roy Thomas Baker," *Trouser Press,* January 1982, 26.

41. This rhythmic emphasis emerged most of all from main songwriter and rhythm guitarist Ric Ocasek's approach to constructing the songs, which began with a strong rhythmic foundation. For more on Ocasek and the band's songwriting style, see J. D. Considine, "The Cars," *Musician Player & Listener,* January 1982, 60–61.

42. Craig Leon, quoted in Mark Cunningham, *Good Vibrations: A History of Record Production* (Chessington, Surrey: Castle Communications, 1996), 278.

43. Leon, quoted in Cunningham, *Good Vibrations,* 278.

44. Robinson is quoted in Jon Pareles, "Power Steering," *Rolling Stone,* January 25, 1979, 61.

45. Judd's particular innovation was that he turned away from "painter's paint" and instead sought to stock his studio with the common metallic colors of the automotive industry. So if solid red and black seemed like a natural fit for a group named the Cars, there was indeed good reason. For more on Judd's use of color, see David Batchelor, "Everything as Colour," in *Donald Judd,* ed. Nicholas Serota (New York: Distributed Art Publishers, 2004), 71. Kraftwerk fully embraced their homage to the Russian Constructivists, even jokingly attributing its album cover design to the long deceased constructivist El Lissitzky.

46. Alan Betrock and Andy Schwartz, "The Future's Gleam: A Rock and Roll Survey," *New York Rocker,* September 1978, 32.

47. Robert Christgau, "Triumph of the New Wave: Results of the Fifth (or Sixth) Annual Pazz and Jop Critics' Poll," *Village Voice,* January 22, 1979, 1, 39–41.

48. Yetnikoff continues: "People used to walk into record stores to buy one album and walk out with three. Now they just buy the one they want." Quoted in Jim Miller, "Is Rock On the Rocks?" *Newsweek,* April 19, 1982, 105.

49. "Record Companies Get Badly Scratched," *Business Week,* August 6, 1979, 27.

50. "Record Company Firings Continue," *Rolling Stone,* January 24, 1980, 27.

51. Denisoff gives a good detailed account of the 1979 depression in *Tarnished Gold: The Record Industry Revisited* (New Brunswick, NJ: Transaction Books, 1986), especially 106–19.

52. Radcliffe Joe, "Dearth of Superstars Dims Industry Future: Producer Rather than Artist is Star," *Billboard,* July 14, 1979, 46, 67, 71.

53. Will Straw, "Popular Music As Cultural Commodity: The American Recorded Music Industries, 1976–1985 (United States)," PhD diss., McGill University, 1990, 269.

54. For more on Hurrah's transformation from discotheque to rock disco, and its place in the perceived rock/disco split, see Tim Lawrence, *Love Saves the Day: A History of American Dance Music Culture, 1970–1979* (Durham, NC: Duke University Press, 2003), 394–95.

55. Roman Kozak, "Rock Disco Pops in N.Y. Houses," *Billboard,* July 14, 1979, 46, 66, 86.

56. In his excellent 1981 overview of the rock disco circuit, Vincent Nicolosi estimates the number of rock discos at more than two hundred. See Nicolosi, "Rock Discos: Why Are They Here? What Do They Want?!" *Trouser Press,* August 1981, 25–27, 57.

57. The prices in this sentence come from the three following sources: $70,000–$100,000, see Frith, *Sound Effects,* 147; $500,000, see Adam White and Dick Nusser, "New Wave Rockers Click in U.S. Mart," *Billboard,* August 18, 1979, 15; $2,000 to $4,000, see David Kahne, "Producing: The Art of Low-Budget Recording," *Music & Sound Output,* December 1982, 106. Kahne produced the 1981 debuts by San Francisco bands Red Rockers and Romeo Void for $2,000 and $4,000 respectively. As he mentions, these prices were more similar to the budgets of the early 1960s than those of the present day.

58. Ian Copeland, *Wild Thing: The Backstage, On the Road, In the Studio, Off the Charts Memoirs of Ian Copeland* (New York: Simon & Schuster, 1995), 237.

59. Don Waller, "Live Reviews: The Knack, Starwood," *New York Rocker,* April–May 1979, 48.

60. Terry Atkinson, "The Knack: Yesterday and Today," *Rolling Stone,* October 18, 1979, 32.

61. Jay Merritt, "Rock Strikes Back!" *Rolling Stone,* March 20, 1980, 23.

62. Jim Green, "Changing Records," *Trouser Press,* March 1980, 26.

63. Cary Darling, "New Wave Wins Programming OK," *Billboard,* November 10, 1979, 1, 28.

64. Timothy White, "Billy Joel is Angry," *Rolling Stone,* September 4, 1980, 40.

65. Richard Grabel, "Déjà Vu: Only the Bands have Changed at the Heatwave Festival," *Trouser Press* (reprinted from the *New Musical Express*), November 1980, 25.

66. James Henke, "Heatwave: Did New Wave Sell Out?" *Rolling Stone*, October 16, 1980, 24.

67. John Sippel, "Profit Push: Execs Cite More Conservative Acquisition & Recording Plans," *Billboard*, May 1, 1982, 10.

68. Ed Harrison, "AOR Cuts New Wave Shows," *Billboard*, September 26, 1981, 1.

69. It was not always the case that AOR stations sought a demographic older than twenty-five-year-olds. As Ken Barnes explains, in the mid-1970s stations were forced to adjust from their "main demographic cell, [of] men between 18 and 24" when they found that the general audience was aging, and becoming more "adult." See his "Top 40 Radio: A Fragment of the Imagination," in *Facing the Music*, ed. Simon Frith (New York: Pantheon, 1988), 28.

70. Harrison, "AOR Cuts," 14.

71. By 1986 college radio had risen in prominence to the point where a critically renowned rock group like R.E.M. (who initially began as part of the new wave) could attribute the gold sales of their latest album, *Life's Rich Pageant*, almost solely to the airplay and support of the college radio network. In appreciation of the gold record status, the band's label, IRS records, sent out a commemorative "thank you" display to many college radio stations.

72. Denisoff, *Tarnished Gold*, 107.

73. Many, however, agreed that it was ridiculous to trace the lost music industry revenues into other entertainment areas. As Robert Christgau pointed out in his excellent examination of the early 1980s music industry, "Rock'n'Roll Roller Coaster: The Music Biz on a Joyride," *Village Voice*, February 7, 1984, "If leisure activities cut into each other that mechanistically, the sports equipment boom of the late '70s would have done music in" (37).

Chapter 2

1. Scott Isler, "The Short and Long of The Ramones," *Trouser Press*, May 1980, 17.

2. On the distinctions between American and British radio at the turn of the 1980s, see Frith, *Sound Effects*, 121–26.

3. Jason Toynbee, "Policing Bohemia, Pinning Up Grunge: The Music Press and Generic Change in British Pop and Rock," *Popular Music* 12, no. 3 (1993): 291.

4. Michael Watts, "A New Dress Code on the British Scene," *Los Angeles Times*, April 5, 1981, Calendar, 72.

5. Bowie's comment comes from a November 1980 *NME* interview. It is quoted in Dave Rimmer, *New Romantics: The Look* (London: Omnibus Press, 2003), 26.

6. Egan's playlist is featured in Rimmer, *New Romantics*, 96–97.

7. Dave Rimmer, "The Human League: Human Nature," *Smash Hits*, December 10, 1981. Reprinted in *Rock's Backpages*, http://www.rocksbackpages.com/article.html?ArticleID=3132.

8. Kurt Loder, "Human League's Pop Dreams," *Rolling Stone*, July 8, 1982, 42.

9. During the second half of 1984, while the circulation for *Smash Hits* was just over half a million, *NME*'s sales had plummeted to 123,192, *Sounds'* to 83,398, and

Melody Maker's to 68,217. See Dave Rimmer, *Like Punk Never Happened: Culture Club and the New Pop* (Boston: Faber and Faber, 1985), 163.

10. For an excellent summary of the "style bibles" and new pop criticism in general, see Ulf Lindberg et al., *Rock Criticism from the Beginning: Amusers, Bruisers and Cool-Headed Cruisers* (New York: Peter Lang, 2005), 218–58.

11. See, for example, Robert Palmer, "Britain's New Pop—Synthetic Bands," *New York Times*, March 7, 1982, D19, 30; Van Gosse, "Electropop," *Music & Sound Output*, March–April 1982, 86–90; Bob Doerschuk, "The New Synthesizer Rock," *Keyboard*, June 1982, 11–18; Kenn Lowy, "A Synth Pop Handbook," *Trouser Press*, December 1982, 32–37; Roman Kozak, "Techno-pop Groups Make Chart Inroads," *Billboard*, December 25, 1982, 3, 89.

12. Andy Schwartz, "Anglophilia: Can it Be Cured?" *New York Rocker*, December 1981, 26.

13. See Nelson George and Paul Grein, "Black Formats Offer More New Act Airplay," *Billboard*, June 5, 1982, 1, 22.

14. Nelson George, "Reverse Crossover," *New York Rocker*, June 1981, 14.

15. Carolyn Baker quoted in R. Serge Denisoff, *Inside MTV* (New Brunswick, NJ: Transaction Books, 1988), 46.

16. Goodwin, *Dancing*, 29–37.

17. Parke Peterbaugh, "Anglomania: America Surrenders to the Brits—But Who Really Wins?" *Rolling Stone*, November 10, 1983, 31.

18. While various journalists were quick to label the explosion of new groups as a second "British Invasion," Robert Christgau rightly pointed out that ever since the Beatles, the American charts had, in general, been occupied by a fair number of British acts. In fact it was only punk rock's failure in 1977 to translate into American business dollars that suspended this British dominance. The new crop of British groups could thus have been seen as simply renewing the occupation that had been in place throughout the late 1960s and early and middle 1970s. See Christgau, "Rock-'n'Roller Coaster," 40–41.

19. "What Is New Music? All That Came Before . . . And More," *Billboard*, July 9, 1983, NM1–12.

20. Will Straw, "Popular Music and Postmodernism in the 1980s," in *Sound and Vision: The Music Video Reader*, ed. Simon Frith, Andrew Goodwin, and Lawrence Grossberg (New York: Routledge, 1993), 3–21.

21. As Straw mentions, this procedure has precedents that date back to the early 1960s, when singles were the focus of attention and albums were released as a secondary item in hopes of expanding on the interest initially generated by the "hit" tracks.

22. Paul D. Lopes, "Innovation and Diversity in the Popular Music Industry, 1969 to 1990," *American Sociological Review* 57, no. 1 (1992): 66.

23. Steven Ward, "Caught with his Trousers Down: The Ira Robbins Interview," *RockCritics.com*, http://rockcriticsarchives.com/interviews/irarobbins/irarobbins .html.

24. Jock Baird, "A Flock of Seagulls: Easy Street Comes to an End," *Musician*, September 1983, 24.

25. Lou O'Neill Jr. and Philip Bashe, "US Festival '83 in Words and Photos," *Circus,* August 31, 1983, 35.

26. Tommy Lee et al., *The Dirt: Confessions of the World's Most Notorious Rock Band* (New York: Harper Collins, 2001), 90.

27. For more on this particular narrative device and its relationship to rock history, see Keir Keightley, "Reconsidering Rock," in *The Cambridge Companion to Pop and Rock,* ed. Simon Frith, Will Straw, and John Street (New York: Cambridge University Press, 2001), 109–42.

28. See, for example, "Celebrity Rate a Record: Molly Hatchet," *Hit Parader,* September 1983, 23. Two years later Dire Straits would similarly position real rock against new music in the parodic hit single "Money for Nothing," which complains about "the little faggot with the earring and the make-up" that had become a staple on MTV.

29. Sam Sutherland, "U2 Edges Forward with its Own Brand of 'New,'" *Billboard,* July 9, 1983, 51.

30. Bill Black, "The Smiths: Keep Young and Beautiful," *Sounds,* November 19, 1983. Reprinted in *Rock's Back Pages,* http://www.rocksbackpages.com/article.html?ArticleID=6282.

31. This quote comes from the band's 1983 song "I Must Not Think Bad Thoughts," which specifically lists other underground American bands like the Minutemen and Black Flag that the new British Invasion had drowned out.

32. David Fricke, "The Declaration of Independents," in *The Rock Yearbook 1985,* ed. Allan Jones (Toronto: Stoddart, 1984), 120.

33. Simon Reynolds, "What's Missing? The State of Pop in 1985," in *Bring the Noise: 20 Years of Writing About Hip Rock and Hip Hop* (London: Faber and Faber, 2007), 7. First published in *Monitor* 3 (July 1985), no page numbers given.

34. Simon Reynolds, "Against Health and Efficiency: Independent Music in the 1980s," in *Zoot Suits and Second-Hand Dresses: An Anthology of Fashion and Music,* ed. Angela McRobbie (Boston: Unwin Hyman, 1988), 245–55.

35. "New Wave," *All Music Guide,* http://www.allmusic.com/cg/amg.dll?p=amg&sql=77:381.

36. Johnny Marr's quote is transcribed from *Seven Ages of Rock,* episode 7, "What the World is Waiting For," dir. Sebastian Barfield (BBC, 2007).

37. Fricke, "The Declaration of Independents," 121.

38. On the "timbral conformity" of the new digital preset instruments, see Andrew Goodwin, "Rationalization and Democratization in the New Technologies of Popular Music," in *Popular Music and Communication,* 2nd ed., ed. James Lull (Newbury Park, CA: Sage, 1991), 84. On the proliferation of the "gated" drum sound, see Greg Milner, *Perfecting Sound Forever: An Aural History of Recorded Music* (New York: Faber and Faber, 2009), 164–70.

39. Bill Flanagan, "The Age of Excess," *Musician,* November 1989, 34.

40. My observations in this paragraph are largely indebted to Reebee Garofalo, *Rockin' Out: Popular Music in the U.S.A.,* 4th ed. (Upper Saddle River, NJ: Pearson Prentice Hall, 2008), especially 333–45.

41. See Sean Ross, "Billboard Debuts Weekly Chart of Alternative Rock," *Billboard,* September 10, 1988, 10.

42. Quoted in David Daley, "In The Light," *Alternative Press,* November 1999, 74.

43. In an era of fragmented radio markets and sales categories, the Hot 100 singles chart of the early 1990s no longer reflected the music of a predominantly white pop and rock mainstream as it had in previous decades. The singles chart was now dominated by artists from the Rhythm & Blues and Dance music charts, while rock music's influence was reflected more in the Album Rock and Modern Rock charts and the Top 200 Album sales charts. That Nirvana's *Nevermind* should eventually top the Album chart was less an anomaly than "Smells Like Teen Spirit" breaking into the Top 10 singles chart.

44. Quoted in Jon Pareles's "Nirvana, The Band That Hates to Be Loved," *New York Times,* November 14, 1993, H44.

45. Of the top twenty Album Rock songs listed on *Billboard*'s January 25, 1992, Album Rock Tracks chart, fifteen were by North American artists.

46. Eric Boehlert, "Modern Rock Radio Roars Ahead: Format's Growth Continues to Surprise," *Billboard,* November 5, 1994, 115.

47. Eric Boehlert, "Modern Rock Comes into its Own: Genre Flexes its Hit-Making Muscle," *Billboard,* April 9, 1994, 69.

48. By the end of 1996 these cynical grumblings had grown even darker and louder as the industry finally witnessed its first substantial decrease in alternative album rock sales. Subsequently, critics began issuing alarms that echoed the dissatisfaction and panic of "The Great Depression of 1979." See, for example: Jon Pareles, "All That Music and Nothing to Listen To," *New York Times,* January 5, 1997, H34, H44, and Christopher John Farley, "Waiting For the Next Big Thing," *Time,* December 16, 1996, 70–71.

49. See Tom Frank, "Alternative to What?" in *Sounding Off! Music as Subversion/Resistance/Revolution,* ed. Ron Sakolsky and Fred Wei-Han Ho (Brooklyn, NY: Autonomedia, 1995), 109–19.

50. As *Billboard*'s chart manager explained, the change from "Album" to "Mainstream" reflected a change in focus away from an album-based format to one that was predominantly singles-oriented. See "Name Changed on Album Rock Tracks: Mainstream Rock List Mirrors Radio Shifts," *Billboard,* April 13, 1996, 6.

51. For more on the emergence of "classic modern rock" stations, see Eric Boehlert, "Modern Rock Radio Branching Out: Format Offshoots Mix Fresh with Familiar," *Billboard,* January 15, 1994, 1, 63.

52. Greg Rule, "Meet the Rentals: Nerds with Moogs . . . And Proud of It!" *Keyboard,* March 1996, 66.

Chapter 3

1. David Byrne quoted in David Gans, *Talking Heads: The Band & Their Music* (New York: Avon, 1985), 114.

2. Carter Ratcliff, "David Byrne and the Modern Self: 'How Do I Work This,'" *Artforum,* May 1985, 95.

3. David Bowman, *This Must Be the Place: The Adventures of Talking Heads in the 20th Century* (New York: HarperCollins, 2001), 262.

4. In choosing nervousness as the subject of this chapter, I will be focusing exclusively on male singers and white masculinity. Largely this is because rock critics

of the era refrained from labeling new wave's female musicians as nervous. Even though singers like Lene Lovich and Dale Bozzio of Missing Persons employed many of the same "nervous" vocal mannerisms as David Byrne, they were often much more controlled in their vocalizations, and the personas they projected were far removed from the repressed white "awkwardness" that Byrne deliberately projected. Lovich, a Detroit native with Eastern European roots, took to the stage in lace, braided hair, and flowing skirts, and was typically portrayed as an exotic gypsy or alien presence. Bozzio, on the other hand, was a former *Playboy* Bunny, who assumed a provocative and commanding highly sexualized image that dominated critical evaluations of the band.

5. Mikal Gilmore, "Talking Heads: Psychodramas You Can Dance To," *Rolling Stone*, November 29, 1979, 24.

6. Lester Bangs, "David Byrne Says 'Boo!'," in *Mainlines, Blood Feasts, and Bad Taste: A Lester Bangs Reader,* ed. John Morthland (New York: Anchor, 2002), 116.

7. Ibid., 118.

8. Ibid., 117.

9. George Beard, *American Nervousness, Its Causes and Consequences* (New York: G. P. Putnam's Sons, 1881), viii–ix.

10. A. D. Rockwell, "Some Causes and Characteristics of Neurasthenia," *New York Medical Journal* 58 (1893): 590. Quoted in F. G. Gosling, *Before Freud: Neurasthenia and the American Medical Community, 1870–1910* (Urbana: University of Illinois Press, 1987), 13.

11. On the sensory overload, and perceived dangers, of the early-twentieth-century city, see Ben Singer, *Melodrama and Modernity: Early Sensational Cinema and Its Contexts* (New York: Columbia University Press, 2001), especially 59–99.

12. Georg Simmel, "The Metropolis and Mental Life," in *The Sociology of Georg Simmel,* trans. and ed. Kurt H. Wolff (New York: Free Press, 1950), 410.

13. Michael O'Malley suggests the comparison between neurasthenia and ADHD in his essay, "That Busyness That is Not Business: Nervousness and Character at the Turn of the Last Century," *Social Research* 72, no. 2 (2005): 384.

14. Megan Barke, Rebecca Fribush, and Peter N. Stearns, "Nervous Breakdown in 20th-Century American Culture," *Journal of Social History* 33, no. 3 (2000): 571.

15. Many articles and essays from the turn of the 1980s address the anxieties accompanying the integration of computers into society. For a concise summary of these concerns, see Thomas B. Sheridan, "Computer Control and Human Alienation," *Technology Review* 83, no. 1 (1980): 60–73.

16. Gosling, *Before Freud,* 10.

17. Beard, *American Nervousness,* 26.

18. Julian B. Carter, *The Heart of Whiteness: Normal Sexuality and Race in America, 1880–1940* (Durham, NC: Duke University Press, 2007), 48.

19. Tom Lutz, *American Nervousness 1903: An Anecdotal History* (Ithaca: Cornell University Press, 1991), 6.

20. On the American glamorization of neuroses and the popularization of psychoanalysis and the psychological in the second and third decades of the twentieth century, see Joel Pfister, "Glamorizing the Psychological: The Politics of the Performances of Modern Psychological Identities," in *Inventing the Psychological: Toward a*

Cultural History of Emotional Life in America, ed. Joel Pfister and Nancy Schnog (New Haven: Yale University Press, 1997), 167–213.

21. Galen Brandt, "Talking Heads," *Trouser Press,* November 1979, 25.

22. Sam Binkley, *Getting Loose: Lifestyle Consumption in the 1970s* (Durham, NC: Duke University Press, 2007).

23. Simon Frith and Angela McRobbie, "Rock and Sexuality," in *On Record: Rock, Pop and the Written Word,* ed. Simon Frith and Andrew Goodwin (New York: Pantheon, 1990), 374.

24. Kevin J. Mumford, "'Lost Manhood' Found: Male Sexual Impotence and Victorian Culture in the United States," in *American Sexual Politics: Sex, Gender, and Race since the Civil War,* ed. John C. Fout and Maura Shaw Tantillo (Chicago: University of Chicago Press, 1993), 84–85.

25. Ibid., 93.

26. Richard Dyer, *White* (New York: Routledge, 1997), 17.

27. See especially Peter N. Stearns, *American Cool: Constructing a Twentieth-Century Emotional Style* (New York: New York University Press, 1994), and *Battleground of Desire: The Struggle for Self-Control in Modern America* (New York: New York University Press, 1999).

28. Nugent draws attention specifically to Costello's December 19, 1977, performance on *Saturday Night Live* as a pivotal moment in the development of the late 1970s nerd archetype. Inspired by Costello's unusual look and style, which she deemed "nerd rock," *SNL* writer Anne Beatts, along with Rosie Shuster, developed a skit for Bill Murray and Gilda Radner in which they portrayed nerds. See Benjamin Nugent, *American Nerd: The Story of My People* (New York: Scribner, 2008), 61–66.

29. Mary Bucholtz, "The Whiteness of Nerds: Superstandard English and Racial Markedness," *Journal of Linguistic Anthropology* 11, no. 1 (2001): 84–100.

30. Will Straw, "Dance Music," in Frith, Straw, and Street, *Cambridge Companion,* 171.

31. Will Straw, "The Booth, The Floor and the Wall: Dance Music and the Fear of Falling," in *Popular Music—Style and Identity,* ed. Will Straw, Stacey Johnson, Rebecca Sullivan, and Paul Friedlander (Montreal: Centre for Research on Canadian Cultural Industries and Institutions, 1995), 252–53.

32. Richard Riegel, "Review of Thompson Twins, *In the Name of Love,*" *Creem,* September 1982, 54.

33. Ira Robbins, "Devo: Maybe!" *Trouser Press,* January 1979, 16.

34. MT Laverty, "Devo: In Search of the Big Enema," *Trouser Press,* April 1978, 12; Barbara Graustark, "Devo's Primal Pop," *Newsweek,* October 30, 1978, 77.

35. In their biography of Devo, *Are We Not Men? We Are Devo!* (London: SAF, 2003), Jade Dellinger and David Giffels trace the crystallization of the "de-evolution" concept and Devo band name back to two primary sources that Casale, Mothersbaugh, and their collaborating friend Bob Lewis had stumbled across in the early 1970s: a *Wonder Woman* comic from March–April 1948 (featured as a reprint in the March 1972 issue of *Adventure Comics* no. 416), whose story centers around a professor with an experimental "devolution" machine capable of transforming monkeys into other animals, and an obscure "religious pamphlet" from the 1920s, B. H. Shadduck's *Jocko-Homo Heavenbound* (Roger, OH: Jocko-Homo, 1924), which claimed that thou-

sands of years of human sin and corruption were signs of a "d-evolution" that had placed mankind on a stairway to hell rather than heaven.

36. For a compelling analysis of Devo's cultural critique, see Bodinger-deUriarte, "Opposition to Hegemony."

37. Gerald Casale quoted in Bodinger-deUriarte, "Opposition to Hegemony," 60.

38. On the relationship between robots and Fordism in the 1920s, see Peter Wollen, *Raiding the Icebox: Reflections on Twentieth-Century Culture* (Bloomington: Indiana University Press, 1993), especially 35–71.

39. Antonio Gramsci, *Selections from the Prison Notebooks,* ed. and trans. Quinton Hoare and Geoffrey Nowell-Smith (New York: International Publishers, 1971), 304–5.

40. David Temperley has observed that such instances, where we encounter an unresolved "divorce" between the melody and harmony, are a normal recurring feature of rock's particular musical syntax. See Temperley, "The Melodic-Harmonic 'Divorce' in Rock," *Popular Music* 26, no. 2 (2007): 323–42. This "divorce" is deliberately exaggerated in "Uncontrollable Urge," in a way that foregrounds the disjunction and encourages the listener to hear the loss of control in Mothersbaugh's voice.

41. I would like to thank Stephen Meyer for pointing this out to me.

42. Richard Middleton, "Rock Singing," in *The Cambridge Companion to Singing,* ed. John Potter (New York: Cambridge University Press, 2000), 29.

43. This is how Andy Partridge of XTC explained his nervous "herky-jerky" vocal style: "My voice hasn't any qualities whatsoever, so the idea is to start from style and work towards stylization as a strength rather than the quality of my voice." Quoted in Jim Green, "The Agony and the XTC," *Trouser Press,* August 1978, 12.

44. For a summary of studies devoted to nervousness and voice, see Petri Laukka et al., "In a Nervous Voice: Acoustic Analysis and Perception of Anxiety in Social Phobics' Speech," *Journal of Nonverbal Behavior* 32, no. 4 (2008): 195–214.

45. The following discussion of communication disorders draws from two main sources: Daniel R. Boone, *Human Communication and its Disorders* (Englewood Cliffs, NJ: Prentice Hall, 1987), and Elena Plante and Pelagie M. Beeson, *Communication and Communication Disorders: A Clinical Introduction* (Boston: Allyn and Bacon, 1999).

46. Boone, *Human Communication,* 318.

47. "Corporate Life Forms on Virgin Territory: DEVO," in *Search & Destroy #7–11: The Complete Reprint,* ed. V. Vale (San Francisco: V/Search, 1997), 6.

48. Ken Tucker, "Africa Calling: Review of Talking Heads *Remain in Light," Rolling Stone,* December 11, 1980, 55.

Chapter 4

1. Frank Rose, "Connoisseurs of Trash in a World Full of It: Review of the B-52's *Wild Planet," Rolling Stone,* October 30, 1980, 54.

2. John Rockwell, "The Pop Life: How the B-52's Cope with the Success Trap," *New York Times,* August 31, 1979, C16.

3. John Rockwell, "B-52's, Rock Band from Georgia," *New York Times,* June 3, 1978, 11.

4. The lyrics are quoted from the band's single "Rock Lobster." The Gertrude Stein allusion comes from Stuart Cohn, "The B-52's: Just Like Us," *Trouser Press,* No-

vember 1979, 8. While the comparison to Stein certainly makes sense, Schneider has admitted that he was influenced more directly by the equally nonsensical writings of Lewis Carroll. Given that Carroll's *Alice's Adventures in Wonderland* contains a chapter that features a "Lobster Quadrille," the connection between Carroll and "Rock Lobster" indeed seems much more suggestive.

5. The band also claimed in early interviews that its name came from some B-52 bomber jackets that they had worn at one point, and that B-52's was also slang for a vitamin.

6. Those who have argued that new wave should be understood most of all as an ironic musical genre include Covach, "Pangs of History," and Bruce J. Shulman, *The Seventies: The Great Shift in American Culture, Society, and Politics* (New York: Free Press, 2002).

7. Linda Hutcheon, *Irony's Edge: The Theory and Politics of Irony* (New York: Routledge, 1994), 19.

8. Jon Savage, "Yesterday's Sound Tomorrow: Review of the B-52's *B-52's,*" *Melody Maker*, June 30, 1979. Reprinted in *Rock's Backpages*, http://www.rocksbackpages .com/article.html?ArticleID=14660.

9. Cohn, "The B-52's," 8.

10. Cynthia Rose, "The B-52's: Hair Today Gone Tomorrow?" *New Musical Express*, January 3, 1981. Reprinted in *Rock's Backpages*, http://www.rocksbackpages.com/arti cle.html?ArticleID=1207.

11. On the dearth of gay rockers at the turn of the 1980s, see Adam Block's essay "The Confessions of a Gay Rocker," *The Advocate*, April 15, 1982, 43–47.

12. This pigeonholing persists to this day. For example, for many years *All Music Guide* placed the singer-songwriter Steven Grossman, whose 1974 debut for Mercury records was the first major label release by an openly gay artist, under a single genre category: "Gay."

13. Cynthia Rose, "The B-52's," *New Musical Express*, June 4, 1983. Reprinted in *Rock's Backpages*, http://www.rocksbackpages.com/article.html?ArticleID=1208.

14. This quote comes from Andy Warhol, describing those images ("all the modern things") that attracted the 1960s pop artists. See Andy Warhol and Pat Hackett, *Popism: The Warhol Sixties* (New York: Harper & Row, 1980), 3.

15. Rose, "The B-52's: Hair Today Gone Tomorrow."

16. Anthony DeCurtis, "The B-52's Return Home," *Rolling Stone*, November 27, 1980, 84.

17. Christin J. Mamiya, *Pop Art and Consumer Culture: American Super Market* (Austin: University of Texas Press, 1992).

18. For a discussion of the link between suburban family home life and its representations in the discourse of 1960s space travel, see Lynn Spigel, "From Theatre to Space Ship: Metaphors of Suburban Domesticity in Postwar America," in *Visions of Suburbia*, ed. Roger Silverstone (New York: Routledge, 1997), 217–39.

19. Susannah Handley, *Nylon: The Story of a Fashion Revolution* (Baltimore: Johns Hopkins University Press, 1999).

20. Tupperware was praised not just for its convenience and durability, but for its elegant modern shapes and machine aesthetic designs. The Museum of Modern Art even featured a Tupperware display in 1956. See Alison J. Clarke, *Tupperware: The*

Promise of Plastic in 1950s America (Washington, DC: Smithsonian Institution Press, 1999), 36–37.

21. Mamiya, *Pop Art*, 26–27.

22. Michael L. Smith, "Selling the Moon: The U.S. Manned Space Program and the Triumph of Commodity Scientism," in *The Culture of Consumption: Critical Essays in American History 1880–1980*, ed. Richard Wightman Fox and T. J. Jackson Lears (New York: Pantheon, 1983), 175–209.

23. Ibid., 186.

24. Sara Doris, *Pop Art and the Contest Over American Culture* (New York: Cambridge University Press, 2007), 183.

25. Ibid.

26. Mark Vail, *Vintage Synthesizers: Groundbreaking Instruments and Pioneering Designers of Electronic Music Synthesizers* (San Francisco: Miller Freeman, 1993), 233.

27. On the "aura" of residual technology and media, see Timothy D. Taylor, *Strange Sounds: Music, Technology & Culture* (New York: Routledge, 2001), and Charles Acland, ed., *Residual Media* (Minneapolis: University of Minnesota Press, 2007).

28. Kennedy Fraser, "On and Off the Avenue: Feminine Fashions," *New Yorker*, April 14, 1975, 84–85.

29. Rose, "The B-52's," in *New Musical Express*.

30. Hebdige, *Subculture*.

31. See Claude Lévi-Strauss, *The Savage Mind* (Chicago: University of Chicago Press, 1966), 16–22.

32. Hebdige's reading of the punk style that results from this bricolage is not unproblematic. He suggests that as appropriated by the punks, a symbol like the swastika no longer functions as a Nazi signifier, but is instead emptied of its original connotations. That the swastika lacks meaning is purportedly what shocks the viewer. Dave Laing refutes this idea, pointing out that while members of the punk subculture may have taken the swastika as an absent signifier, some brought violence upon themselves precisely because observers took the symbol not as being "empty" of meaning but as a literal political statement. A signifier, as such, is always *multiaccentual*. "That is, there is always within it a tension between different potential meanings, the result, it could be said, of the pull of different discourses to have it read as part of their own meaning-system." See Laing, *One Chord Wonders*, 96.

33. Sylvie Simmons, "The Go-Go's: Ready Steady Go-Go's," *Sounds*, April 12, 1980. Reprinted in *Rock's Backpages*, http://www.rocksbackpages.com/article.html?ArticleID=13067.

34. Mitch Cohen, "The B-52's: Climate Control in the Land of 16 Dances," *Creem*, December 1979, 37; James Henke, "The B-52's," *Rolling Stone*, December 11, 1980, 10; Rosalind Russell, "Cindy Wilson / Kate Pierson," in *New Women In Rock*, ed. Liz Thompson (New York: Delilah/Putnam, 1982), 23.

35. Karen Bettez Halnon, "Poor Chic: The Rationalization Consumption of Poverty," *Current Sociology* 50, no. 4 (2002): 501–16.

36. Gael Sweeney, "The King of White Trash Culture: Elvis Presley and the Aesthetics of Excess," in *White Trash: Race and Class in America*, ed. Matt Wray and Annalee Newitz (New York: Routledge, 1997), 249–66.

37. See, for example, Karen Schoemer, "At Home in the Top 40 and Still Full of Kitsch," *New York Times,* December 31, 1989, H27.

38. Mancini is credited as one of the writers on "Planet Claire." On "crime jazz" and "jazz exotica," see Phil Ford, "Jazz Exotica and the Naked City," *Journal of Musicological Research* 27, no. 2 (2008): 113–33.

39. Mats Sexton, *The B-52's Universe: The Essential Guide to the World's Greatest Party Band* (Minneapolis: Plan-B Books, 2002), 152.

40. The Plymouth Satellite was first introduced in 1964, in the wake of the American "space race" craze.

41. Rick Anderson, "Rock Lobster," *All Music Guide,* http://www.allmusic.com/song/rock-lobster_+2049401 (accessed November 22, 2010).

42. Eddy took the emphasis on the guitar's "bass" end even further by playing some of his lead lines on an actual bass guitar. For more on the specifics of the surf guitar style, see John Blair, "Chairmen of the Board: The Surf Guitar Summit," *Guitar Player,* September 1996, 68–82.

43. Michael Shore, "Athens' Golden Age: New Sounds from a Georgia Town," *Music Sound & Output,* January–February 1983, 95.

44. Wilson plays the third note of the chord progression on the sixth scale degree (a flat), and one could arguably hear the accompanying chord as based on either F minor or A major. "Out of Limits," however, is unambiguous in its i–III–iv–V ascending chord progression. The B-52's would return to a similar ascending chord progression on 1980's "Private Idaho," this time adding the chromatic organ line from the *The Twilight Zone,* which only added to the association with "Out of Limits."

45. Jonathan Cott, "John Lennon: A Conversation," *Rolling Stone,* January 22, 1981, 37.

46. Clement Greenberg, "Avant-Garde and Kitsch," *Partisan Review* 6, no. 5 (1939): 34–49. Greenberg's essay was issued on the eve of World War II, and clearly intended to provide a sober analysis of the dire artistic circumstances in totalitarian states such as Germany, where avant-garde art was denounced as "degenerate music," or the Soviet Union, where artists were issued mandates to produce state-approved works of positive "socialist realism." Kitsch had completely obliterated the avant-garde in these states, as art had devolved into works of mass-produced propaganda. This political dimension added a certain weight to Greenberg's arguments.

47. Dwight MacDonald, "Masscult and Midcult," in *Against the American Grain: Essays on the Effects of Mass Culture* (New York: Random House, 1962), 29.

48. Ibid.

49. Gillo Dorfles, ed., *Kitsch: The World of Bad Taste* (New York: Bell, 1969).

50. Mark Mazzulo, "Fans and Critics: Greil Marcus's *Mystery Train* as Rock'n'Roll History," *Musical Quarterly* 81, no. 2 (1997): 145–69.

51. Jim Miller, ed., *The Rolling Stone Illustrated History of Rock & Roll* (New York: Rolling Stone Press / Random House, 1976).

52. Carl Belz, "The Expansion of Rock Style: 1957 through 1963," in *The Story of Rock* (New York: Oxford University Press, 1969), 60–117. In his article "The Girl Groups" for the *Rolling Stone* history, Greil Marcus refers to the period between 1958 and 1965 as "fallow years for rock and roll" (154).

53. Michael Thompson, "An Anatomy of Rubbish," in *Arts in Society,* ed. Paul Barker (London: Fontana, 1977), 42.

54. Andrew Ross, "Uses of Camp" in *No Respect: Intellectuals and Popular Culture* (New York: Routledge, 1989), 145–46.

55. Susan Sontag, "Notes on 'Camp,'" *Partisan Review* 31, no. 4 (1964): 515–30.

56. Richard Dyer, "It's Being So Camp as Keeps Us Going," in *Camp: Queer Aesthetics and the Performing Subject,* ed. Fabio Cleto (Ann Arbor: University of Michigan Press, 1999), 114.

57. On camp and the "transformation of the sign," see Laura Christian, "The Sign's Send-Up: Camp and the Performing Subject of Semiosis," *Semiotica* 137 (2001): 117–38.

58. See John Fiske, "Reading the Beach," in *Reading Popular Culture* (Boston: Unwin Hyman, 1989), 43–76; Joan Ormrod, "*Endless Summer* (1964): Consuming Waves and Surfing the Frontier," *Film & History* 25, no. 1 (2005): 39–51; Suzanne Clisby, "Summer Sex: Youth, Desire and the Carnivalesque at the English Seaside," in *Transgressive Sex: Subversion and Control in Erotic Encounters,* ed. Hastings Donnan and Fiona Magowan (New York: Berghahn, 2009), 47–68.

59. Sexton, *The B-52's Universe,* 36.

60. Gillian G. Gaar, *She's a Rebel: The History of Women in Rock & Roll* (Seattle: Seal Press, 1992), 257.

61. Joan Ormrod, "Issues of Gender in *Muscle Beach Party* (1964)," *Scope,* December 2002, http://www.scope.nottingham.ac.uk/article.php?issue=dec2002&id=270&section=article.

62. Rudolf P. Gaudio, "Sounding Gay: Pitch Properties in the Speech of Gay and Straight Men," *American Speech* 69, no. 1 (1994): 30–57; Erez Levon, "Hearing Gay: Prosody, Interpretation, and the Affective Judgments of Men's Speech," *American Speech* 81, no. 1 (2006): 56–78; Benjamin Munson, "The Acoustic Correlates of Perceived Masculinity, Perceived Femininity, and Perceived Sexual Orientation," *Language and Speech* 50, no. 1 (2007): 125–42.

63. DeCurtis, "The B-52's Return Home," 84.

64. My thanks to Vincent Stephens for this observation.

65. The term "clean teen" comes from Thomas Doherty's *Teenagers and Teenpics: The Juvenilization of American Movies in the 1950s* (Boston: Unwin Hyman, 1988).

66. Henke, "The B-52's," 10.

67. R. L. Rutsky, "Surfing the Other: Ideology on the Beach," *Film Quarterly* 52, no. 4 (1999): 12–23.

68. Discussing the song in a 2008 interview, B-52's drummer Keith Strickland acknowledged that he had always considered "Rock Lobster" to have a "middle eastern" quality. See "Q&A: What's the Story Behind 'Rock Lobster'," *AolMusic,* http://music.aol.com/video/qanda-whats-the-story-behind-rock/the-b-52s/2116949.

69. Clifford Chase, "Am I Getting Warmer: The B-52's: *The B-52's,*" in *Heavy Rotation: Twenty Writers on the Albums that Changed Their Lives,* ed. Peter Terzian (New York: Harper Perennial, 2009), 161.

70. Aaron Fricke, *Reflections of a Rock Lobster: A Story about Growing Up Gay* (Boston: Alyson, 1981).

71. Kirse Granat May, *Golden State, Golden Youth: The California Image in Popular Culture, 1955–1966* (Chapel Hill: University of North Carolina Press, 2002), 122.

Chapter 5

"(I Wish It Could Be) 1965 Again" is the title of a 1979 song by the Barracudas.

1. White and Nusser, "New Wave Rockers," 1.

2. Jim Green, "Green Circles," *Trouser Press,* September 1979, 32.

3. Roy Carr, "The Highly Original Thoughts of Chairman Fieger," *New Musical Express,* March 22, 1980, 19.

4. White and Nusser, "New Wave Rockers," 15.

5. Terry Atkinson, "The Knack: Yesterday and Today," *Rolling Stone,* October 18, 1979, 32.

6. By referring to the Beatles as modern, I do not mean to imply that they were a mod group. The Beatles carried little currency with the British mod subculture itself and in many instances were viewed with disdain. Rather, they were "modern" to the extent that they embodied a new pop aesthetic, one that was seen as ushering in an entire new movement—the British Invasion.

7. For a good discussion of the Knack's biography and their position as "the undisputed kings of the L.A. rock scene," see Ken Sharp and Doug Sulpy's interview with singer-guitarist Doug Fieger and guitarist Berton Averre in *Power Pop! Conversations with the Power Pop Elite* (Willow Grove, PA: Poptomes, 1997), 238–49. More than just heading a general "L.A. rock scene," the Knack were at the commercial forefront of a nationally recognized L.A. power pop scene that included bands like 20/20, the Plimsouls, the Pop, and the Bangs (Bangles).

8. Waller, "Live Reviews," 48.

9. Deena Weinstein, "Art Versus Commerce: Deconstructing a (Useful) Romantic Illusion," in *Stars Don't Stand Still in the Sky: Music and Myth,* ed. Karen Kelly and Evelyn McDonnell (New York: New York University Press, 1999). For all the examples that Weinstein cites to deflate this "romantic illusion," she concludes that the myth will continue to persist "because too many people gain too many different things—money, identity, prestige, or a common critical standard—from it to give it up" (68).

10. Mark Coleman, "The Knack," in *The Rolling Stone Album Guide,* ed. Anthony DeCurtis and James Henke, with Holly George-Warren (New York: Random House, 1992), 404.

11. Carr, "Highly Original Thoughts," 19.

12. Ibid.

13. From an interview with Peter Case of the Plimsouls, in Sharp and Sulpy, *Power Pop!* 233.

14. Poptopia is the name of a power pop festival that was held annually in Los Angeles in the late 1990s. It also is the name of Rhino Records' three-volume 1997 power pop retrospective.

15. Many power pop bands claimed that their endeavors were "artistic." Few insisted upon this more persistently than Shoes, one of the early groups to lead the mid-1970s power pop insurgence. See, for example, their comments in Carl Cafarelli's "The Kids Are Alright! The History of Power Pop," *Goldmine,* January 1996,

32. Critics and fans have likewise constantly couched power pop music in the language of artistic description. In a review of the dB's' album *Stands for Decibels*, Marjorie Karp likens the group's efforts of working with a "received convention" to "the way a painter uses sienna and ocher, or a poet the sonnet form." See Karp, "Album Reviews: The db's 'Stands For Decibels,'" *New York Rocker*, May 1981, 44.

16. Wilfrid Mellers, *Twilight of the Gods: The Music of the Beatles* (New York: Viking, 1973).

17. "Pete Townshend on 'Lily,'" *Hit Parader*, October 1967, 44.

18. One finds many blanket statements crediting Pete Townshend of the Who as the first to use the label *power pop*. Some power pop aficionados, such as the musician Marshall Crenshaw (in the liner notes to *Poptopia: Power Pop Classics of the '80s*, Rhino R2 72729), specifically date the phrase to a 1966 Townshend interview with *Hit Parader* magazine. Crenshaw's memory may be slightly off, however, for the earliest mention of *power pop* I have uncovered is in the 1967 article cited in the previous footnote. Describing the Who's music of that time—songs such "Pictures Of Lily," "Substitute," and "I Can't Explain"—Townshend proclaims that "power pop is what we play—what the *Small Faces* used to play, and the kind of pop the *Beach Boys* played in the days of 'Fun, Fun, Fun.'"

19. From a 1985 interview quoted in John M. Borack, *Shake Some Action: The Ultimate Power Pop Guide* (Fort Collins, CO: Not Lame Recording, 2007), 11.

20. The pop art style of Stout's cover illustration has provided a point of departure for numerous power pop compilations, such as Bomp! Records' 1996 compilation *The Roots of Power Pop* and Rhino Records' 1997 three-volume *Poptopia* series. Even more directly, the October–November 2002 issue of *Magnet* magazine copied the cover art directly for its own special on the history of power pop.

21. Greg Shaw, "Editorial," *Bomp!* March 1978, 5.

22. Greg Shaw, "Editorial: In Defense of Rock Theory," *Bomp!* November 1977, 29.

23. In particular, see Shaw, "It All Came Back."

24. Shaw, "Defense of Rock Theory," 29.

25. See Bernard Gendron, *Between Montmartre*, 227–47.

26. Legs McNeil's quote is transcribed from *The History of Rock'n'Roll*, vol. 9, *Punk*, prod. and dir. Ted Haimes, 60 min., Time/Life Warner Home Video, 1995, videocassette.

27. Gendron, *Between Montmartre*, 231.

28. A similar revival took place in the U.K., where new groups like Showaddywaddy and Darts mined the rockabilly and vocal harmony group style of the late 1950s and early 1960s rock and roll era, releasing popular cover versions of songs like Buddy Holly's "Heartbeat" (1958) and Gene Chandler's "Duke of Earl" (1962).

29. Fred Davis, *Yearning for Yesterday: A Sociology of Nostalgia* (New York: Free Press, 1979), 104. For a comprehensive examination of America's nostalgic engagements and obsessions during the 1970s, see Michael Kammen's exhaustive study *Mystic Chords of Memory: The Transformation of Tradition in American Culture* (New York: Alfred A. Knopf, 1991), especially 618–704.

30. Gendron, *Between Montmartre*, 236.

31. Shaw, "Editorial," *Bomp!* March 1978, 4.

32. Ibid.

33. Ira Robbins, "Power Pop Primer, *Trouser Press,* April 1978, 22–27.

34. Robbins, "New Wave R.I.P."

35. Robbins, "Power Pop Primer," 22.

36. Ibid., 22.

37. Davis, *Yearning for Yesterday,* 56–64.

38. See Howard Schuman and Jacqueline Scott, "Generations and Collective Memory," *American Sociological Review* 54, no. 3 (1989): 359–81.

39. Susan Stewart, *On Longing: Narratives of the Miniature, the Gigantic, the Collection* (Baltimore: John Hopkins University Press, 1984); Morris B. Holbrook, "On the New Nostalgia: 'These Foolish Things' and Echoes of the Dear Departed Past," in *Continuities in Popular Culture: The Present in the Past & the Past in the Present and Future,* ed. Ray B. Browne and Ronald J. Ambrosetti (Bowling Green, OH: Bowling Green State University Press, 1993), 74–120; Janelle L. Wilson, *Nostalgia: Sanctuary of Meaning* (Lewisburg, PA: Bucknell University Press, 2005).

40. Mitch Easter, liner notes to *Poptopia: Power Pop Classics of the '80s,* Rhino R2 72729.

41. See, in particular, Simon Frith, "Art Ideology and Pop Practice," in *Marxism and the Interpretation of Culture,* ed. Cary Nelson and Lawrence Grossberg (Urbana: University of Illinois Press, 1988), 461–75, and Frith, "Pop Music," in Frith, Straw, and Street, *Cambridge Companion,* 93–108. Timothy Warner also summarizes the differences between pop and rock in *Pop Music.*

42. The myth of the "three minute" single prevails throughout power pop lingo old and new. Ruth Polsky's *Trouser Press* feature on the Beat ran under the heading "3-Minute Supremacists," March 1980, 10. Phil Davis's 1981 *New York Rocker* interview with Shoes was titled "Three Minutes with Shoes," February 1981, 28, 38. Nineties Seattle power pop group Tubetop carried on the tradition, naming its 1997 CD *Three Minute Hercules.*

43. Sharp and Sulpy, *Power Pop!* 221.

44. Daisann McLane, "Rubinoos: The Brain Children of Pop," *Rolling Stone,* May 31, 1979, 19.

45. Asked about his adopted British accent, 20/20 singer and bassist Ron Flynt admitted to suffering from "Beatle damage." See the interview with 20/20 in Sharp and Sulpy, *Power Pop!* 212.

46. For a specific discussion of how the Bangles used the Rickenbacker as a symbolic device, see Peter Mercer-Taylor, "Songs From the Bell Jar: Autonomy and Resistance in the Music of The Bangles," *Popular Music* 17, no. 2 (1998): 187–204.

47. Johnny Angel, "Skinny Ties & Spiky Hair: The Guitarists of the New Wave Remember," *Guitar Player,* August 1995, 48.

48. Mick Berry and Jason Gianni, *The Drummer's Bible: How to Play Every Drum Style from Afro-Cuban to Zydeco* (Tucson: See Sharp Press, 2004), 133. Berry and Gianni place the origins of the "Mersey Beat" drum pattern in Liverpool with groups like Cliff Richard and the Shadows, after which it supposedly disseminated to surf music. This attribution seems too narrow, however, as this particular drum pattern was circulating throughout the early 1960s in a number of different rock and pop styles.

49. Jacqueline Warwick, *Girl Groups, Girl Culture: Popular Music and Identity in the 1960s.* (New York: Routledge, 2007), 35.

50. John Storm Roberts, *The Latin Tinge: The Impact of Latin American Music on the United States* (New York: Oxford University Press, 1979); Ned Sublette, "The Kingsmen and the Cha Cha Chá," in *Listen Again: A Momentary History of Pop Music*, ed. Eric Weisbard (Durham, NC: Duke University Press, 2007), 69–94.

51. Roy Brewer, "The Use of Habanera Rhythm in Rockabilly Music," *American Music* 17, no. 3 (1999): 303.

52. There are, of course, exceptions. John Bonham embellishes the backbeat of Led Zeppelin's "D'yer Mak'er" (1973) with an occasional double snare hit.

53. Kathleen Stewart, "Nostalgia—A Polemic," in *Rereading Cultural Anthropology*, ed. George E. Marcus (Durham, NC: Duke University Press, 1992), 259.

54. Michael Schudson, *Watergate in American Memory: How We Remember, Forget, and Reconstruct the Past* (New York: Basic Books, 1992), 52.

55. Frith, "Pop Music," 96.

56. Greg Shaw, "20/20: The End of All Songs," *Bomp!* March 1978, 35.

57. Davis, "Three Minutes with Shoes," 38.

58. Jay Schwartz, "The dB's," *New York Rocker*, September 1978, 21.

59. Robert Gjerdingen, *A Classic Turn of Phrase: Music and the Psychology of Convention* (Philadelphia: University of Pennsylvania Press, 1988), 267.

60. Power pop historian Ken Sharp, quoted in Andrew Earles, "The '70s: The Birth of Uncool," *Magnet*, October–November 2002, 42.

61. Mitch Cohen, "Review of The Romantics' *The Romantics*," *Creem*, April 1980, 54.

62. Ibid.

63. Robert Christgau, "Christgau Consumer Guide," *Creem*, May 1983, 12.

64. Dave Marsh, "Review of the Knack . . . *but the little girls understand*," *Rolling Stone*, April 3, 1980, 62.

65. Charles Shaar Murray, "Review of The Knack . . . *but the Little Girls Understand*," *New Musical Express*, March 15, 1980, 40.

66. Quoted in Sharp and Sulpy, *Power Pop!* 246.

67. Ibid.

68. Ibid., 244.

69. Fieger invokes the "art" descriptive in Sharp and Sulpy, *Power Pop!* 245.

Chapter 6

1. Doerschuk, "The New Synthesizer Rock," 14.

2. The phrase "keys to the future" appears as one of the headings to Jon Young's article, "Roll Over Guitar Heros [*sic*]: Synthesizers are Here," *Trouser Press*, May 1982, 22.

3. Trevor Pinch, "Giving Birth to New Users: How the Minimoog Was Sold to Rock & Roll," in *How Users Matter: The Co-Construction of Users and Technology*, ed. Nelly Oudshoorn and Trevor Pinch (Cambridge: MIT Press, 2003), 259.

4. Young, "Roll Over Guitar Heros," 27.

5. Ibid., 24.

6. Ibid.

7. "Hello It's Me," *Trouser Press*, August 1982, 6.

8. Carl Rhodes, "Outside the Gates of Eden: Utopia and Work in Rock Music," *Group & Organization Management* 32, no. 1 (2007): 24.

9. For a particularly nuanced reading of the relationship between rock music, work, and professionalism, see Chris McDonald's chapter "The Work of Gifted Hands" in *Rush: Rock Music and the Middle Class* (Bloomington: Indiana University Press, 2009), 101–33.

10. See in particular Charles Keil, "Motion and Feeling Through Music," in Keil and Steven Feld, *Music Grooves* (Chicago: University of Chicago Press, 1994), 53–76; Tricia Rose, *Black Noise: Rap Music and Black Culture in Contemporary America* (Hanover, NH: Wesleyan University Press, 1994); Steve Waksman, *Instruments of Desire: The Electric Guitar and the Shaping of Musical Experience* (Cambridge: Harvard University Press, 1999), 167–206; Susan Fast, *In the Houses of the Holy: Led Zeppelin and the Power of Rock Music* (New York: Oxford University Press, 2001); Elisabeth Le Guin, *Boccherini's Body: An Essay in Carnal Musicology* (Berkeley: University of California Press, 2006); Glenn Pillsbury, *Damage Incorporated: Metallica and the Production of Musical Identity* (New York: Routledge, 2006); Anthony Gritten and Elaine King, eds., *Music and Gesture* (Burlington, VT: Ashgate, 2006).

11. Richard Leppert and Stephen Zank, "The Concert and the Virtuoso," in *Piano Roles: Three Hundred Years of Life with the Piano,* ed. James Parakilas (New Haven: Yale University Press, 1999), 267.

12. Paul Théberge, "Technology," in *Key Terms in Popular Music and Culture,* ed. Bruce Horner and Thomas Swiss (Malden, MA: Blackwell, 1999), 217.

13. Trevor Pinch and Frank Trocco detail the Moog's entry into the late 1960s rock world in vivid detail in *Analog Days: The Invention and Impact of the Moog Synthesizer* (Cambridge: Harvard University Press, 2002).

14. Edward Macan, *Rocking the Classics: English Progressive Rock and the Counterculture* (New York: Oxford University Press, 1997), 34–36.

15. I take the label "one-handed piano player" from keyboardist David Paich of Toto, quoted in Bob Doerschuk, "High on the Charts with Toto," *Contemporary Keyboard,* May 1979, 48.

16. The *Keyboard* staff, "The Power and the Glory of the Lead Synthesizer," *Keyboard,* February 1984, 62.

17. Ibid., 60.

18. On the keyboard's feminine associations, see Arthur Loesser, *Men, Women & Pianos: A Social History* (New York: Simon and Schuster, 1954).

19. Bob Doerschuk, ed., *Rock Keyboard* (New York: Quill, 1985), 5.

20. On the history of male radio hobbyists, see Susan Douglas, *Listening In: Radio and the American Imagination, from Amos'n'Andy and Edward R. Murrow to Wolfman Jack and Howard Stern* (New York: Times Books, 1999). On the rise of male hi-fi enthusiasts and social space of the 1950s suburbs, see Keir Keightley, " 'Turn It Down!' She Shrieked: Gender, Domestic Space, and High Fidelity, 1948–59," *Popular Music* 15, no. 2 (1995): 149–77. On the importance of male hobbyists like Bill Gates to the rise of the personal computer in the 1970s, see Paul E. Ceruzzi, *A History of Modern Computing* (Cambridge: MIT Press, 1998).

21. Eric Gaer, "Emerson, Lake and Palmer: A Force to be Reckoned With," *Downbeat,* May 9, 1974, 15.

22. Pinch, "Giving Birth," 259.

23. David Crombie, *The Synthesizer and Electronic Keyboard Handbook* (New York: Alfred A. Knopf, 1984), 12.

24. As one of the early American new wave synthesizer players, Gear of the Los Angeles band Screamers, explained in a 1978 interview, "We want to push the synthesizer and make it as dynamic as the guitar but without the symbolism attached to it, which is very sexual and phallic." See Evan Hosie, "Are We New Wave? We Are Eno," *New York Rocker,* July–August 1978, 22.

25. Kevin Holm-Hudson, "'Come Sail Away' and the Commodification of 'Prog Lite,'" *American Music* 23, no. 3 (2005): 377–94.

26. Doerschuk's use of the phrase "new romantics" should not be confused with the British movement of the same name (described in chapter 2) that emerged in the early 1980s centered on Spandau Ballet and other bands.

27. Doerschuk, *Rock Keyboard,* 145. It is worth noting that Doerschuk praises the new wave at the expense of the "new romantics" in order to dramatize a juncture in his narrative. In the book's preceding chapter, Doerschuk celebrates these very same supposedly bombastic "new romantics," lavishing attention on their musical approach and style.

28. Ibid., 147.

29. Russ Summers, "Greg Hawkes: Rock in the Fast Lane With The Cars," *Contemporary Keyboard,* April 1980, 8–9.

30. John Diliberto, "Ultravox," *Down Beat,* May 1983, 20.

31. Summers, "Greg Hawkes," 12.

32. Quoted in *Keyboard* staff, "Power and Glory," 62.

33. Doerschuk, *Rock Keyboard,* 149.

34. John Covach, *What's That Sound? An Introduction to Rock and its History,* 2nd ed. (New York: Norton, 2009), 440. Covach's description occurs in a discussion of Wright's "Dream Weaver."

35. Tim Barr, *Kraftwerk: From Düsseldorf to the Future (with Love)* (London: Ebury Press, 1998), 3; Jason Ankeny, "Kraftwerk Biography," *All Music Guide,* http://www.allmusic.com/cg/amg.dll?p=amg&sql=11:kifpxqe5ldde~T1.

36. Gary Numan, with Steve Malins, *Praying to the Aliens (An Autobiography)* (London: Andre Deutsch, 1998), 48.

37. Myles Palmer, *New Wave Explosion: How Punk Became New Wave Became the 80s* (New York: Proteus, 1981), 51.

38. Ray Coleman, "The Numan Who Fell to Earth," *Melody Maker,* October 18, 1980, 33.

39. Ray Coleman, *Gary Numan: The Authorised Biography* (Great Britain: Sidgwick and Jackson, 1982), 38.

40. Numan, *Praying to the Aliens,* 51.

41. Bruce Dancis, "Gary Numan: Britain's New Wave Techno-Rocker," *Contemporary Keyboard,* August 1980, 39.

42. "Letters," *Contemporary Keyboard,* October 1980, 4.

43. The "This is a chord" statement first appeared in *Sideburns,* a British "Stranglerzine" from December 1976. It is reprinted in Savage, *England's Dreaming,* 280.

44. Numan, *Praying to the Aliens,* 49–50.

45. Ibid., 64, 66.

46. Quoted in Steven Grant, "Is Gary Numan Eclectic?" *Trouser Press,* May 1980, 6.

47. Numan, *Praying to the Aliens,* 64.

48. Paul Lester, "When Gary Numan Met Little Boots," *Guardian,* December 3, 2009, http://www.guardian.co.uk/music/2009/dec/03/gary-numan-little-boots-fea ture.

49. Phil Sutcliffe, "Do Sheep Dream of Electric Androids? The Gary Numan Enigma," *Sounds,* October 6, 1979. Reprinted in *Rock's Backpages,* http://www.rocks backpages.com/article.html?ArticleID=3529; Coleman, "Numan Who Fell."

50. On the connection between aliens, androids, and otherness in popular music, see Ken McLeod, "Space Oddities: Aliens, Futurism and Meaning in Popular Music," *Popular Music* 22, no. 3 (2003): 337–55.

51. Numan, *Praying to the Aliens,* 57.

52. Numan uses the parentheses around "Friends" to indicate that they are not real humans, but androids.

53. Numan admits in his autobiography that part of the song's appeal is a main hook that consists of a "wrong note" that he accidentally hit and decided to keep while writing the song on the piano. While he does not reveal *where* in the synthesizer line this occurs, it is reasonable to assume that he is referring to the recurring tritone. Numan, *Praying to the Aliens,* 63.

54. Indeed, it does seem to be the case that "Are 'Friends' Electric?" stemmed not simply from Numan's science fiction imagination, but from his personal experiences. As he explained of the song in a 1979 interview, "That was inspired by living in towerblocks in England, where it's very hip to say that, because we live in towerblocks, we don't need neighbors anymore. I was feeling very depersonalized at the time. It was a time when some friends had turned on me. I was very angry with them, and with not being in contact anymore." Quoted in Grant, "Is Gary Numan Eclectic?" 6.

55. For a particularly compelling look at the contradictory nature of celebrity and stardom as it relates to another musical performer, see Pamela Wilson, "Mountains of Contradictions: Gender, Class, and Region in the Star Image of Dolly Parton," in *Reading Country Music: Steel Guitars, Opry Stars, and Honky-Tonk Bars,* ed. Cecelia Tichi (Durham, NC: Duke University Press, 1998), 98–120.

56. Chris Bohn, "Alone in a Crowd," *Melody Maker,* June 9, 1979, 28–29.

57. Jon Savage, "Gary Numan: In Every Dream Car, a Heart-throb," in *Time Travel: Pop, Media and Sexuality 1976–96* (London: Chatto & Windus, 1996), 106.

58. Quoted in Steve Malins, notes for Tubeway Army, *Replicas,* Beggars Banquet BBL 7 CD.

59. On the prominence of doubles, artificial intelligence, and their relationship to the synthesizer in new wave, see Massimiano Bucchi and Andrea Lorenzet, "Before and After Science: Science and Technology in Pop Music, 1970–1990," in *Communicating Science in Social Contexts: New Models, New Practices,* ed. Donghong Cheng, Michel Claessens, Toss Gascoigne, Jenni Metcalfe, Bernard Schiele, and Shunke Shi (New York: Springer, 2008), 139–50.

60. Quoted in Malins, introduction to Numan, *Praying to the Aliens,* xi.

61. E. L. Widmer, "Crossroads: The Automobile, Rock and Roll and Democracy," in *Autopia: Cars and Culture,* ed. Peter Wollen and Joe Kerr (London: Reaktion, 2002), 65, 68.

62. Gerri Hirshey, "Pink Cadillacs, Little Red Corvettes, Paradise by the Dashboard Light: A Fast, Loud History of Rock & Rap Rides," *Rolling Stone,* May 11, 2000, 91. It should be noted that Hirshey does not include Numan's "Cars" within her historical survey.

63. Scott Isler, "Gary Numan Finds Safety in 'Cars,'" *Rolling Stone,* May 1, 1980, 22.

64. Numan, *Praying to the Aliens,* 73.

65. Don Shewey, "Review of Gary Numan, *The Pleasure Principle," Rolling Stone,* March 20, 1980, 58.

66. Ira Robbins, "Review of Gary Numan, *The Pleasure Principle," Trouser Press,* February 1980, 38.

67. Sutcliffe, "Do Sheep Dream?"

68. Alec Ross, "Human League," *Trouser Press,* November 1980, 12.

69. Bob Doerschuk, "Orchestral Manoeuvres in the Dark," *Keyboard,* April 1982, 30.

70. Freff, "Missing Persons," *Musician,* April 1983, 82.

71. Alan DiPerna, "Musicmaking: Yaz's 'Situation,'" *Music & Sound Output,* February 1983, 98.

72. Robert Walser quotes one such instance in *Running With The Devil: Power, Gender, and Madness in Heavy Metal* (Hanover, NH: Wesleyan University Press, 1993), where the drummer for heavy metal group Anthrax denounces the synthesizer as a "gay" instrument. Walser includes the quote (130) as part of a more extensive discussion addressing the politics of androgyny in 1980s glam metal (124–36).

Chapter 7

1. Mary Harron, "Adam and the Ants," in *The Rock Yearbook 1982,* ed. Al Clark (New York: St. Martin's Press, 1981), 112.

2. All told, the album would stay in the Top 10 for an astounding thirty-three weeks.

3. David Byrne, press kit for Talking Heads, *Remain in Light,* Sire Records SRK 6095.

4. David Breskin, "Talking Heads," in *The Year in Rock 1981–82,* ed. John Swenson (New York: Delilah, 1981), 134.

5. On the terms of, and debates surrounding, "global modernity," see John Tomlinson, *Globalization and Culture* (Chicago: University of Chicago Press, 1999).

6. Steven Feld, "A Sweet Lullaby for World Music," *Public Culture* 12, no. 1 (2000): 146.

7. The term was coined in the early 1980s by Austin, Texas, bandleader and DJ Dan Del Santo.

8. Andrew Goodwin and Joe Gore, "World Beat and the Cultural Imperialism Debate," in Sakolsky and Ho, *Sounding Off!* 122.

9. Keil and Feld, *Music Grooves,* 266.

10. Reebee Garofalo, "Crossing Over: 1939–1989," in *Split Image: African Americans*

in the Mass Media, ed. Janette L. Dates and William Barlow (Washington, DC: Howard University Press, 1990), 57.

11. Vivien Goldman, "Jah Punk: New Wave Digs Reggae," *Sounds,* September 3, 1977. Reprinted in *Rock's Backpages,* http://www.rocksbackpages.com.article.html?ArticleID=8504.

12. Ibid.

13. Much of this positive assessment is based on the activities and live concerts of punk and reggae artists who joined together in 1976–77 in the formation of Rock Against Racism, an organization "set up to combat racial discrimination in rock music and British society in general," especially as spread by the National Front party. For summaries and analyses of Rock Against Racism, see Ian Goodyear, "Rock Against Racism: Multiculturalism and Political Mobilization, 1976–1981," *Immigrants and Minorities* 22, no. 1 (2003): 44–62; Ashley Dawson, "'Love Music, Hate Racism': The Cultural Politics of the Rock Against Racism Campaigns, 1976–1981," *Postmodern Culture* 16, no. 1 (2005), http://muse.jhu.edu/journals/pmc/v016/16.1dawson.html.

14. Richard Grabel, "Live Review: The Slits," *New Musical Express,* January 12, 1980, 35.

15. Marcus, "Wake Up!" 41.

16. Dick Hebdige, *Cut'n'Mix: Culture, Identity and Caribbean Music* (New York: Routledge, 1990), 106.

17. For example, in *Hole In Our Soul: The Loss of Beauty and Meaning in American Popular Music* (New York: Free Press, 1994), Martha Bayles condemns the whole of British punk rock as a mere vessel for McLaren's "perverse modernist" desires. See especially 305–15.

18. Bromberg, *Wicked Ways,* 214.

19. Quoted in Tom Vague's 1981 interview, "Bow-Wow-Wow: I Was a Stowaway By the C-Side," reprinted in *The Great British Mistake: Vague 1977–92* (San Francisco: AK Press, 1994), 25.

20. Robert Palmer, "Latest British Invasion: 'The New Tribalism,'" *New York Times,* November 25, 1981, C13.

21. It should be noted that the phrase *king of the wild frontier* has another, more specific association as well. It is also part of the title from the 1950s Walt Disney theme song for the television series *Davy Crockett.*

22. Roger Wallis and Krister Malm, *Big Sounds from Little People: The Music Industry in Small Countries* (New York: Pendagron Press, 1984), 190–91.

23. Quoted from Adele-Marie Cherrison's interview with Ant in *Sounds,* July 25, 1980. A small portion of the interview is reprinted in George Gimarc's *Post Punk Diary: 1980–1982* (New York: St. Martin's Griffin, 1997), 65.

24. Ant and Pirroni were not the first Western pop musicians to adopt the "Burundi Beat" for their own financial gain. For her 1975 album, *The Hissing of Summer Lawns,* Joni Mitchell, like Mike Steiphenson before her with the original "Burundi Black" single, composed a song, "The Jungle Line," which she laid on top of the track from Vuylsteke's recording. In the album's liner notes she thanks "Burundi," but claims the composer credits exclusively in her own name.

25. R. Murray Schafer, *The Tuning of the World* (New York: Alfred A. Knopf, 1977), 90.

26. Keil and Feld, *Music Grooves,* 259.

27. Ibid., 263.

28. Echo and the Bunnymen later released a recording of the WOMAD performance under the title of "Zimbo" as a flipside to their 1983 single "The Cutter." On the record, singer Ian McCulloch announces the group as "Echo and the Burundi-men."

29. Peter Jowers, "Beating New Tracks: WOMAD and the British World Music Movement," in *The Last Post: Music After Modernism,* ed. Simon Miller (Manchester: Manchester University Press, 1993), 74; Thomas Brooman and Bob Hooton, liner notes for *Raindrops Pattering on Banana Leaves and Other Tunes: A WOMAD Benefit L.P.,* WOMAD records, WOMAD: 001.

30. Ronnie Graham, *The Da Capo Guide to Contemporary African Music* (New York: Da Capo Press, 1988), 230.

31. Richard Harrington, "Who Invited The Ants to America's Rock Picnic?" *Washington Post,* April 12, 1981, H1 and H5.

32. Quoted in Mablen Jones, *Getting it On: The Clothing of Rock 'n' Roll* (New York: Abbeville Press, 1987), 191.

33. While "twang" may seem a rather loose descriptive, this is in fact the adjective by which Eddy was known throughout his career. His first album in 1958, for example, was entitled *Have "Twangy" Guitar Will Travel.*

34. Tim Sommer, "Adam and the Ants," *Trouser Press,* July 1981, 13.

35. Rimmer, *Like Punk Never Happened,* 9. For an extensive and provocative explication of Ant's "theories" and "attitudes" see Fred and Judy Vermorel's *Adam and the Ants* (New York: Omnibus Press, 1981).

36. Fredric Jameson, *Postmodernism, or, The Cultural Logic of Late Capitalism* (Durham, NC: Duke University Press, 1991), 19. Jameson's key pessimistic arguments are sketched on pp. 16–25.

37. The American frontier was never "officially" closed, but in a series of papers and talks in the 1890s the American historian Frederick Jackson Turner offered the results from the census of 1890 as proof that geographically the "open" frontier had by that point ceased to exist. He posed his influential "frontier thesis," that American society had been weaned on the promises of the frontier, and would be in crisis until a new frontier (one that might be found in educational and marketplace ambition and competition) had been found to supplant the one of old. See Turner's *The Frontier in American History* (New York: Henry Holt, 1920). Richard Slotkin has traced, in exhaustive fashion, the expansion of this American frontier myth as a twentieth-century political, media, and cinematic phenomenon in *Gunfighter Nation: The Myth of the Frontier in Twentieth-Century America* (New York: Atheneum, 1992).

38. Richard Slotkin, *The Fatal Environment: The Myth of the Frontier in the Age of Industrialization 1800–1890* (New York: Atheneum, 1985), 53.

39. Roy Harvey Pearce, *The Savages of America: A Study of the Indian and the Idea of Civilization* (Baltimore: John Hopkins Press, 1953), 242.

40. See "Adam, Ants in Heap Big Trouble," *Trouser Press,* June 1981, 4.

41. John Tobler, *Adam and the Ants: Superstar* (Knutsford, Cheshire: Stafford Pemberton, 1982), 53.

42. Wendy Rose, "The Great Pretenders: Further Reflections on Whiteshaman-

ism," in *The State of Native America: Genocide, Colonization, and Resistance*, ed. M. Annette Jaimes (Boston: South End Press, 1992), 413.

43. Harrington, "Who Invited The Ants," H1.

44. "Adam Smokes Peace Pipe," *Trouser Press* (August 1981), 5.

45. Adam Ant, *Stand & Deliver: The Autobiography* (London: Pan Books, 2007), 167.

46. Harrington, "Who Invited The Ants," H5.

47. Vermorel and Vermorel, *Adam and the Ants*, 23.

48. Many studies have examined how Western societies historically have characterized American Indians and other tribal "primitives" as overly sexualized. See, in particular, Raymond William Stedman, *Shadows of the Indian: Stereotypes in American Culture* (Norman: University of Oklahoma Press, 1982); Marianna Torgovnick, *Gone Primitive: Savage Intellects, Modern Lives* (Chicago: University of Chicago Press, 1990); Peter Van Lent, "Her Beautiful Savage: The Current Sexual Image of the Native American Male," in *Dressing in Feathers: The Construction of the Indian in American Popular Culture*, ed. S. Elizabeth Bird (Boulder, CO: Westview Press, 1996), 211–28.

49. Andy Bennett, "Subcultures or Neo-Tribes? Rethinking the Relationship between Youth, Style and Musical Taste," *Sociology* 33, no. 3 (1999): 599–617.

50. This paragraph draws heavily from Peter Stallybrass and Allon White, "Bourgeois Hysteria and the Carnivalesque," in *The Politics and Poetics of Transgression* (Ithaca: Cornell University Press, 1986), 171–90.

51. Torgovnick, *Gone Primitive*, 37.

52. Steve Keaton, "Album Review: Kings of the Wild Frontier," *Sounds*, November 6, 1980. Quoted in Gimarc, *Post Punk Diary*.

53. Jon Young, "Hot Spots," *Trouser Press*, August 1981, 62.

54. Ant, *Stand & Deliver*, 151.

55. Robert Payes, "Review of Thompson Twins *In the Name of Love*," *Trouser Press*, October 1982, 35.

56. Quoted in Ted Fox, *In The Groove: The People Behind the Music* (New York: St. Martin's Press, 1986), 306.

57. See especially Paul Gilroy's comments on the Police in *"There Ain't No Black in the Union Jack": The Cultural Politics of Race and Nation* (Chicago: University of Chicago Press, 1991), 171, and Mike Alleyne, "White Reggae: Cultural Dilution in the Record Industry," *Popular Music and Society* 24, no. 1 (2000): 15–30.

58. George, "Reverse Crossover," 14.

59. Michael Hill, "Basic Black, Off-White," *New York Rocker*, June 1981, 12.

60. See Hebdige's commentary in *Subculture*, 46–50.

61. Eno's comments come from a radio interview with Charles Amirkhanian, "Eno at KPFA: 2 Feb. 1980, 13 March 1980, 2 April 1980," quoted in Eric Tamm, *Brian Eno: His Music and the Vertical Color of Sound*, rev. ed. (New York: Da Capo Press, 1995), 32.

62. Krista Reese, *The Name of This Book is Talking Heads* (New York: Proteus, 1982), 53–54.

63. Mikal Gilmore and Spottswood Erving, "Brian Eno," in Swenson, *Year in Rock 1981–82*, 80.

64. Amirkhanian, "Eno at KPFA," quoted in Tamm, *Brian Eno*, 161.

65. See, for example, Jon Pareles, "Does this Global Village have Two-Way Traffic? Review of David Byrne and Brian Eno *My Life in the Bush of Ghosts*," *Rolling Stone*, April 2, 1981, 60.

66. Tamm, *Brian Eno*, 6.

67. Cynthia Rose, "Brian Eno," *New Musical Express*, July 26, 1980. Reprinted in *Rock's Backpages*, http://www.rocksbackpages.com.article.html?ArticleID=1197.

68. David Sheppard, *On Some Faraway Beach: The Life and Times of Brian Eno* (Chicago: Chicago Review Press, 2009), 341.

69. Frances Lass, "Talking Heads," in *The Rock Yearbook 1982*, ed. Al Clark (New York: St. Martin's Press, 1981), 127.

70. Gans, *Talking Heads*, 87.

71. Alan Merriam, "Review of *African Rhythm and African Sensibility: Aesthetics and Social Action in African Musical Idiom*, by John Miller Chernoff," *Ethnomusicology* 24, no. 3 (1980): 559–61.

72. Gilmore and Erving, "Brian Eno," 83.

73. Bill Milkowski, "Brian Eno: Excursions in the Electronic Environment," *Down Beat*, June 1983, 57.

74. Gans, *Talking Heads*, 78.

75. John Miller Chernoff, *African Rhythm and African Sensibility: Aesthetics and Social Action in African Musical Idioms* (Chicago: University of Chicago Press, 1979), 154.

76. In 1986 the members of Los Lobos would find themselves in a scenario similar to that of the Talking Heads's rhythm section, recording the song "All Around the World" with Paul Simon for inclusion on his *Graceland* album. Cesar Rosas and Louis Perez of the band describe how the song transpired: "So we got into the studio, there were no songs. After a while we started feeling like idiots: 'when is he going to show us the song?' . . . We expected him to have a song ready for us to interpret when we met him in Los Angeles, but he said, 'You guys just play,' and we said 'Play what?' We just worked up a bunch of stuff that he eventually got a song out of, and that was it." On the album Simon would claim sole songwriting credit for both the lyrics and the music. Rosas's and Perez's quotes are from an April 1987 interview with *Musician* magazine, quoted in Steven Feld, "Notes on World Beat," *Public Culture* 1, no. 1 (1988): 35.

77. John Rockwell, *All American Music: Composition in the Late Twentieth Century* (New York: Vintage, 1983), 240.

78. Tucker, "Africa Calling," 55.

79. Ibid.

80. Other critics had commended the Talking Heads for uniting "dancing" and "thinking" prior to *Remain in Light*. See, for example, Michael Shore's review of *Fear of Music*, in *New York Rocker*, August 1979, 40: "[The] Talking Heads are funkier than ever. *But*, while it's all quite danceable, it's the kind of stuff that's sure to provoke disturbing thoughts while you boogie."

81. Mitchell Cohen, "Play That Funky Music White Boy: Review of Talking Heads *Remain in Light*," *Creem*, January 1981, 52.

82. Frith, *Sound Effects*, 19, 21.

83. For more on the moral panic surrounding ragtime, see David Joyner's "The Ragtime Controversy," in *America's Musical Pulse*, ed. Kenneth J. Bindas (Westport, CT: Greenwood Press, 1992), 239–47. For the historical connection between black music and black rhythm, see Ronald Radano, "Hot Fantasies: American Modernism and the Idea of Black Rhythm," in *Music and the Racial Imagination*, ed. Ronald Radano and Philip V. Bohlman (Chicago: University of Chicago Press, 2000), 459–80.

84. Philip Tagg, "Open Letter: 'Black Music,' 'Afro-American Music' and 'European Music,'" *Popular Music* 8, no. 3 (1989): 285–98.

85. Breskin, "Talking Heads," 134.

86. Hill, "Basic Black, Off-White," 12.

87. Ibid.

88. Ibid.

89. Ibid.

90. Feld, "Notes on World Beat," 37.

Epilogue

1. Simon Reynolds, "The 70's are so 90's. The 80's are the Thing Now," *New York Times*, May 5, 2002, A1.

2. Gina Arnold, "So New, It's Old," *Metroactive*, April 25–May 1, 1996. Reprinted at *Metroactive.com*, http://www.metroactive.com/papers/metro/04.25.96/new-wave-9617.html.

3. Andrew Essex, "'70s vs '80s," *Entertainment Weekly*, March 13, 1998, *EW.com*, http://www.ew.com/ew/article/0,,282160,00.html.

4. Reynolds, "The 70's are so 90's," A48. Reynolds refers to these groups as "electro," but one also commonly finds them lumped under the label of "electroclash."

5. Elizabeth Guffey, *Retro: The Culture of Revival* (London: Reaktion, 2006), 133.

6. Musicologist Timothy Taylor has applied the label of "technostalgia" to 1990s groups like Stereolab whose use of vintage keyboards evoked the "space age pop" of the late 1950s and early 1960s. See Taylor, *Strange Sounds*, 96–114.

7. Stuart Borthwick and Ron Moy, *Popular Music Genres: An Introduction* (New York: Routledge, 2004).

8. It should be noted that part of the book's bias toward synthpop reflects its British origins. While *new wave* and *new music* were popular terms in North America throughout the early 1980s, British journalists and music critics largely abandoned these labels during this time and instead tended to categorize bands in subgenres like synthpop.

9. George Lipsitz, *Time Passages: Collective Memory and American Popular Culture* (Minneapolis: University of Minnesota Press, 1990), 99–132.

10. This phrase is borrowed from George Melly's *Revolt into Style: The Pop Arts* (Garden City, NY: Anchor, 1971).

11. Elizabeth Goodman, "The Lady Killers," *Spin*, November 2004, 73.

12. I am borrowing the label "therapy rock" from Michael Azzerad's article "Punk's Earnest New Mission," *New York Times*, January 4, 2004, AR1, AR32.

13. Reynolds, "The 70's are so 90's," A48.

14. "The Modern Biography," http://www.ilikemusic.com/features/The_Modern-1252.

15. "Black Tie Dynasty, *Movements*," http://www.idolrecords.com/onesheets/index.php?ID=62.

16. Neil McCormick, "La Roux, Lady Gaga, Mika, Little Boots: The 80s are Back," *Telegraph.co.uk*, August 5, 2009, http://www.telegraph.co.uk/culture/music/rockandpopfeatures/5978573/La-Roux-Lady-Gaga-Mika-Little-Boots-the-80s-are-back.html.

Bibliography

Acland, Charles, ed. *Residual Media*. Minneapolis: University of Minnesota Press, 2007.

"Adam, Ants in Heap Big Trouble." *Trouser Press,* June 1981, 4.

"Adam Smokes Peace Pipe." *Trouser Press,* August 1981, 5.

Alleyne, Mike. "White Reggae: Cultural Dilution in the Record Industry." *Popular Music and Society* 24, no. 1 (2000): 15–30.

Altman, Billy. "Review of *The Cars.*" *Creem,* September 1978, 61.

Anderson, Rick. "Rock Lobster." *All Music Guide,* http://www.allmusic.com/song/rock-lobster_+2049401 (accessed November 22, 2010).

Angel, Johnny. "Skinny Ties & Spiky Hair: The Guitarists of the New Wave Remember." *Guitar Player,* August 1995, 42–48.

Ankeny, Jason. "Kraftwerk Biography." *All Music Guide,* http://www.allmusic.com/cg/amg.dll?p=amg&sql=11:kifpxqe5ldde~T1 (accessed May 17, 2010).

Ant, Adam. *Stand & Deliver: The Autobiography.* London: Pan Books, 2007.

Arnold, Gina. "So New, It's Old." *Metroactive,* April 25–May 1, 1996. Reprinted at *Metroactive.com,* http://www.metroactive.com/papers/metro/04.25.96/new-wave-9617.html.

Atkinson, Terry. "The Knack: Yesterday and Today." *Rolling Stone,* October 18, 1979, 9, 32, 36–37.

Azzerad, Michael. "Punk's Earnest New Mission." *New York Times,* January 4, 2004, AR1, AR32.

Baird, Jock. "A Flock of Seagulls: Easy Street Comes to an End." *Musician,* September 1983, 22–30, 114.

Baker, Glenn A., and Stuart Coupe. *The New Music.* New York: Harmony Books, 1981.

Ballard, J. G. "The Sound-Sweep." In *The Voices of Time,* 41–79. London: Victor Gollancz, 1985.

Bangs, Lester. "David Byrne Says 'Boo!'" In *Mainlines, Blood Feasts, and Bad Taste: A Lester Bangs Reader,* ed. John Morthland, 115–18. New York: Anchor, 2002.

Barke, Megan, Rebecca Fribush, and Peter N. Stearns. "Nervous Breakdown in 20th-Century American Culture." *Journal of Social History* 33, no. 3 (2000): 565–84.

Barnes, Ken. "Top 40 Radio: A Fragment of the Imagination." In *Facing the Music*, ed. Simon Frith, 8–50. New York: Pantheon, 1988.

Barr, Tim. *Kraftwerk: From Düsseldorf to the Future (with Love)*. London: Ebury Press, 1998.

Batchelor, David. "Everything as Colour." In *Donald Judd*, ed. Nicholas Serota, 64–75. New York: Distributed Art Publishers, 2004.

Bayles, Martha. *Hole In Our Soul: The Loss of Beauty and Meaning in American Popular Music*. New York: Free Press, 1994.

Beard, George. *American Nervousness, Its Causes and Consequences*. New York: G. P. Putnam's Sons, 1881.

Belz, Carl. *The Story of Rock*. New York: Oxford University Press, 1969.

Bennett, Andy. "Subcultures or Neo-Tribes? Rethinking the Relationship between Youth, Style and Musical Taste." *Sociology* 33, no. 3 (1999): 599–617.

Berry, Mick, and Jason Gianni. *The Drummer's Bible: How to Play Every Drum Style from Afro-Cuban to Zydeco*. Tucson: See Sharp Press, 2004.

Betrock, Alan, and Andy Schwartz. "The Future's Gleam: A Rock and Roll Survey." *New York Rocker*, September 1978, 30–33.

Bianco, David. *Who's New Wave in Music: An Illustrated Encyclopedia 1976–1982 (The First Wave)*. Ann Arbor, MI: Pierian Press, 1985.

Binkley, Sam. *Getting Loose: Lifestyle Consumption in the 1970s*. Durham, NC: Duke University Press, 2007.

Bisch, Louis E. *Be Glad You're Neurotic*. New York: Whittlesey House, 1936.

Black, Bill. "The Smiths: Keep Young and Beautiful." *Sounds*, November 19, 1983. Reprinted in *Rock's Back Pages*, http://www.rocksbackpages.com/article.html?ArticleID=6282.

"Black Tie Dynasty, *Movements*." http://www.idolrecords.com/onesheets/index.php?ID=62 (accessed May 23, 2010).

Blair, John. "Chairmen of the Board: The Surf Guitar Summit." *Guitar Player*, September 1996, 68–82.

Block, Adam. "The Confessions of a Gay Rocker." *Advocate*, April 15, 1982, 43–47.

Bodinger-deUriarte, Christina. "Opposition to Hegemony in the Music of Devo: A Simple Matter of Remembering." *Journal of Popular Culture* 18, no. 4 (1984–85): 56–71.

Boehlert, Eric. "Modern Rock Comes into its Own: Genre Flexes its Hit-Making Muscle." *Billboard*, April 9, 1994, 1, 69.

Boehlert, Eric. "Modern Rock Radio Branching Out: Format Offshoots Mix Fresh with Familiar." *Billboard*, January 15, 1994, 1, 63.

Boehlert, Eric. "Modern Rock Radio Roars Ahead: Format's Growth Continues to Surprise." *Billboard*, November 5, 1994, 5, 115.

Bohn, Chris. "Alone in a Crowd." *Melody Maker*, June 9, 1979, 28–29.

Boone, Daniel R. *Human Communication and its Disorders*. Englewood Cliffs, NJ: Prentice Hall, 1987.

Borack, John M. *Shake Some Action: The Ultimate Power Pop Guide*. Fort Collins, CO: Not Lame Recording Co., 2007.

Borthwick, Stuart, and Ron Moy. *Popular Music Genres: An Introduction*. New York: Routledge, 2004.

Bowman, David. *This Must Be the Place: The Adventures of Talking Heads in the 20th Century*. New York: HarperCollins, 2001.

Brandt, Galen. "Talking Heads." *Trouser Press,* November 1979, 21–26.

Breskin, David. "Talking Heads." In *The Year in Rock 1981–82,* ed. John Swenson, 128–35. New York: Delilah, 1981.

Breward, Christopher. *The Culture of Fashion: A New History of Fashionable Dress.* New York: Manchester University Press, 1994.

Brewer, Roy. "The Use of Habanera Rhythm in Rockabilly Music." *American Music* 17, no. 3 (1999): 300–17.

Bromberg, Craig. *The Wicked Ways of Malcolm McLaren.* New York: Harper & Row, 1989.

Brooman, Thomas, and Bob Hooton. Notes for *Raindrops Pattering on Banana Leaves and Other Tunes: A WOMAD Benefit L.P.* WOMAD records, WOMAD: 001.

Bucholtz, Mary. "The Whiteness of Nerds: Superstandard English and Racial Markedness." *Journal of Linguistic Anthropology* 11, no. 1 (2001): 84–100.

Bucchi, Massimiano, and Andrea Lorenzet. "Before and After Science: Science and Technology in Pop Music, 1970–1990." In *Communicating Science in Social Contexts: New Models, New Practices,* ed. Donghong Cheng, Michel Claessens, Toss Gascoigne, Jenni Metcalfe, Bernard Schiele and Shunke Shi, 139–50. New York: Springer, 2008.

Byrne, David. Press Kit for Talking Heads, *Remain in Light.* Sire Records SRK 6095.

Cafarelli, Carl. "The Kids Are Alright! The History of Power Pop." *Goldmine,* January 5, 1996, 20–44, 130–32, 137–40.

Carr, Roy. "The Highly Original Thoughts of Chairman Fieger." *New Musical Express,* March 22, 1980, 19, 63.

Carter, Julian B. *The Heart of Whiteness: Normal Sexuality and Race in America, 1880–1940.* Durham, NC: Duke University Press, 2007.

Cateforis, Theo. "Performing the Avant-Garde Groove: Devo and the Whiteness of the New Wave." *American Music* 22, no. 4 (2004): 564–88.

"Celebrity Rate a Record: Molly Hatchet." *Hit Parader,* September 1983, 23.

Ceruzzi, Paul E. *A History of Modern Computing.* Cambridge: MIT Press, 1998.

Chase, Clifford. "Am I Getting Warmer: The B-52's: *The B-52's.*" In *Heavy Rotation: Twenty Writers on the Albums that Changed Their Lives,* ed. Peter Terzian, 142–71. New York: Harper Perennial, 2009.

Chernoff, John Miller. *African Rhythm and African Sensibility: Aesthetics and Social Action in African Musical Idioms.* Chicago: University of Chicago Press, 1979.

Christgau, Robert. "Christgau Consumer Guide." *Creem,* May 1983, 12.

Christgau, Robert. "Rock'n'Roller Coaster: The Music Biz on a Joyride." *Village Voice,* February 7, 1984, 37–45.

Christgau, Robert. "Triumph of the New Wave: Results of the Fifth (or Sixth) Annual Pazz and Jop Critics' Poll." *Village Voice,* January 22, 1979, 1, 39–41.

Christian, Laura. "The Sign's Send-Up: Camp and the Performing Subject of Semiosis." *Semiotica* 137 (2001): 117–38.

Clarke, Alison J. *Tupperware: The Promise of Plastic in 1950s America.* Washington, DC: Smithsonian Institution Press, 1999.

Clisby, Suzanne. "Summer Sex: Youth, Desire and the Carnivalesque at the English Seaside." In *Transgressive Sex: Subversion and Control in Erotic Encounters,* ed. Hastings Donnan and Fiona Magowan, 47–68. New York: Berghahn, 2009.

Cohen, Mitch. "The B-52's: Climate Control in the Land of 16 Dances." *Creem*, December 1979, 36–37, 59–60.

Cohen, Mitchell. "Play That Funky Music White Boy: Review of Talking Heads *Remain in Light*." *Creem*, January 1981, 52.

Cohen, Mitch. "Review of *The Romantics*." *Creem*, April 1980, 54.

Cohen, Mitch. "What Price Glory? Ramones Soldier On." *Creem*, June 1980, 24–25, 58–59.

Cohn, Stuart. "The B-52's: Just Like Us." *Trouser Press*, November 1979, 8.

Coleman, Mark. "The Knack." In *The Rolling Stone Album Guide*, ed. Anthony DeCurtis and James Henke, with Holly George-Warren, 404–5. New York: Random House, 1992.

Coleman, Ray. *Gary Numan: The Authorised Biography*. London: Sidgwick and Jackson, 1982.

Coleman, Ray. "The Numan Who Fell to Earth." *Melody Maker*, October 18, 1980, 32–34.

Considine, J. D. "The Cars." *Musician Player & Listener*, January 1982, 52–61.

Coon, Caroline. "If the Kids are United . . ." *Sounds*, June 3, 1978. Reprinted in *Rock's Backpages* http://www.rocksbackpages.com/article.html?ArticleID=11035.

Coon, Caroline. "Punk Alphabet." *Melody Maker*, November 27, 1976, 33.

Copeland, Ian. *Wild Thing: The Backstage, On the Road, In the Studio, Off the Charts Memoirs of Ian Copeland*. New York: Simon & Schuster, 1995.

"Corporate Life Forms on Virgin Territory: DEVO." In *Search & Destroy #7–11: The Complete Reprint*, ed. V. Vale, 6, 37. San Francisco: V/Search, 1997. Originally published in *Search & Destroy* 7 (1978).

Cott, Jonathan. "John Lennon: A Conversation." *Rolling Stone*, January 22, 1981, 37–39.

Covach, John. "Pangs of History in Late 1970s New-Wave Rock." In *Analyzing Popular Music*, ed. Allan Moore, 173–95. New York: Cambridge University Press, 2003.

Covach, John. *What's That Sound: An Introduction to Rock and its History*, 2nd ed. New York: Norton, 2009.

Crenshaw, Marshall. Notes for *Poptopia! Power Pop Classics of the '80s*, Rhino compact disc, R2 72729.

Crombie, David. *The Synthesizer and Electronic Keyboard Handbook*. New York: Alfred A. Knopf, 1984.

Cunningham, Mark. *Good Vibrations: A History of Record Production*. Chessington, Surrey: Castle Communications, 1996.

Daley, David. "In The Light." *Alternative Press*, November 1999, 68–78.

Dancis, Bruce. "Gary Numan: Britain's New Wave Techno Rocker." *Contemporary Keyboard*, August 1980, 38–46.

Darling, Cary. "New Wave Wins Programming OK." *Billboard*, November 10, 1979, 1, 28.

Davis, Fred. *Fashion, Culture and Identity*. Chicago: University of Chicago Press, 1992.

Davis, Fred. *Yearning for Yesterday: A Sociology of Nostalgia*. New York: The Free Press, 1979.

Davis, Phil. "Three Minutes with Shoes." *New York Rocker*, February 1981, 28, 38.

Dawson, Ashley. "'Love Music, Hate Racism': The Cultural Politics of the Rock

Against Racism Campaigns, 1976–1981." *Postmodern Culture* 16, no. 1 (2005), http://muse.jhu.edu/journals/pmc/v016/16.1dawson.html.

The Decline of Western Civilization: Original Soundtrack. Slash audio recording, SR 105.

DeCurtis, Anthony. "The B-52's Return Home." *Rolling Stone,* November 27, 1980, 84.

Dellinger, Jade, and David Giffels. *Are We Not Men? We Are Devo!* London: SAF, 2003.

Denisoff, R. Serge. *Inside MTV.* New Brunswick, NJ: Transaction Books, 1988.

Denisoff, R. Serge. *Tarnished Gold: The Record Industry Revisited.* New Brunswick, NJ: Transaction Books, 1986.

de Whalley, Chas. "Jam: Maximum New Wave." *Sounds,* March 5, 1977. Reprinted in *Rock's Backpages,* http://www.rocksbackpages.com/article.html?ArticleID=8292.

Diliberto, John. "Ultravox." *Down Beat,* May 1983, 18–21, 54.

DiPerna, Alan. "Musicmaking: Yaz's 'Situation.'" *Music & Sound Output,* February 1983, 98, 102.

Doerschuk, Bob. "High on the Charts with Toto." *Contemporary Keyboard,* May 1979, 12, 48.

Doerschuk, Bob. "The New Synthesizer Rock: Stripped-Down Dance Music for an Electronic World." *Keyboard,* June 1982, 11–18.

Doerschuk, Bob. "Orchestral Manoeuvres in the Dark." *Keyboard,* April 1982, 30–36.

Doerschuk, Bob, ed. *Rock Keyboard.* New York: Quill, 1985.

Doherty, Thomas. *Teenagers & Teenpics: The Juvenilization of American Movies in the 1950s.* Boston: Unwin Hyman, 1988.

Dorfles, Gillo, ed. *Kitsch: The World of Bad Taste.* New York: Bell, 1969.

Doris, Sara. *Pop Art and the Contest Over American Culture.* New York: Cambridge University Press, 2007.

Douchet, Jean. *French New Wave.* Trans. Robert Bonnono. New York: Distributed Art Publishers, 1999.

Douglas, Susan. *Listening In: Radio and the American Imagination, from Amos'n'Andy and Edward R. Murrow to Wolfman Jack and Howard Stern.* New York: Times Books, 1999.

Dyer, Richard. "It's Being So Camp as Keeps Us Going." In *Camp: Queer Aesthetics and the Performing Subject,* ed. Fabio Cleto, 110–16. Ann Arbor: University of Michigan Press, 1999.

Dyer, Richard. *White.* New York: Routledge, 1997.

Earles, Andrew. "The '70s: The Birth of Uncool." *Magnet,* October–November 2002, 42–43.

Easter, Mitch. Notes for *Poptopia! Power Pop Classics of the '80s,* Rhino compact disc, R2 72729.

Eden, Kevin S. *Wire . . . Everybody Loves A History.* Wembley: SAF, 1991.

Elms, Robert. "B-52's." *New Styles New Sounds Magazine,* April 1982. Reprinted in *The Third Pyramid: The B-52's Archive,* http://www.btinternet.com/~roc.lobsta/new sounds.html.

Essex, Andrew. "'70s vs '80s'." *Entertainment Weekly,* March 13, 1998. *EW.com,* http://www.ew.com/ew/article/0,,282160,00.html.

Fallows, David. "Ars Nova." *The New Grove Dictionary of Music and Musicians.* Vol. 2, ed. Stanley Sadie, 80–81. London: Macmillan, 2001.

Farley, Christopher John. "Waiting For the Next Big Thing." *Time,* December 16, 1996, 70–71.

Fast, Susan. *In the Houses of the Holy: Led Zeppelin and the Power of Rock Music.* New York: Oxford University Press, 2001.

Feld, Steven. "Notes on World Beat." *Public Culture* 1, no. 1 (1988): 31–37.

Feld, Steven. "A Sweet Lullaby for World Music." *Public Culture* 12, no. 1 (2000): 145–71.

Fiske, John. *Reading Popular Culture.* Boston: Unwin Hyman, 1989.

Flanagan, Bill. "The Age of Excess." *Musician,* November 1989, 30–40.

Flanagan, Bill. "Cookin' With Roy Thomas Baker." *Trouser Press,* January 1982, 25–28.

Ford, Phil. "Jazz Exotica and the Naked City." *Journal of Musicological Research* 27, no. 2 (2008): 113–33.

Fox, Ted. *In The Groove: The People Behind the Music.* New York: St. Martin's Press, 1986.

Frank, Tom. "Alternative to What?" In *Sounding Off!: Music as Subversion/Resistance/Revolution,* ed. Ron Sakolsky and Fred Wei-Han Ho, 109–19. Brooklyn, NY: Autonomedia, 1995.

Fraser, Kennedy. "On and Off the Avenue: Feminine Fashions." *New Yorker,* April 14, 1975, 80–89.

Freff. "Missing Persons." *Musician,* April 1983, 80–83.

Fricke, Aaron. *Reflections of a Rock Lobster: A Story about Growing Up Gay.* Boston: Alyson Publications, Inc., 1981.

Fricke, David. "The Declaration of Independents." In *The Rock Yearbook 1985,* ed. Allan Jones, 120–22. Toronto: Stoddart, 1984.

Friedman, Susan Stanford. "Definitional Excursions: The Meanings of *Modern/Modernity/Modernism.*" *MODERNISM/modernity* 8, no. 3 (2001): 493–513.

Frith, Simon. "Art Ideology and Pop Practice." In *Marxism and the Interpretation of Culture,* ed. Cary Nelson and Lawrence Grossberg, 461–75. Urbana: University of Illinois Press, 1988.

Frith, Simon. "Pop Music." In *The Cambridge Companion to Pop and Rock,* ed. Simon Frith, Will Straw, and John Street, 93–108. New York: Cambridge University Press, 2001.

Frith, Simon. "The Return of Passion." *New Statesman,* October 2, 1981, 24–25.

Frith, Simon. *Sound Effects: Youth, Leisure and the Politics of Rock'n'Roll.* New York: Pantheon, 1981.

Frith, Simon, and Angela McRobbie. "Rock and Sexuality." In *On Record: Rock, Pop, and the Written Word,* ed. Simon Frith and Andrew Goodwin, 371–89. New York: Pantheon, 1990.

Gaar, Gillian G. *She's a Rebel: The History of Women in Rock & Roll.* Seattle: Seal Press, 1992.

Gaer, Eric. "Emerson, Lake and Palmer: A Force to be Reckoned With." *Downbeat,* May 9, 1974, 14–15, 31.

Gans, David. *Talking Heads: The Band & Their Music.* New York: Avon, 1985.

Garofalo, Reebee. "Crossing Over: 1939–1989." In *Split Image: African Americans in the Mass Media,* ed. Janette L. Dates and William Barlow, 57–121. Washington, DC: Howard University Press, 1990.

Garofalo, Reebee. *Rockin' Out: Popular Music in the USA.* 4th ed. Upper Saddle River, NJ: Pearson Prentice Hall, 2008.

Gaudio, Rudolf P. "Sounding Gay: Pitch Properties in the Speech of Gay and Straight Men." *American Speech* 69, no. 1 (1994): 30–57.

Gendron, Bernard. *Between Montmartre and the Mudd Club: Popular Music and the Avant-Garde*. Chicago: University of Chicago Press, 2002.

George, Nelson. "Reverse Crossover." *New York Rocker*, June 1981, 14.

George, Nelson, and Paul Grein. "Black Formats Offer More New Act Airplay." *Billboard*, June 5, 1982, 1, 22.

Gilmore, Mikal. "Talking Heads: Psychodramas You Can Dance To." *Rolling Stone*, November 29, 1979, 9, 20, 23–24.

Gilmore, Mikal, and Spottswood Erving. "Brian Eno." In *The Year in Rock 1981–82*, ed. John Swenson, 80–85. New York: Delilah, 1981.

Gilroy, Paul. *"There Ain't No Black in the Union Jack": The Cultural Politics of Race and Nation*. Chicago: University of Chicago Press, 1991.

Gimarc, George. *Post Punk Diary: 1980–1982*. New York: St. Martin's Griffin, 1997.

Gjerdingen, Robert. *A Classic Turn of Phrase: Music and the Psychology of Convention*. Philadelphia: University of Pennsylvania Press, 1988.

Goldman, Vivien. "Jah Punk: New Wave Digs Reggae." *Sounds*, September 3, 1977. Reprinted in *Rock's Backpages*, http://www.rocksbackpages.com/article.html?ArticleID=8504.

Goodman, Elizabeth. "The Lady Killers." *Spin*, November 2004, 72–74.

Goodwin, Andrew. *Dancing in the Distraction Factory: Music Television and Popular Culture*. Minneapolis: University of Minnesota Press, 1992.

Goodwin, Andrew. "Popular Music and Postmodern Theory." In *The Postmodern Arts: An Introductory Reader*, ed. Nigel Wheale, 80–100. New York: Routledge, 1995.

Goodwin, Andrew. "Rationalization and Democratization in the New Technologies of Popular Music." In *Popular Music and Communication*, 2nd ed., ed. James Lull, 75–100. Newbury Park, CA: Sage, 1991.

Goodwin, Andrew, and Joe Gore. "World Beat and the Cultural Imperialism Debate." In *Sounding Off! Music as Subversion/Resistance/Revolution*, ed. Ron Sakolsky and Fred Wei-Han Ho, 121–31. Brooklyn, NY: Autonomedia, 1995.

Goodyear, Ian. "Rock Against Racism: Multiculturalism and Political Mobilization, 1976–1981." *Immigrants and Minorities* 22, no. 1 (2003): 44–62.

Gore, Joe, and Andrew Goodwin. "Your Time is Gonna Come: Talking about Led Zeppelin." *One Two Three Four* 4 (Winter 1987): 4–11.

Gosse, Van. "Electropop." *Music & Sound Output*, March–April 1982, 86–90.

Gosling, F. G. *Before Freud: Neurasthenia and the American Medical Community, 1870–1910*. Urbana: University of Illinois Press, 1987.

Grabel, Richard. "Déjà Vu: Only the Bands have Changed at the Heatwave Festival." *Trouser Press*, November 1980, 25–27.

Grabel, Richard. "Live Reviews: The Slits." *New Musical Express*, January 12, 1980, 35.

Graham, Ronnie. *The Da Capo Guide to Contemporary African Music*. New York: Da Capo Press, 1988.

Gramsci, Antonio. *Selections from the Prison Notebooks*. Ed. and trans. Quinton Hoare and Geoffrey Nowell-Smith. New York: International Publishers, 1971.

Grant, Steven. "Is Gary Numan Eclectic?" *Trouser Press*, May 1980, 6, 44.

Graustark, Barbara. "Devo's Primal Pop." *Newsweek,* October 30, 1978, 77.

Green, Jim. "The Agony and the XTC." *Trouser Press,* August 1978, 12.

Green, Jim. "Blondie: Progress Report from the Power Station." *Trouser Press,* September 1979, 12–18.

Green, Jim. "Changing Records." *Trouser Press,* March 1980, 24–27, 41.

Green, Jim. "Green Circles." *Trouser Press,* September 1979, 32.

Greenberg, Clement. "Avant-Garde and Kitsch." *Partisan Review* 6, no. 5 (1939): 34–49.

Gritten, Anthony, and Elaine King, eds. *Music and Gesture.* Burlington, VT: Ashgate, 2006.

Guffey, Elizabeth. *Retro: The Culture of Revival.* London: Reaktion, 2006.

Halnon, Karen Bettez. "Poor Chic: The Rationalization Consumption of Poverty." *Current Sociology* 50, no. 4 (2002): 501–16.

Handley, Susannah. *Nylon: The Story of a Fashion Revolution.* Baltimore: Johns Hopkins University Press, 1999.

Harrington, Richard. "Who Invited The Ants to America's Rock Picnic?" *Washington Post,* April 12, 1981, H1, H5.

Harrison, Ed. "AOR Cuts New Wave Shows." *Billboard,* September 26, 1981, 1, 14.

Harron, Mary. "Adam and the Ants." In *The Rock Yearbook 1982,* ed. Al Clark, 112. New York: St. Martin's Press, 1981.

Hebdige, Dick. *Cut'n'Mix: Culture, Identity and Caribbean Music.* New York: Routledge, 1990.

Hebdige, Dick. *Subculture: The Meaning of Style.* London: Methuen, 1979.

"Hello It's Me." *Trouser Press,* December 1980, 2.

"Hello It's Me." *Trouser Press,* August 1982, 6.

Henke, James. "The B-52's." *Rolling Stone,* December 11, 1980, 9–13.

Henke, James. "Heatwave: Did New Wave Sell Out?" *Rolling Stone,* October 16, 1980, 24–25.

Heylin, Clinton. *Babylon's Burning: From Punk to Grunge.* New York: Canongate, 2007.

Heylin, Clinton. *From The Velvets to the Voidoids: A Pre-Punk History for a Post-Punk World.* New York: Penguin, 1993.

Hill, Michael. "Basic Black, Off-White." *New York Rocker,* June 1981, 12–13.

Hirshey, Gerri. "Pink Cadillacs, Little Red Corvettes, Paradise by the Dashboard Light: A Fast, Loud History of Rock & Rap Rides." *Rolling Stone,* May 11, 2000, 87–114.

The History of Rock'n'Roll. Vol. 9, *Punk.* Produced and directed by Ted Haimes. 60 min. Time Life Warner Home Video, 1995. Videocassette.

Holbrook, Morris B. "On the New Nostalgia: 'These Foolish Things' and Echoes of the Dear Departed Past." In *Continuities in Popular Culture: The Present in the Past & the Past in the Present and Future,* ed. Ray B. Browne and Ronald J. Ambrosetti, 74–120. Bowling Green, OH: Bowling Green State University Press, 1993.

Holm-Hudson, Kevin. "'Come Sail Away' and the Commodification of 'Prog Lite.'" *American Music* 23, no. 3 (2005): 377–94.

Hosie, Evan. "Are We New Wave? We Are Eno." *New York Rocker,* July–August 1978, 22–23.

Hutcheon, Linda. *Irony's Edge: The Theory and Politics of Irony.* New York: Routledge, 1994.

Isler, Scott. "Gary Numan Finds Safety in 'Cars.'" *Rolling Stone,* May 1, 1980, 22.

Isler, Scott. "The Short and Long of the Ramones." *Trouser Press,* May 1980, 16–19.

Jameson, Fredric. "The Politics of Theory: Ideological Positions in the Postmodernism Debate." *New German Critique* 33 (Autumn 1984): 53–65.

Jameson, Fredric. *Postmodernism, or, The Cultural Logic of Late Capitalism.* Durham, NC: Duke University Press, 1991.

Joe, Radcliffe. "Dearth of Superstars Dims Industry Future: Producer Rather than Artist is Star." *Billboard,* July 14, 1979, 46, 67, 71.

Jones, Mablen. *Getting it On: The Clothing of Rock 'n' Roll.* New York: Abbeville Press, 1987.

Jowers, Peter. "Beating New Tracks; WOMAD and the British World Music Movement." In *The Last Post: Music After Modernism,* ed. Simon Miller, 52–87. New York: Manchester University Press, 1993.

Joyner, David. "The Ragtime Controversy." In *America's Musical Pulse,* ed. Kenneth J. Bindas, 239–47. Westport, CT: Greenwood Press, 1992.

Kahne, David. "Producing: The Art of Low-Budget Recording." *Music & Sound Output,* December 1982, 104–6.

Kammen, Michael. *Mystic Chords of Memory: The Transformation of Tradition in American Culture.* New York: Alfred A. Knopf, 1991.

Karp, Marjorie. "Album Reviews: The db's 'Stands For Decibels.'" *New York Rocker,* May 1981, 44.

Keightley, Keir. "Reconsidering Rock." In *The Cambridge Companion to Pop and Rock,* ed. Simon Frith, Will Straw, and John Street, 109–42. New York: Cambridge University Press, 2001.

Keightley, Keir. "'Turn It Down!' She Shrieked: Gender, Domestic Space, and High Fidelity, 1948–59." *Popular Music* 15, no. 2 (1995): 149–77.

Keil, Charles, and Steven Feld. *Music Grooves.* Chicago: University of Chicago Press, 1994.

Kent, Nick. "New York: The Dark Side of Town." *New Musical Express,* May 5, 1973. Reprinted in *Rock's Backpages,* http://www.rocksbackpages.com/article.html?ArticleID=16007.

The *Keyboard* Staff. "The Power and the Glory of Lead Synthesizer." *Keyboard,* February 1984, 60–69.

Kozak, Roman. "Punk Music Analyzed, Praised and Blasted at N.Y. Session." *Billboard,* March 25, 1978, 26.

Kozak, Roman. "Punk Rock Grows in N.Y." *Billboard,* November 20, 1976, 1, 66, 86.

Kozak, Roman. "Rock Disco Pops in N.Y. Houses." *Billboard,* July 14, 1979, 46, 66, 86.

Kozak, Roman. "Techno-pop Groups Make Chart Inroads." *Billboard,* December 25, 1982, 3, 89.

Kronengold, Charles. "Exchange Theories in Disco, New Wave, and Album-Oriented Rock." *Criticism* 50, no. 1 (2008): 43–82.

Laing, Dave. *One Chord Wonders: Power and Meaning in Punk Rock.* Philadelphia: Open University Press, 1985.

Lass, Frances. "Talking Heads." In *The Rock Yearbook,* ed. Al Clark, 126–27. New York: St. Martin's Press, 1981.

Laukka, Petri, Clas Linnman, Fredrik Åhs, Anna Pissiota, Örjan Frans, Vanda Faria, Åsa Michelgård, Lieuwe Appel, Mats Fredrikson, and Tomas Furmark. "In a Nervous Voice: Acoustic Analysis and Perception of Anxiety in Social Phobics' Speech." *Journal of Nonverbal Behavior* 32, no. 4 (2008): 195–214.

Laverty, MT. "Devo: In Search of the Big Enema." *Trouser Press,* April 1978, 12, 54.

Lawrence, Tim. *Love Saves the Day: A History of American Dance Music Culture, 1970–1979.* Durham, NC: Duke University Press, 2003.

Leblanc, Lauraine. *Pretty in Punk: Girls' Gender Resistance in a Boys' Subculture.* New Brunswick, NJ: Rutgers University Press, 1999.

Lee, Tommy, Vince Neil, Mick Mars, Nicki Sixx, and Neil Strauss. *The Dirt: Confessions of the World's Most Notorious Rock Band.* New York: Harper Collins, 2001.

Le Guin, Elisabeth. *Boccherini's Body: An Essay in Carnal Musicology.* Berkeley: University of California Press, 2006.

Leppert, Richard, and Stephen Zank. "The Concert and the Virtuoso." In *Piano Roles: Three Hundred Years of Life with the Piano,* ed. James Parakilas, 237–81. New Haven: Yale University Press, 1999.

Lester, Paul. "When Gary Numan Met Little Boots." *Guardian,* December 3, 2009, http://www.guardian.co.uk/music/2009/dec/03/gary-numan-little-boots-feature.

"Letters." *Contemporary Keyboard,* October 1980, 4.

Lévi-Strauss, Claude. *The Savage Mind.* Chicago: University of Chicago Press, 1966.

Levon, Erez. "Hearing Gay: Prosody, Interpretation, and the Affective Judgments of Men's Speech." *American Speech* 81, no. 1 (2006): 56–78.

Lindberg, Ulf, Gestur Gudmundsson, Morten Michelsen, and Hans Weisethaunet. *Rock Criticism from the Beginning: Amusers, Bruisers and Cool-Headed Cruisers.* New York: Peter Lang, 2005.

Lipsitz, George. *Time Passages: Collective Memory and American Popular Culture.* Minneapolis: University of Minnesota Press, 1990.

Loder, Kurt. "Human League's Pop Dreams." *Rolling Stone,* July 8, 1982, 33, 40–42.

Loesser, Arthur. *Men, Women & Pianos: A Social History.* New York: Simon and Schuster, 1954.

Lopes, Paul D. "Innovation and Diversity in the Popular Music Industry, 1969 to 1990." *American Sociological Review* 57, no. 1 (1992): 56–71.

Lowy, Kenn. "A Synth Pop Handbook." *Trouser Press,* December 1982, 32–37.

Lutz, Tom. *American Nervousness 1903: An Anecdotal History.* Ithaca: Cornell University Press, 1991.

Macan, Edward. *Rocking the Classics: English Progressive Rock and the Counterculture.* New York: Oxford University Press, 1997.

MacDonald, Dwight. "Masscult and Midcult." In *Against the American Grain: Essays on the Effects of Mass Culture,* 3–75. New York: Random House, 1962.

Malins, Steve. Introduction to *Praying to the Aliens (an Autobiography),* by Gary Numan with Steve Malins. London: André Deutsch Limited, 1998.

Malins, Steve. Notes for Gary Numan, *Replicas,* Beggars Banquet compact disc, BBL 7 CD.

Mamiya, Christin J. *Pop Art and Consumer Culture: American Super Market.* Austin: University of Texas Press, 1992.

Marcus, Greil. "The Girl Groups." In *The Rolling Stone Illustrated History of Rock & Roll,* ed. Jim Miller, 154–57. New York: Rolling Stone Press / Random House, 1976.

Marcus, Greil. *Lipstick Traces: A Secret History of the Twentieth Century.* Cambridge: Harvard University Press, 1989.

Marcus, Greil. "Wake Up! It's Fab, It's Passionate. It's Wild, It's Intelligent! It's the Hot New Sound of England Today!" *Rolling Stone,* July 24, 1980, 38–43.

Marsh, Dave. "Review of the Knack . . . *but the little girls understand.*" *Rolling Stone,* April 3, 1980, 62.

Marsh, Dave. "Various: New York New Wave." *Melody Maker,* October 6, 1973. Reprinted in *Rock's Backpages,* http://www.rocksbackpages.com/article.html?ArticleID=9049.

May, Kirse Granat. *Golden State, Golden Youth: The California Image in Popular Culture, 1955–1966.* Chapel Hill: University of North Carolina Press, 2002.

Mazullo, Mark. "Fans and Critics: Greil Marcus's *Mystery Train* as Rock'n'Roll History." *Musical Quarterly* 81, no. 2 (1997): 145–69.

McCormick, Neil. "La Roux, Lady Gaga, Mika, Little Boots: The 80s are Back." *Telegraph.co.uk,* August 5, 2009, http://www.telegraph.co.uk/culture/music/rockandpopfeatures/5978573/La-Roux-Lady-Gaga-Mika-Little-Boots-the-80s-are-back.html.

McDonald, Chris. *Rush: Rock Music and the Middle Class.* Bloomington: Indiana University Press, 2009.

McLane, Daisann. "Rubinoos: The Brain Children of Pop." *Rolling Stone,* May 31, 1979, 19.

McLeod, Ken. "Space Oddities: Aliens, Futurism and Meaning in Popular Music." *Popular Music* 22, no. 3 (2003): 337–55.

Mellers, Wilfrid. *Twilight of the Gods: The Music of the Beatles.* New York: Viking, 1973.

Melly, George. *Revolt into Style: The Pop Arts.* Garden City, NY: Anchor, 1971.

Mercer-Taylor, Peter. "Songs From the Bell Jar: Autonomy and Resistance in the Music of The Bangles." *Popular Music* 17, no. 2 (1998): 187–204.

Merriam, Alan P. "Review of *African Rhythm and African Sensibility: Aesthetics and Social Action in African Musical Idiom,* by John Miller Chernoff." *Ethnomusicology* 24, no. 3 (1980): 559–61.

Merritt, Jay. "Rock Strikes Back!" *Rolling Stone,* March 20, 1980, 19–23.

Middleton, Richard. "Rock Singing." In *The Cambridge Companion to Singing,* ed. John Potter, 28–41. New York: Cambridge University Press, 2000.

Milkowski, Bill. "Brian Eno: Excursions in the Electronic Environment." *Down Beat,* June 1983, 14–17, 57.

Miller, Jim, ed. "Is Rock On the Rocks?" *Newsweek,* April 19, 1982, 104–7.

Miller, Jim, ed. *The Rolling Stone Illustrated History of Rock & Roll.* New York: Rolling Stone Press / Random House, 1976.

Milner, Greg. *Perfecting Sound Forever: An Aural History of Recorded Music.* New York: Faber and Faber, 2009.

"The Modern Biography." http://www.ilikemusic.com/features/The_Modern-1252 (accessed May 23, 2010).

Mumford, Kevin J. "'Lost Manhood' Found: Male Sexual Impotence and Victorian Culture in the United States." In *American Sexual Politics: Sex, Gender, and Race since the Civil War*, ed. John C. Fout and Maura Shaw Tantillo, 75–99. Chicago: University of Chicago Press, 1993.

Munson, Benjamin. "The Acoustic Correlates of Perceived Masculinity, Perceived Femininity, and Perceived Sexual Orientation." *Language and Speech* 50, no. 1 (2007): 125–42.

Murray, Charles Shaar. "Review of The Knack . . . *but the Little Girls Understand*." *New Musical Express*, March 15, 1980, 40.

"Name Changed on Album Rock Tracks: Mainstream Rock List Mirrors Radio Shifts." *Billboard*, April 13, 1996, 6.

Nehring, Neil. *Flowers in the Dustbin: Culture, Anarchy and Postwar England*. Ann Arbor: University of Michigan Press, 1993.

"New Wave." *All Music Guide*, http://www.allmusic.com/cg/amg.dll?p=amg&sql=77:381 (accessed April 3, 2010).

"The New Wave Coming of Age: A Billboard Spotlight." *Billboard*, January 14, 1978, 47–67.

Nicolosi, Vincent. "Rock Discos: Why Are They Here? What Do They Want?!" *Trouser Press*, August 1981, 25–27, 57.

Nugent, Benjamin. *American Nerd: The Story of My People*. New York: Scribner, 2008.

Numan, Gary, with Steve Malins. *Praying to the Aliens (An Autobiography)*. London: André Deutsch, 1998.

O'Malley, Michael. "That Busyness That is Not Business: Nervousness and Character at the Turn of the Last Century." *Social Research* 72, no. 2 (2005): 371–406.

O'Neill, Lou, Jr., and Philip Bashe. "US Festival '83 in Words and Photos." *Circus*, August 31, 1983, 33–47.

Ormrod, Joan. "*Endless Summer* (1964): Consuming Waves and Surfing the Frontier." *Film & History* 25, no. 1 (2005): 39–51.

Ormrod, Joan. "Issues of Gender in *Muscle Beach Party* (1964)." *Scope* (December 2002), http://www.scope.nottingham.ac.uk/article.php?issue=dec2002&id=270&section=article.

Palmer, Myles. *New Wave Explosion: How Punk Became New Wave Became the 80s*. New York: Proteus, 1981.

Palmer, Robert. "Britain's New Pop—Synthetic Bands." *New York Times*, March 7, 1982, D19, 30.

Palmer, Robert. "Latest British Invasion: 'The New Tribalism.'" *New York Times*, November 25, 1981, C13.

Pareles, Jon. "All That Music and Nothing to Listen To." *New York Times*, January 5, 1997, H34, H44.

Pareles, Jon. "Does this Global Village have Two-Way Traffic? Review of David Byrne and Brian Eno *My Life in the Bush of Ghosts*." *Rolling Stone*, April 2, 1981, 60.

Pareles, Jon. "Nirvana, The Band That Hates To Be Loved." *New York Times*, November 14, 1993, H32, H44.

Pareles, Jon. "Power Steering." *Rolling Stone*, January 25, 1979, 58–61.

Payes, Robert. "Review of Thompson Twins *In The Name of Love*." *Trouser Press*, October 1982, 35.

Pearce, Roy Harvey. *The Savages of America: A Study of the Indian and the Idea of Civilization.* Baltimore: John Hopkins Press, 1953.

Perry, Mark. *Sniffin' Glue: The Essential Punk Accessory.* London: Sanctuary House, 2000.

Peterbaugh, Parke. "Anglomania: America Surrenders to the Brits—But Who Really Wins?" *Rolling Stone,* November 10, 1983, 31–32.

"Pete Townshend on 'Lily.'" *Hit Parader,* October 1967, 44.

Pfister, Joel. "Glamorizing the Psychological: The Politics of the Performances of Modern Psychological Identities." In *Inventing the Psychological: Toward a Cultural History of Emotional Life in America,* ed. Joel Pfister and Nancy Schnog, 167–213. New Haven: Yale University Press, 1997.

Pillsbury, Glenn. *Damage Incorporated: Metallica and the Production of Musical Identity.* New York: Routledge, 2006.

Pinch, Trevor. "Giving Birth to New Users: How the Minimoog Was Sold to Rock & Roll." In *How Users Matter: The Co-Construction of Users and Technology,* ed. Nelly Oudshoorn and Trevor Pinch, 247–70. Cambridge: MIT Press, 2003.

Pinch, Trevor, and Frank Trocco. *Analog Days: The Invention and Impact of the Moog Synthesizer.* Cambridge: Harvard University Press, 2002.

Plante, Elena, and Pelagie M. Beeson. *Communication and Communication Disorders: A Clinical Introduction.* Boston: Allyn and Bacon, 1999.

Polsky, Ruth. "The Beat: 3-Minute Supremacists." *Trouser Press,* March 1980, 10.

"Q&A: What's the Story Behind 'Rock Lobster.'" *AolMusic,* http://music.aol.com/video/qanda-whats-the-story-behind-rock/the-b-52s/2116949 (accessed August 6, 2009).

Radano, Ronald. "Hot Fantasies: American Modernism and the Idea of Black Rhythm." In *Music and the Racial Imagination,* ed. Ronald Radano and Philip V. Bohlman, 459–80. Chicago: University of Chicago Press, 2000.

Ratcliff, Carter. "David Byrne and the Modern Self: 'How Do I Work This.'" *Artforum,* May 1985, 95–96.

"Record Companies Get Badly Scratched." *Business Week,* August 6, 1979, 26–30.

"Record Company Firings Continue." *Rolling Stone,* January 24, 1980, 27.

Reese, Krista. *The Name of This Book is Talking Heads.* New York: Proteus, 1982.

Reynolds, Simon. "Against Health and Efficiency: Independent Music in the 1980s." In *Zoot Suits and Second-Hand Dresses: An Anthology of Fashion and Music,* ed. Angela McRobbie, 245–55. Boston: Unwin Hyman, 1988.

Reynolds, Simon. *Rip It Up and Start Again: Postpunk 1978–1984.* London: Faber and Faber, 2005.

Reynolds, Simon. "The 70's Are So 90's. The 80's Are the Thing Now." *New York Times,* May 5, 2002, A1, 48.

Reynolds, Simon. "What's Missing? The State of Pop in 1985." In *Bring the Noise: 20 Years of Writing About Hip Rock and Hip Hop,* 1–8. London: Faber and Faber, 2007.

Riegel, Richard. "Review of Thompson Twins, *In the Name of Love.*" *Creem,* September 1982, 54.

Rhodes, Carl. "Outside the Gates of Eden: Utopia and Work in Rock Music." *Group & Organization Management* 32, no. 1 (2007): 22–49.

Rimmer, Dave. "The Human League: Human Nature." *Smash Hits,* December 10,

1981. Reprinted in *Rock's Backpages,* http://www.rocksbackpages.com/article
.html?ArticleID=3132.

Rimmer, Dave. *Like Punk Never Happened: Culture Club and the New Pop.* Boston: Faber and Faber, 1985.

Rimmer, Dave. *New Romantics: The Look.* London: Omnibus Press, 2003.

Robbins, Ira. "Devo: Maybe!" *Trouser Press,* January 1979, 16.

Robbins, Ira, ed. *The New Trouser Press Record Guide.* 2nd ed. New York: Charles Scribner's Sons, 1985.

Robbins, Ira, ed. *The New Trouser Press Record Guide.* 3rd ed. New York: Collier, 1989.

Robbins, Ira. "New Wave R.I.P.: Nails in the Coffin." *Trouser Press,* October 1977, 20–22, 32.

Robbins, Ira. "Power Pop Primer." *Trouser Press,* April 1978, 22–27.

Robbins, Ira. "Review of Gary Numan, *The Pleasure Principle.*" *Trouser Press,* February 1980, 38–39.

Robbins, Ira, ed. *The Trouser Press Guide to New Wave Records.* New York: Charles Scribner's Sons, 1983.

Roberts, John Storm. *The Latin Tinge: The Impact of Latin American Music on the United States.* New York: Oxford University Press, 1979.

Rockwell, John. *All American Music: Composition in the Late Twentieth Century.* New York: Vintage, 1983.

Rockwell, John. "B-52's, Rock Band from Georgia." *New York Times,* June 3, 1978, 11.

Rockwell, John. "The Pop Life: How the B-52's Cope with the Success Trap." *New York Times,* August 31, 1979, C16.

Rodger, Gillian. "Drag, Camp and Gender Subversion in the Music and Videos of Annie Lennox." *Popular Music* 23, no. 1 (2004): 17–29.

Romanowski, Patricia, and Holly George-Warren, eds. *The New Rolling Stone Encyclopedia of Rock & Roll.* New York: Fireside, 1995.

Rose, Cynthia. "Brian Eno." *New Musical Express,* July 26, 1980. Reprinted in *Rock's Backpages,* http://www.rocksbackpages.com/article.html?ArticleID=1197.

Rose, Cynthia. "The B-52's." *New Musical Express,* June 4, 1983. Reprinted in *Rock's Backpages,* http://www.rocksbackpages.com/article.html?ArticleID=1208.

Rose, Cynthia. "The B-52's: Hair Today Gone Tomorrow?" *New Musical Express,* January 3, 1981. Reprinted in *Rock's Backpages,* http://www.rocksbackpages.com/article.html?ArticleID=1207.

Rose, Frank. "Connoisseurs of Trash in a World Full of It: Review of the B-52's *Wild Planet.*" *Rolling Stone,* October 30, 1980, 54–55.

Rose, Tricia. *Black Noise: Rap Music and Black Culture in Contemporary America.* Hanover, NH: Wesleyan University Press, 1994.

Rose, Wendy. "The Great Pretenders: Further Reflections on Whiteshamanism." In *The State of Native America: Genocide, Colonization, and Resistance,* ed. M. Annette Jaimes, 403–21. Boston: South End Press, 1992.

Ross, Alec. "Human League." *Trouser Press,* November 1980, 12.

Ross, Andrew. *No Respect: Intellectuals and Popular Culture.* New York: Routledge, 1989.

Ross, Sean. "Billboard Debuts Weekly Chart of Alternative Rock." *Billboard,* September 10, 1988, 1, 10.

Rule, Greg. "Meet the Rentals: Nerds with Moogs . . . And Proud of It!" *Keyboard*, March 1996, 66–67.

Russell, Rosalind. "Cindy Wilson / Kate Pierson." In *New Women in Rock*, ed. Liz Thompson, 23. New York: Delilah/Putnam, 1982.

Rutsky, R. L. "Surfing the Other: Ideology on the Beach." *Film Quarterly* 52, no. 4 (1999): 12–23.

Savage, Jon. *England's Dreaming: Anarchy, Sex Pistols, Punk Rock, and Beyond*. New York: St. Martin's Press, 1992.

Savage, Jon. *Time Travel: Pop, Media and Sexuality, 1977–96*. London: Chatto & Windus, 1996.

Savage, Jon. "Yesterday's Sound Tomorrow: Review of the B-52's *B-52's*." *Melody Maker*, June 30, 1979. Reprinted in *Rock's Backpages*, http://www.rocksback pages.com/article.html?ArticleID=14660.

Schafer, R. Murray. *The Tuning of the World*. New York: Alfred A. Knopf, 1977.

Schoemer, Karen. "At Home in the Top 40 and Still Full of Kitsch." *New York Times*, December 31, 1989, H27.

Schudson, Michael. *Watergate in American Memory: How We Remember, Forget, and Reconstruct the Past*. New York: Basic Books, 1992.

Schuman, Howard, and Jacqueline Scott. "Generations and Collective Memory." *American Sociological Review* 54, no. 3 (1989): 359–81.

Schwartz, Andy. "Anglophilia: Can it Be Cured?" *New York Rocker*, December 1981, 26–27.

Schwartz, Jay. "The dB's." *New York Rocker*, September 1978, 20–22.

Seven Ages of Rock. Episode 7, "What the World is Waiting For." Produced and directed by Sebastian Barfield. BBC, 2007.

Sexton, Mats. *The B-52's Universe: The Essential Guide to the World's Greatest Party Band*. Minneapolis: Plan-B Books, 2002.

Sharp, Ken, and Doug Sulpy. *Power Pop! Conversations with the Power Pop Elite*. Willow Grove, PA: Poptomes, 1997.

Shaw, Greg. "Editorial." *Bomp!* March 1978, 4–5, 57.

Shaw, Greg. "Editorial: In Defense of Rock Theory." *Bomp!* November 1977, 4–5, 29.

Shaw, Greg. "'It All Came Back': A Trenchant Analysis of the Pop Revival." *Who Put the Bomp* 12 (Spring 1975), 4, 16.

Shaw, Greg. "20/20: The End of All Songs." *Bomp!* March 1978, 35.

Sheppard, David. *On Some Faraway Beach: The Life and Times of Brian Eno*. Chicago: Chicago Review Press, 2009.

Sheridan, Thomas B. "Computer Control and Human Alienation." *Technology Review* 83, no. 1 (1980): 60–73.

Shewey, Don. "Review of Gary Numan *The Pleasure Principle*." *Rolling Stone*, March 20, 1980, 58.

Shore, Michael. "Athens' Golden Age: New Sounds from a Georgia Town." *Music Sound & Output*, January–February 1983, 90–96.

Shore, Michael. "Review of Talking Heads *Fear of Music*." *New York Rocker*, August 1979, 40.

Shulman, Bruce J. *The Seventies: The Great Shift in American Culture, Society, and Politics*. New York: Free Press, 2002.

Simmel, George. "The Metropolis and Mental Life." In *The Sociology of Georg Simmel*, trans. and ed. Kurt H. Wolff, 409–24. New York: Free Press, 1950.

Simmons, Sylvie. "The Go-Go's: Ready Steady Go-Go's." *Sounds*, April 12, 1980. Reprinted in *Rock's Backpages*, http://www.rocksbackpages.com/article.html?ArticleID=13067.

Singer, Ben. *Melodrama and Modernity: Early Sensational Cinema and Its Contexts*. New York: Columbia University Press, 2001.

Sippel, John. "Profit Push: Execs Cite More Conservative Acquisition & Recording Plans." *Billboard*, May 1, 1982, 10.

Slotkin, Richard. *Fatal Environment: The Myth of the Frontier in the Age of Industrialization 1800–1890*. New York: Atheneum, 1985.

Slotkin, Richard. *Gunfighter Nation: The Myth of the Frontier in Twentieth-Century America*. New York: Atheneum, 1992.

Smith, Michael L. "Selling the Moon: The U.S. Manned Space Program and the Triumph of Commodity Scientism." In *The Culture of Consumption: Critical Essays in American History 1880–1980*, ed. Richard Wightman Fox and T. J. Jackson Lears, 175–209. New York: Pantheon, 1983.

Sommer, Tim. "Adam and the Ants." *Trouser Press*, July 1981, 13.

Sommer, Tim. "The Sound of the Sinceros." *Trouser Press*, February 1980, 12.

Sontag, Susan. "Notes on 'Camp.'" *Partisan Review* 31, no. 4 (1964): 515–30.

Spigel, Lynn. "From Theatre to Space Ship: Metaphors of Suburban Domesticity in Postwar America." In *Visions of Suburbia*, ed. Roger Silverstone, 217–39. New York: Routledge, 1997.

Stallybrass, Peter, and Allon White. *The Politics and Poetics of Transgression*. Ithaca: Cornell University Press, 1986.

Stearns, Peter N. *American Cool: Constructing a Twentieth-Century Emotional Style*. New York: New York University Press, 1994.

Stearns, Peter N. *Battleground of Desire: The Struggle for Self-Control in Modern America*. New York: New York University Press, 1999.

Stedman, Raymond William. *Shadows of the Indian: Stereotypes in American Culture*. Norman: University of Oklahoma Press, 1982.

Stein, Seymour. "Assault on the Industry!" In "The New Wave Coming of Age: A Billboard Spotlight." *Billboard*, January 14, 1978, 49, 58.

Stewart, Kathleen. "Nostalgia—A Polemic." In *Rereading Cultural Anthropology*, ed. George E. Marcus, 252–66. Durham, NC: Duke University Press, 1992.

Stewart, Susan. *On Longing: Narratives of the Miniature, the Gigantic, the Collection*. Baltimore: John Hopkins University Press, 1984.

Stratton, Jon. "Beyond Art: Postmodernism and the Case of Popular Music." *Theory, Culture & Society* 6, no. 1 (1989): 31–57.

Straw, Will. "The Booth, The Floor and the Wall: Dance Music and the Fear of Falling." In *Popular Music—Style and Identity*, ed. Will Straw, Stacey Johnson, Rebecca Sullivan, and Paul Friedlander, 249–54. Montreal: Centre for Research on Canadian Cultural Industries and Institutions, 1995.

Straw, Will. "Dance Music." In *The Cambridge Companion to Pop and Rock*, ed. Simon Frith, Will Straw, and John Street, 158–75. New York: Cambridge University Press, 2001.

Straw, Will. "Popular Music and Postmodernism in the 1980s." In *Sound and Vision: The Music Video Reader,* ed. Simon Frith, Andrew Goodwin, and Lawrence Grossberg, 3–21. New York: Routledge, 1993.

Straw, Will. "Popular Music as Cultural Commodity: The American Recorded Music Industries, 1976–1985 (United States)." PhD diss., McGill University, 1990.

Sublette, Ned. "The Kingsmen and the Cha Cha Chá." In *Listen Again: A Momentary History of Pop Music,* ed. Eric Weisbard, 69–94. Durham, NC: Duke University Press, 2007.

Summers, Russ. "Greg Hawkes: Rock in the Fast Lane With The Cars." *Contemporary Keyboard,* April 1980, 8–12.

Sutcliffe, Phil. "Do Sheep Dream of Electric Androids? The Gary Numan Enigma." *Sounds,* October 6, 1979. Reprinted in *Rock's Backpages,* http://www.rocksback pages.com/article.html?ArticleID=3529.

Sutherland, Sam. "U2 Edges Forward with its Own Brand of 'New.'" *Billboard,* July 9, 1983, 51, 53.

Sweeney, Gael. "The King of White Trash Culture: Elvis Presley and the Aesthetics of Excess." In *White Trash: Race and Class in America,* ed. Matt Wray and Annalee Newitz, 249–66. New York: Routledge, 1997.

Tagg, Philip. "Open Letter: 'Black Music,' 'Afro-American Music' and 'European Music.'" *Popular Music* 8, no. 3 (1989): 285–98.

Tamm, Eric. *Brian Eno: His Music and the Vertical Color of Sound.* Rev. ed. New York: Da Capo Press, 1995.

Taylor, Steven. *False Prophets: Field Notes from the Underground.* Hanover, NH: Wesleyan University Press, 2004.

Taylor, Timothy D. *Strange Sounds: Music, Technology & Culture.* New York: Routledge, 2001.

Temperley, David. "The Melodic-Harmonic 'Divorce' in Rock." *Popular Music* 26, no. 2 (2007): 323–42.

Théberge, Paul. "Technology." In *Key Terms in Popular Music and Culture,* ed. Bruce Horner and Thomas Swiss, 209–24. Malden, MA: Blackwell, 1999.

Thompson, Michael. "An Anatomy of Rubbish." In *Arts in Society,* ed. Paul Barker, 36–42. London: Fontana, 1977.

Tobler, John. *Adam and the Ants: Superstar.* Knutsford, Cheshire: Stafford Pemberton Publishing, 1982.

Tomlinson, John. *Globalization and Culture.* Chicago: University of Chicago Press, 1999.

Torgovnick, Marianna. *Gone Primitive: Savage Intellects, Modern Lives.* Chicago: University of Chicago Press, 1990.

Toynbee, Jason. "Policing Bohemia, Pinning Up Grunge: The Music Press and Generic Change in British Pop and Rock." *Popular Music* 12, no. 3 (1993): 289–300.

Truffaut, François. "A Certain Tendency of the French Cinema." In *Movies and Methods: An Anthology,* ed. Bill Nichols, 224–37. Berkeley: University of California Press, 1976.

Tucker, Ken. "Africa Calling: Review of Talking Heads *Remain in Light.*" *Rolling Stone,* December 11, 1980, 55.

Turner, Frederick Jackson. *The Frontier in American History.* New York: Henry Holt, 1920.

Vague, Tom. "Bow Wow Wow: I Was a Stowaway By the C-Side." In *The Great British Mistake: Vague 1977–92*, 23–26. San Francisco: AK Press, 1994.

Vail, Mark. *Vintage Synthesizers: Groundbreaking Instruments and Pioneering Designers of Electronic Music Synthesizers*. San Francisco: Miller Freeman, 1993.

Van Lent, Peter. "Her Beautiful Savage: The Current Sexual Image of the Native American Male." In *Dressing in Feathers: The Construction of the Indian in American Popular Culture*, ed. S. Elizabeth Bird, 211–28. Boulder, CO: Westview Press, 1996.

Vermorel, Fred, and Judy Vermorel. *Adam and the Ants*. New York: Omnibus Press, 1981.

Waksman, Steve. *Instruments of Desire: The Electric Guitar and the Shaping of Musical Experience*. Cambridge: Harvard University Press, 1999.

Waller, Don. "Live Reviews: The Knack, Starwood." *New York Rocker*, April–May 1979, 48.

Wallis, Roger, and Krister Malm. *Big Sounds From Little People: The Music Industry in Small Countries*. New York: Pendragon Press, 1984.

Walser, Robert. *Running With the Devil: Power, Gender, and Madness in Heavy Metal Music*. Hanover, NH: Wesleyan University Press, 1993.

Ward, Steven. "Caught with his Trousers Down: The Ira Robbins Interview." *RockCritics.com*, http://rockcriticsarchives.com/interviews/irarobbins/irarobbins.html (accessed June 29, 2009).

Warhol, Andy, and Pat Hackett. *Popism: The Warhol Sixties*. New York: Harper & Row, 1980.

Warner, Timothy. *Pop Music—Technology and Creativity: Trevor Horn and the Digital Revolution*. Burlington, VT: Ashgate, 2003.

Warwick, Jacqueline. *Girl Groups, Girl Culture: Popular Music and Identity in the 1960s*. New York: Routledge, 2007.

Watts, Michael. "A New Dress Code on the British Scene." *Los Angeles Times*, April 5, 1981, Calendar, 72–73.

Weinstein, Deena. "Art Versus Commerce: Deconstucting a (Useful) Romantic Illusion." In *Stars Don't Stand Still In the Sky: Music and Myth*, ed. Karen Kelly and Evelyn McDonnell, 56–69. New York: New York University Press, 1999.

"What Is New Music? All That Came Before . . . And More." *Billboard*, July 9, 1983, NM1-12.

White, Adam, and Dick Nusser. "New Wave Rockers Click in U.S. Mart." *Billboard*, August 18, 1979, 1, 15.

White, Timothy. "Billy Joel is Angry." *Rolling Stone*, September 4, 1980, 37–40.

Widmer, E. L. "Crossroads: The Automobile, Rock and Roll and Democracy." In *Autopia: Cars and Culture*, ed. Peter Wollen and Joe Kerr, 65–74. London: Reaktion, 2002.

Williams, Raymond. *Marxism and Literature*. New York: Oxford University Press, 1977.

Wilson, Janelle L. *Nostalgia: Sanctuary of Meaning*. Lewisburg, PA: Bucknell University Press, 2005.

Wilson, Pamela. "Mountains of Contradictions: Gender, Class, and Region in the Star Image of Dolly Parton." In *Reading Country Music: Steel Guitars, Opry Stars, and Honky-Tonk Bars*, ed. Cecelia Tichi, 98–120. Durham, NC: Duke University Press, 1998.

Wolf, Johannes. *Geschichte der Mensural Notation von 1250–1460*. Hildesheim: George Olms; Weisbaden: Breitkopf & Härtel, 1965.

Wollen, Peter. *Raiding the Icebox: Reflections on Twentieth-Century Culture*. Bloomington: Indiana University Press, 1993.

Wood, Robert T. *Straightedge Youth: Complexity and Contradictions of a Subculture*. Syracuse, NY: Syracuse University Press, 2006.

Yack, Bernard. *The Fetishism of Modernities: Epochal Self-Consciousness in Contemporary Social and Political Thought*. Notre Dame: University of Notre Dame Press, 1997.

Young, Jon. "Hot Spots." *Trouser Press*, August 1981, 62.

Young, Jon. "Roll Over Guitar Heros [*sic*], Synthesizers Are Here." *Trouser Press*, May 1982, 22–27.

Index